Little Farm On Brown Road

* * *

By

Joe Brown

Haystack Press
1042 Bona Court
Kernersville, NC 27284
2005

Little Farm On Brown Road

* * * * * * *

Published by:

Joe Brown
Haystack Press
1042 Bona Court
Kernersville, NC 27284

Telephone: (336) 996-7752
Website: www.HaystackPress.com
Email: Joe@HaystackPress.com

Library of Congress Control Number
2005930368
ISBN: 0-9769106-8-3

In Memory

This book is dedicated to the memory of my Grandma, Nellie Vestal Proctor, who along with my Mom made the best biscuits in the whole world; my school principal and hero, Mr. C. C. Wright; and long time family friend, Mr. Claude Shore.

A Note of Appreciation

Thanks to my brothers and sisters who daily gave me plenty to write about over the years. Elmer (1934), Wayne (1936), Rose (1939), John (1943), Jane (1945), and Danny (1949) each helped with valuable information and encouragement. Our memories of the past and our faith in God help us to continue the family tradition to be close and to treasure not only the old memories, but also the memories we continue to make.

Thanks to my wife Sherry, my sons Joey and Daniel, and my daughters Megan and Morgan for their support and encouragement.

Contents

Contents

Introduction

Little Farm on Brown Road is a sequel to *Memories: Farm Days, Farm Ways* which covered the first 11 ½ years of my life on the small tobacco farm in the Cycle community of Yadkin County, North Carolina.

Dad's youngins had grown into a highly productive work crew. With better equipment on Mr. Claude Shore's farm, the crew would continue to grow. Close working relationships with Mr. Shore and with Dad's brother Nelson would help make ends meet.

Life on the farm was a good life, but it was hard work with long hours. Tobacco was the cash crop, even though many other crops were grown too.

Dad's work crew would start to leave the farm one at a time, beginning with Elmer in 1954, Wayne in 1955, and Rose in 1957. Dad knew that the small farm could not compete with public jobs for the high school graduate. The small farm was being squeezed out.

Mom and Dad had taught their children how to work and to trust God each day. The children would all leave the farm for jobs in the city, but their hearts would stay in the rolling hills of Yadkin County better known as the Little Farm on Brown Road.

Joe Brown
July 2005

Chapter 1
The Well

The Indian summer was staying on longer this year. It was Thursday, October 2, 1952. The temperature was in the mid 80's. Old #63 came to a screeching halt at the bus stop at Grandpa Brown's tobacco barn. It seemed that everything squeaked or rattled on this old bus. Surely this bus would be replaced soon.

Wayne, Rose, Joe, John, and Jane stuck their head in the door of Grandpa Brown's packhouse to say hey to Mom, Dad, Elmer, and Danny.

"Hey, ya'll," Wayne said as all of the school youngins looked around the room at the stacks of graded tobacco, which was ready to be tied.

"Hey, youngins. Ya'll hurry on to the house and get your old clothes on so you can help us," Dad said. "I would like to get finished by week after next."

"Ya'll look at the contraption at work down at the house. We're digging a well," Elmer said.

Dad had been talking recently about getting a well dug so we could have our own water supply. Today was the day that Pea Ridge Well Drilling Company started drilling. They first used their modern equipment to pick out a place to drill.

"Why didn't we let Grandpa Brown show us where to dig?" Joe asked. He remembered all the many times that Grandpa had helped so many people find water.

"The modern gadgets are supposed to be more reliable," Dad said. "The drilling company guarantees they will get us an abundant supply of water or they will not charge us."

"I still like Grandpa's simple method," Joe said as he and the rest of the school youngins headed down the winding driveway towards the plain country house that was in the front of the 22 rolling acres of land in the foothills of Yadkin County. Dad's farm was within hollering distance of Wilkes County, which had the name of being the "moonshine capital of the world."

"Boy, that machine sure is loud, ain't it?" Rose said as they all gawked at the rattling, smoking drilling machine.

"It sure is, Rose," Jane said. Jane was getting ready to have her seventh birthday next week. She had just recently started to school.

"I'd really like to run that machine," John spoke up over the racket of the drilling. "That would be neat." John was in the 4th grade this year.

"I wouldn't want to run it," Joe said. "I think I'd hear that racket all night long in my sleep." Joe was now in the 6th grade.

"I guess you'd get used to the noise, but I'm with you, Joe. I don't care for all that racket," Wayne added. He was the older of the school youngins since Elmer had graduated this past May. Wayne was in the 10th grade. He was always careful to comb his wavy hair as he had girls on his mind all the time.

"We'd better get changed and get on back up to the packhouse before Dad gives us a whistle," Joe said. They all knew that a whistle from Dad was a warning that they would be in big trouble soon if they didn't get moving.

Soon the school crew was back at the packhouse to help for a couple of hours before supper and then until about 9:00 p.m. after supper. "I was getting ready to give ya'll a whistle," Dad said as he showed them which stack of tobacco to tie.

"Wayne, you and Joe go ahead and put all we have tied on sticks."

The sticks of tobacco would then be packed and covered up to keep the tobacco in case until it was ready to go to the market.

"How long is it going to take to get our well dug, Dad?" Joe asked as he was holding the tobacco stick for Wayne.

"It'll probably take about a week if their equipment has them digging in the right place," Dad said.

"I'll sure be glad when we have our own water source," Mom said. "We use so much more water now than we did a few years ago. I don't know how much longer the spring is going to keep up with our house and Lamar's house, too."

Lamar was Dad's oldest brother. His family had been sharing the spring with our family since Dad built our house in 1945. At times, the relationship between Dad and Uncle Lamar was strained because of the spring. Dad figured he could help relations if he got his own water supply. The two families had always been close and Dad wanted to do all possible to help. The spring was located at the branch that was the property line between the two brothers.

Grandpa Brown, James Henry Brown, stuck his head in the door. "Hey there, youngins. How're ya'll doing today?" he asked.

"We're doing good," the packhouse crew rang out together.

"We're getting us a well dug, Grandpa," Joe said happily. "Pretty soon we'll have plenty of water."

"That's good, Joe. I hope you get all the water you need, but my peach tree limb did not like the place they are digging. Maybe they're right and I am wrong. We'll have to wait and see," Grandpa said as he spit a big stream of Brown Mule chewing tobacco at a bumble bee that was perched on a nearby bush.

"Don't ya'll forget this Sunday is reunion day," Grandpa continued. "Remember last year. Boy, was that a day to remember!"

Last year's reunion was remembered because of the tornado that blew through in mid evening and caused severe damage all around the community. Grandpa's house and other buildings were spared with minimal damage when the twister paid a visit. The 1951 reunion, which was on Jane's 6th birthday, was a birthday to remember, along with the house fire that Dad fought on Joe's 7th birthday.

"Well, I'll see ya'll later. I've got to get my cow milked and fed. It's about suppertime," Grandpa said as he slowly went down the steep bank of Brown Road and on up to his feed barn. Grandpa was slowing down. He was now 68 years old and was continually troubled by an old rupture that he had been living with for years. Grandpa was a tough cookie, but the rupture definitely was bothering him.

"I've got to go and get my cornbread to cooking," Mom said as she moved quickly down the winding driveway to her house. Mom is a pretty lady, sweet and kind as you would want to see. She was now 36 years old, having worked hard all her life, going back to when she was a second mother to her younger brothers and sisters at home. She had bore seven children that she loved dearly and whom loved her in return with all their hearts. Mom also had a stillborn baby in 1947. She was a real trooper who continued to do her job over the many years of tough, hard country life. Mom loved this life and enjoyed cooking for her family and for her preacher more than anyone Joe had ever seen. She was happiest when she cooked a big meal and in turn heard all the many good and kind remarks about her food. All the time she was cooking for nine people, she continued to go to work in the field every day.

"We'd better get on to the house and get our chores done, youngins," Dad said. "We'll come back up for a couple hours after supper."

Dad's crew made quick work of the chores. Dad, Elmer, and Wayne milked and fed the cows. They also fed Old Bill, our trusty horse. Joe and John gathered the eggs while Rose helped Mom with supper.

Joe and John again checked out the well drilling equipment. The well was being drilled close to the waterline from the spring so it would be simple to tap into that line when the well was finished.

"How far do you think they will have to drill, John?" Joe asked as they were analyzing the situation.

"I think it will be over 100 feet," John said with a serious look on his face.

"Supper's on!" Rose hollered from the back steps of the house. Nobody had to be called a second time. Everyone was ready to eat.

The kitchen table was over in the back section of the room. Mom and Dad sat out front. Elmer and Wayne sat at the ends of the table. Rose, Joe, John, and Jane sat in back on the homemade bench. Danny sat beside Mom where she could help him as needed. Danny was now a little over 3 ½ years old.

Mom prayed, "Heavenly Father, thank you for this good day you've given us. Thank you for health and strength you provide for us. Thank you for this food. May it be used to nourish and strengthen us. Be with the sick and shut-in. Bless those who are bereaved. Help us to live for you each day. We thank you in Jesus' name. Amen."

Mom poured milk all around as they ate a Brown's Supper Special cornbread and milk. All her family loved this meal. Leftover pinto beans and taters were on the table also, but Joe, like his dad, just made a meal out of cornbread and milk. Who could possibly want anything any better? Joe did not know of anything close to this meal.

"Dad, what happens if the well drillers don't find water?" Joe asked in between big spoon bites of cornbread and milk.

"No water, no pay," Dad replied.

"Will they drill somewhere else if they don't find water there, Dad?" Rose asked.

"I don't think so," Dad said. "They checked all around with their water finding gadget and settled on the best possible place. I guess they will leave if they don't find water. Let's hope they find water. Be positive."

No water was found on Friday. The drilling continued for a half of a day on Saturday. The drillers were now down to 100 feet with no sign of water. Hopefully, Monday would be a better day.

Mom cooked all day on Saturday for the big reunion on Sunday at Grandpa Brown's. Joe chopped the heads off two hens that had quit laying. Mom would fix fried chicken for the reunion. Hens that quit laying did not usually live very long.

On Sunday morning, Dad drove his family to Mineral Springs Baptist Church in Jonesville. We had been going to this church for over two years now.

Pastor Myers greeted us at the door. He always had a smile on his face and a twinkle in his eyes.

"Good morning, Brown family. What a beautiful day!" Pastor Myers said as he shook hands with the whole family. He scratched his bald head and adjusted his glasses.

"Did you bring that toy cow with you, Danny?" Pastor Myers always kidded Danny about a brown looking toy cow that Danny had.

"Does your cow give chocolate milk since it is brown?" Pastor Myers would ask. Danny would just giggle when teased about his cow.

Pastor Myers preached on Heaven this morning. The choir sang the old song about Heaven before his message:

"How beautiful Heaven must be!
Sweet home of the happy and free,
Fair haven of rest for the weary,
How beautiful Heaven must be!"

Amen's rang out from all over and Aunt Callie Foster leaped to her feet shouting and waving her little white handkerchief. Aunt Callie was about 90 years old and was subject to get happy just about any time, especially when Heaven was mentioned.

"Can you imagine a place without heartache, without pain, without tears, without sin? That's what Heaven will be. Make sure you are ready to go. All you have to do is ask Jesus to come into your heart. You cannot make it alone. There's only one way. That's through Jesus Christ. Accept Him today," Pastor Myers said in closing.

Brown Reunion

After church, Dad headed his crew back home and to the James Henry Brown reunion. The crowd was gathering quickly. Ralph Winters came home with Joe and John as he usually did about every other week. The three of them were good buddies and usually played all Sunday evenings.

In addition to our family, others in attendance were Grandpa, Grandma, Aunt Annie Sue, Troy, Aunt Mary Lee, Allen, Aunt Daisy, Uncle Bill and their family, Uncle Lamar, Aunt Ivy, Lyman, Jimmy, Lorene, Avalon, Elaine, Tim, Uncle Nelson, Aunt Jo, cousin Gray who was the same age as Danny, Fay, Uncle Johnny, Uncle Lonnie, Aunt Stella, Farmer Brown, Aunt Lucy Pardue, Leck and Ida Groce with their twins, Nadine and Justine, and a whole bunch of cousins from Statesville who Joe did not know.

Uncle Guy and Aunt Rosemary did not make it home this year from Pennsylvania. It seems that last year's storm scared Aunt Rosemary who did not ever come back to North Carolina.

The makeshift tables were loaded with good country food. You name it and it was here. Joe made his rounds spying the food so he would know where to start. He always wanted to get a country ham biscuit, a chicken leg, and, of course, plenty of sweets.

Grandpa Brown welcomed everyone. "It's good to see such a good turnout this year. We certainly hope we do not have any of the foul weather this year. We got our fill of that last year. Everyone make themselves at home and eat up. Johnny will bless the food and then we'll eat."

Uncle Johnny prayed, "Heavenly Father, thank you for your goodness, for health and strength. Thank you for our family. We pray you'll bless this food now in Jesus' precious name. Amen. Amen."

As soon as he finished praying, Uncle Johnny went around taking pictures with his moving picture camera. He got such a thrill out of taking pictures and then coming back to show them.

There was a mad dash for the food. Joe scooted in and got his plate filled up quickly. Ralph and John were right behind Joe. Soon, they found a shady spot under the old apple tree and sat down to eat up.

"You just can't beat this, Ralph. Did you ever see so much food? If you can't get filled up here, I don't think you are trying. There's enough food to feed an army," Joe said.

"There's plenty of food, alright," Ralph said between bites.

After the meats, Joe worked his way through the sweet table. He got a big piece of chocolate pie, chocolate pound cake, and topped it off with a big helping of Mom's sweet potato saunker. He was full to the top.

It was baseball time. Joe, John, and Ralph tossed the baseball with Lyman, Jimmy, Elmer, and Wayne. The yard was too crowded to get a game going, but it was fun to fire the ball around to see who could catch the hot potato.

Slowly the crowd was leaving. Another Brown reunion was over. Mom and Dad made their way back down the winding driveway to spend a few minutes at the house before Sunday night church services. At precisely 5:15 p.m., Dad hurried everyone to get started to church. We had a real load tonight as Jimmy wanted to go with us, as he often did on Sunday nights. With Ralph, that made a real car full, eleven people. Mom, Dad, John, Jane, and Danny sat in the front seat while Elmer, Wayne, Rose, Joe, Ralph, and Jimmy were in the back seat. What a carload!

It was a sleepy night at church. Everyone had missed their evening naps. Pastor Myers was a good preacher, but Joe doesn't remember too much he said. He was plumb tired out. He certainly would sleep good tonight.

It was back to the packhouse Monday evening after school and also after supper. Dad still planned on getting all the tobacco ready by the middle of next week. There was still a bunch of tobacco to tie.

Monday was another bad day at the well drilling. Tuesday was ended with the same results, 200 feet deep and still no water of any substance was found. Happy birthday #7 for Jane. This birthday was a little quieter than last year. Wednesday would be a critical day. The drillers would have to reach water today or it would be time to call it quits.

When Joe and the other youngins got home from school, the drilling equipment was quiet. After 250 feet and no water, the rigger was pulling out. They were in disbelief that they did not find water."What will we do now, Dad?" Joe asked. "Maybe we need to dig our own well the old fashioned way."

"I don't know, son. I've been thinking of running pipe from the old spring down near the old home place," Dad said. "But that would be about ¼ mile. That's a lot of pipe."

"We can do it if that's what you decide, Dad," Elmer said. "Just give us the word. I know we need to do something."

Joe could not get the well out of his mind. He thought about it through chores and supper. He was so preoccupied that Mom thought he was not feeling well.

"Joe, do you feel all right?" Mom asked. "You've been awfully quiet all evening."

"I'm concerned about the well, Mom. I know we need to get something done about it," Joe said.

After working in the packhouse until 9:00 p.m., everyone was worn out and in bed immediately. Joe was asleep even before his head hit the pillow. It was another no-brainer dream night for Joe.

The Well Dream

Grandpa Brown was making a sweep through the back yard with his peach tree limb loaded down with a new 1952 dime in the end. Grandpa thought he would find water near the back door. After two or three walks across the back yard, the peach tree limb jumped indicating Grandpa had found our well site. It was right outside the back door, close enough to enclose and have a well with a shelter as Grandpa and Grandma Proctor does. How neat that would be.

Grandpa marked the area and soon the digging started in earnest. Grandpa, Dad, Elmer, Wayne, Joe, and John got to work with their picks and shovels. Dad figured it would take about a week to dig, depending, of course, on how soon they would find water. Dad planned a 36″ diameter well. Joe was excited about digging. He couldn't believe that Dad listened to him and used the old method to find a site and then to dig by hand.

The blisters were appearing on all hands, despite using gloves. This kind of digging was tough, hard work. By late evening of the first day, Dad rigged up a pulley to lift the dirt bucket up out of the hole. Dad's crew worked in teams to rest each other and to keep the work going. Dad rotated often to keep a fresh digger down in the hole. Dad paid close attention to the sides of the well. He did not want to chance a cave in. At quitting time of day #1, the well was 10 feet deep. It sounds slow, but was actually good progress.

After a good night's rest, Dad's crew was hard at it at first light. Dad wanted to get this well finished and was keeping Wayne, Joe, and John out of school to help. Grandpa was on hand to advise, more than anything else, as he had dug many wells. Grandpa sent down a candle in a bucket first thing to make sure it was safe to send the diggers down. All seemed to be okay. This procedure would be repeated throughout the day. By the end of day #2, the well was 20 feet deep. It was good to see progress.

At supper tonight, Dad's crew was talking about the well.

"I think we're going to find water at 50 feet," Elmer said. "What do ya'll think?"

"I think it will be 55 feet," Wayne said.

"I think it will be 60 feet," Rose jumped in the well talk.

"I think it will be 65 feet," John said.

"I think it will be 68 feet," Jane said.

"It'll be 70 feet," Dad said in between giant sized bites of cornbread and milk.

"I think it will be more like 90 feet," Mom said. "What do you think, Joe? You've been very quiet again."

"It will be 75 feet, I think," Joe said as he chowed down with his favorite supper, cornbread and milk.

Day #3 started again at first light. Grandpa repeated the candle test with no problems again today. Digging was slowed somewhat today by a patch of rocks. Dad hoped he would not have to use dynamite this close to the house. Slowly the rock problem passed. The progress was slower today. The well was 28 feet deep. The depth was still encouraging.

Day #4 showed a slight problem with some sort of gas as the candlelight flickered slightly for the first time. The procedure was repeated more often today to insure the safety of the diggers. Today was the best digging day so far, as the day ended with the well being 40 feet deep. Everyone was encouraged with this good news.

"Boy, this sure is a job, isn't it, Grandpa?" Joe said as he sat down on the doorstep after spending a 15 minute shift in the hole.

"Yes, Joe. It is some of the hardest work you will ever do. It will wear you out fast," Grandpa said.

Day #5 began with a little more flickering of the candle light. Grandpa said we needed to have the digger attach a rope to his waist while in the well digging. That way the digger could be pulled out quickly if he was overcome by gas.

"Tie the rope around your waist snug enough to let us get you out," Grandpa said as Elmer was headed down into the well to start the day. "Keep talking to us while you're working. That way we'll know you're alright."

It was another productive day as well as a safe day. Safety would be watched even more closely as the well increased in depth. Day #5 ended with the well at 50 feet. Joe noticed some moisture under his feet on his last trip in the hole today. He also noticed it was a little harder to breathe.

"It's getting closer to our water, Grandpa. I don't think it will be too much longer. It's harder to breathe, too," Joe said as he took his seat next to Grandpa on the doorstep.

Day #6 began with the usual candle light check. Everything seemed to be about the same as yesterday. The dirt was getting heavier with the moisture. The pulley squeaked loudly with each bucket of dirt that came out. Dad had more turns in the well today, as he was getting anxious to get to the water.

"You can't rush it, Clyde. Just take your time. It won't be long now," Grandpa said as he noticed Dad's weary look after a longer than normal shift in the well. The depth of the well was now 60 feet at the day's end.

Day #7 was filled with excitement and anxiousness of all the diggers being ready to get this well finished. The candle test was more severe today. The candle light went out for the first time indicating that there were gases at the bottom. Elmer, being the oldest youngin and small in size, volunteered to go down to check out the problem. After a thorough candle check, everything was okay. Digging resumed on the same organized shifts. Dad, Elmer, Wayne, and Joe would work in the well while John and the others would keep the dirt emptied and out of the way.

Joe noticed a considerable amount of water on the well floor on his last two or three trips down. It was close now. Just before dark on Wayne's last turn in the well for the day, he suddenly got quiet.

"Something's wrong!" Dad hollered as he shined the flashlight down into the well. "Help me, Elmer. We need to pull Wayne up. I think he is out cold."

Grandpa and Joe jumped up to help. Soon they had pulled Wayne out. He was okay, just a little groggy, shaking his head. He lay down in the yard for a minute, but was alright. We had fished him out just in time.

"We'll wait till daylight to go back down," Dad said. "It looks like we're at about 70 feet now. We'll do a good candle check in the morning."

Day #8 started out with a thorough candle check. There was flickering, but the candle did not go out. "It could have been just a small amount of gases in there yesterday. I think it could also be that Wayne was dog tired at the time, too. That certainly could have affected him," Grandpa analyzed.

Dad agreed. "I think that could be it, Dad. Elmer, how about going down for a quick check?" Dad lowered Elmer down into the murky darkness of the well. A check with the candle proved that no problems seemed to be down there today.

The digging continued tirelessly by Dad's well crew. They really were a fast moving crew. Dad also spent time making sure that the well walls were firm. He would later get some reinforced concrete pipe for the top portion of the well. But first things first, as we had to find water before we wasted money on pipe.

It was about 10:00 a.m. on Joe's fourth shift in the well that the vein was hit. Water gushed all over Joe. He struggled mightily against the surging water.

"Help! Help!" Joe screamed as he struggled. The crew at ground level had seen what happened and were trying to rescue Joe from the rushing water. Joe continued to struggle as he splashed water furiously.

"Joe ! Joe! Wake up!" Elmer grabbed Joe by the shoulders. Joe had been flailing away in the bed and knocked over Elmer's full glass of water and got soaked. A glass of water can really get you good and wet. Elmer had already slipped out of bed and was dressing as Joe was finishing his dream. Elmer had forgotten to move his glass of water.

"Oh, no!" Joe said dejectedly. "Everything was so real. I was dreaming about digging our new well. We had just struck water."

"You struck water alright. My glass of water," Elmer said with a chuckle. Everyone got a big laugh out of Joe's dream at the breakfast table. Joe laughed with them as it was pretty funny, but deep down he was very disappointed.

"Thanks for the thought, Joe," Dad said. "Don't you worry about our water problem. We'll work it out."

Chapter 2
Mr. Madison

At school today, Joe and his classmates got to play baseball, an extra long recess period, as the weather was beautiful. It was 75 degrees, but Mr. Madison, Joe's teacher, knew that this weather would not last much longer.

Joe loved playing baseball. Mr. Madison's room would choose up and play. Joe always wanted to play on the team with Billy Swisher, who was nicknamed "Bull" or "Baby Bull." He was big and strong like a bull and could really smack the baseball farther than anyone else. Joe used to be the catcher. He could catch anything. If James Allen Shore was pitching, he did not want anyone else catching. James was wild and other catchers could not handle his wildness.

"I want "Bouncy" to catch for me," James said. "He can catch anything I throw and he never complains of my wildness." James had given Joe the nickname of "Bouncy" because James said that Joe bounced around like a ball all over the place. A team with Joe, James, and Billy would usually win. Joe had the speed and defense. James was the best pitcher and "Baby Bull" provided the power to keep the bases emptied.

Mr. Madison was a good teacher and loved to watch us play baseball. He would always umpire for us and settle any disputes without question. He was in charge of our class. No one ever questioned his authority. He was an imposing figure of about 6' 6" tall. Mr. Madison also was the assistant principal of the school.

After school, it was on to the packhouse to work on the tobacco. Dad's crew was making good progress and looked forward to finishing next week. The Ashburn crop and the Aunt Lucy crop along with Grandpa's crop were finished. All that remained were the upper leaves of Dad's crop. Dad updated his projection that all tobacco would be finished by Monday, October 13. That would mean Gurn Johnson would take the final load to market in Winston on Tuesday, October 14.

A long day at the packhouse on Friday and Saturday left only a few of the tips to complete Monday. When old #63 brought the school youngins home Monday, Gurn Johnson was backed up to Dad's packhouse loading up for an early trip to Winston on Tuesday.

"Boy, am I glad to see the last of this tobacco go!" Joe said as Gurn and Dad were putting the heavy tarp on the truck.

"Me, too," Dad said. "I just hope it keeps on selling good."

"I think it will, Clyde. This is good looking tobacco," Gurn said. "Maybe we can afford to get Joe some of that good coconut candy for his girlfriend."

"I don't have a girlfriend, Gurn. I told you that already," Joe said. Gurn was always teasing Joe.

Just as Gurn and Dad finished tarping the load, Wayne came running from the feed barn.

"Dad, you need to come and look at Thunder and Lightning. Something is wrong with them," Wayne said in an out-of-breath voice. The two hound dogs belonged to Elmer and Wayne. They had trained them to run rabbits. Thunder and Lightning made a good team. It was fun to hear them run a cottontail over the nearby hills.

Dad hurried to the area just past the feed barn to check on the two hounds.

"They've gone mad, Wayne! Run to the house and get my rifle. I'll have to shoot them," Dad said. "You youngins stay back out of their way. See how they're foaming at the mouth?"

Joe had never seen a dog go mad before, but had heard Dad and Grandpa Brown talk about mad dogs. He sure did not want to get bit by a mad dog. That would be a serious problem.

Wayne came running with Dad's rifle. Dad followed the two hounds down towards the big maple tree where he quickly shot each one of them through the head. It was sad, but it could not be helped. Thank God, Sandy had stayed away from the two hounds. The family sure did not want to lose their cow dog. He was like one of the family.

"Elmer, you and Wayne need to get your shovels and bury your dogs," Dad said. "I hate to have to shoot them, but they were dangerous to Sandy and to all of us. I hope you both understand."

"We understand, Dad," Elmer said and Wayne nodded his head. Joe and John went along to help Elmer and Wayne with the burying.

Dad left out at 3:00 a.m. on Tuesday morning with Gurn to sell the last of the 1952 crop of tobacco. Dad and Gurn were old buddies who used to play baseball together. Gurn married Mitt Pardue, Dad's cousin. Mom and Dad used to double date with Gurn and Mitt years ago. It would be an all day trip for Dad and Gurn. They probably would be home about 9:00 p.m. tonight.

Supper was finished and all the youngins were in bed before Dad got home a few minutes past 9:00 p.m. The famous coconut candy would have to wait until tomorrow after school.

"The tobacco sold real good," Dad told Mom as he ate a late supper that Mom had warmed up for him. "I wish we had some more to sell." Soon Mom and Dad turned in after a long day. There were lots of long days on the farm.

Molasses Time

On Wednesday morning, Dad, Elmer, and Grandpa Brown started on their cane fields after the youngins had left for school. The cane week was a fun time around Grandpa Brown's. Dad and Grandpa went in together to raise cane which when it was finished would be that natural sweetener called molasses. Joe loved the few days of getting the cane ready to become molasses.

After school, Wayne, Rose, Joe, and John joined Grandpa, Dad, and Elmer in stripping the leaves or fodder off the cane stalks. The stalks had been cut and hauled to Grandpa's cane mill area to strip. It took over two full days to get the cane stripped and through the mill to turn the cane stalks into juice to cook.

Dad's crew quit early on Wednesday night as they went to prayer meeting at Mineral Springs Baptist Church. Mom and Dad were faithful to church and set a good example for their youngins.

Early Thursday morning, the cane crew was back at it. By the time the school youngins got home, the cane pile was almost gone. Much of the cane had been juiced by the one horse mill, which was pulled by Grandpa's faithful horse, Old Sam. Cooking would start at first light on Friday and would cook nonstop until late Saturday evening.

On Friday morning as the school youngins were getting on the bus, they could smell the molasses starting to cook. Elmer was feeding the last cane stalks through the mill. The hard work was over now. The rest of the cane-molasses annual cooking would be waiting around for the sweet smell to get sweeter. Grandpa's mill was set up close to Brown Road and everyone who drove by got a whiff of the 'lasses cooking and usually stopped to talk. Farm folks were just plain good people.

As custom was, Grandpa Brown stayed with the cooking until Friday night at midnight. He had plenty of help keeping wood to the fire. Wayne, Joe, John, and cousins Lyman and Jimmy stayed with Grandpa and loved every minute of it. What fun it was to spend time with Grandpa! We all thought that Grandpa was the smartest person in the world. He certainly was the funniest man when he got to telling his stories.

At midnight, Dad, Uncle Nelson, and Elmer took over the cooking of the 'lasses. Grandpa and all the tired youngins went home and hit the sack to get at least a few hours of sleep before the big day tomorrow, or was it today? It was now past midnight.

"See ya'll in the morning," Dad said as he stirred the cooking and skimmed off some of the foam over the top.

Saturday was a big day. Joe stayed around the cooking with Grandpa after he had finished his chores. Dad, Elmer, and Wayne worked until noon around the barn. There was always plenty of work to do.

By noontime Grandpa's place was getting crowded. It was about the same crowd every year, but a few new faces would show up each year. In addition to Grandpa, Grandma, and Dad's family, others in attendance were Annie Sue, Troy and their one year old Terry, Mary Lee, Allen and their two year old Betty Jo and baby Nickey, Uncle Lamar's family, Uncle Nelson, Aunt Jo, Gray, Fay, Wiley Pinnix, Paul Dobbins, Leck and Ida Groce, Ferd and Mattie Cheek, Gurn and Mitt Johnson, Aunt Lucy Pardue, Uncle Johnny Brown, Uncle Lonnie Brown, Farmer Brown, Mr. and Mrs. Shore, and Bobbie Jane. Pastor Myers came by for a few minutes later in the evening as Dad had promised him a big jar of molasses. What a good day it turned out to be for the cooking and socializing! Just call it good country fun.

Grandpa was happy as the 'lasses were dipped out of the vat and put into gallon jars. He would divide the cooking with Dad and then start selling immediately. Grandpa lit up one of his long cigars and enjoyed himself. He always had a chew of Brown Mule chewing tobacco in his jaw, but the cigar seemed to be a sort of "well done" to the end of the cane-molasses week. A lot of hard work was now being enjoyed.

"Thank you all for coming by to visit with us. I hope you enjoy your molasses as much as I enjoy mine. Come on back when you need some more. We have plenty," Grandpa said as he was making his rounds telling everyone goodbye. It was getting late, past bedtime for hardworking country folks.

Dad's crew made their way down the winding driveway to the house. It was bath time, being today was Saturday.

"Can we wait till tomorrow for our baths, Mom?" Joe asked as he was beat.

"No, we need to get our baths quickly," Mom said. "We don't want to go to church tomorrow dirty. Do we?"

Soon the baths were finished and no one had to be told to go to bed. Lights were out and the whole crowd was asleep right away

It was Sunday morning and Joe looked forward to a day of rest. He planned to snooze this evening after church. He had a hard time staying awake during preaching which brought about a thump on the head from Dad. It certainly got your attention when Dad thumped you with his thumping finger. Dad's hands were huge and when he thumped you like a watermelon, you would sit up and take note.

"I think we all need a long nap this evening," Dad said on the way home. "We were sleepy in church this morning, weren't we?"

"I know I was," Joe admitted. He was glad for one time that Ralph Winters hadn't mentioned coming home with them today. Joe was too tired and the cool wind with a threat of rain made for a perfect afternoon nap.

Mom served a tasty Sunday dinner of pinto beans, taters, and biscuits topped off with an all time favorite of Joe's, a sweet potato saunker. Everyone carried on about how good this plain country dinner was. The pinto beans and biscuits were enough for Joe, but the saunker filled him all the way to the top.

"This saunker sure is musty," Dad said. "I must have some more." This saying was one of Dad's favorites. "I can't get enough of them sweet taters."

"It's my favorite saunker, Mom," Elmer said.

"Mine, too!" rang out from all around the table. It seems like all of Mom's family thought as Joe did about the saunker.

"I'm glad you like it," Mom said with a smile. She loved to cook and simply bubbled over when her family bragged on her cooking.

We always appreciated Mom's cooking and made a point to tell her often.

"Mom, I bet you could get a job cooking for the President as good as you cook," Rose said.

"We sure don't want her to do that," John spoke up. "She has a fulltime job here with us. The President would probably want her to move to Washington, D.C."

"I don't have any plans to move anywhere," Mom said, as she seemed to be enjoying this conversation a whole lot. "I have a fulltime job here with my family."

Chapter 3
1952 Elections

"Wonder who is going to be our next president?" Wayne asked. The presidential election was a little over two weeks off. "We'll definitely have a new president 'cause Truman could not run again."

"President Truman is not running, but he could have run," Elmer corrected Wayne. "A president can be elected for two terms. Mr. Truman's first term was when he served the last three years of President Roosevelt's term. Mr. Truman was only elected one time in 1948."

"Oh, I forgot that," Wayne said.

"I think it will be a tight race," Joe said. "General Dwight Eisenhower and Governor Adali Stevenson of Illinois both think they're going to win. I think President Truman shot himself in the foot about the Korean War, especially when he fired my hero General MacArthur. I think that move alone kept him from running again."

The presidential race was a struggle within the Brown and Proctor families. Grandpa Brown was a die hard Republican and Grandpa Proctor was a die hard Democrat. They simply would not give on their convictions. They voted for the party and not for the man.

Joe grew up siding with the Democrats because Mom and Dad voted democratic, but Joe didn't usually think too much of the liberal candidates the democrats ran. He also did not like General Eisenhower. He saw him as another politician who would always want to negotiate or give away rather than stand firm in our beliefs. "Ike", as General Eisenhower was called, promised to end the war in

Korea. That promise also scared Joe. Ike's fast climb through the ranks was too political and was not achieved through military accomplishments as was General MacArthur's.

The election was the subject of many discussions at school in Mr. Madison's class. The class was about evenly divided between General Eisenhower and Governor Stevenson. Joe always argued his point about not liking General Eisenhower's point about ending the war.

"What will General Eisenhower give up to end the war?" Joe asked. "We have lost too many lives over there to give in to the Communist demands."

"You have a good argument there, Joe," Mr. Madison replied. "What do you think Governor Stevenson would do?"

"That's the tough part of it, Mr. Madison. I don't think Governor Stevenson knows what he would do," Joe said. "I'm not very excited about him. My man, General MacArthur, would be firm and strong in his pro-American views, but, of course, he was not nominated, so we will never know what he would have done."

Joe continued, "I think General Eisenhower will probably win simply because of the promise of ending the war. It does not help the democratic cause that Governor Stevenson did not campaign and only agreed to run after the democrats could not agree on any other candidate during their convention."

"You make some very good points, Joe. It sounds like you have been listening to Gabriel Heater on the radio news. We all need to keep up on the current events and especially this important election," Mr. Madison said.

Over the next two weeks, the presidential election was discussed at school, at home, at church, and about everywhere people would gather. It was a hot topic. As Election Day got nearer, most people were predicting a win by the Ike-Dick ticket. General Eisenhower's running mate was Richard Nixon. Their campaign definitely had more energy and seemed to be more appealing.

On Tuesday, November 4, 1952, the people spoke and elected a new president. Mom and Dad drove down to West Yadkin School to vote. They allowed all the youngins to stay up a little later tonight to see if we could get any word on how the election was shaping up.

Gabriel Heater was reporting that General Eisenhower was in the lead and would be hard to catch. At 9:00 p.m., Mom and Dad told the youngins to turn off the radio and get to bed.

"You can find out who won in the morning," Mom said. "I'm sure we'll have a winner by then."

Sure enough, at breakfast, Gabriel Heater was telling about the decisive victory by General Eisenhower. Governor Stevenson had made a concession speech during the night. All that was left now was to see what the final margin of victory would be for the republicans.

When Joe got to school, Mr. Madison greeted him. "Well, you had the election figured out, Joe. I'm sure the results did not surprise you any."

"No, it turned out about the way I thought it would. The democrats did not stand much of a chance. Their candidate simply did not get out and get the exposure that they needed to win," Joe said.

The election was discussed in detail by the class. The classmates who had brothers in Korea and in other places in service seemed to be happy. They hoped that President Eisenhower would make good his promise to end the war. But they, like most of the rest of the class, were leery of any promise that a politician made on the campaign trail. Promises seemed to be forgotten once the election was over.

Corn Harvest

It was corn harvesting time again. Dad had his work crew on the move early after a hardy breakfast of biscuits, gravy, eggs, and some good store bought canned sausage. Joe counted six biscuits and was filled up for a hard morning of work. Mom always did a good job of getting Dad's crew a good nourishing meal before they hit the fields to work.

Dad drove the wagon with Old Bill laboring faithfully as he made the way down by the big maple tree and up on the hill to the 4 acres of corn. It was a good crop. Rainfall had been plentiful this year. Dad had a full crew of corn pickers: Elmer, Wayne, Rose, Joe, John, and Jane. As usual, it would take two Saturdays to pull all the corn. The pulling was becoming more and more of a production line type harvesting each year. With 7 people pulling, it did not take as long to get the wagon full. Dad's crew worked happily as they talked and joked with each other constantly.

"Why does this ear of corn have all this smutty stuff in it, Dad?" Jane asked as she had the black powdery substance al over her hands. She did not like the looks of this stuff.

"That's a disease that gets on the stalk, honey. The ear that has this stuff in it is not any good," Dad said.

"Is it true that Indians used this stuff as war paint in the old days, Dad?" Joe asked with a serious face.

"It could be, Joe, but I'm not sure. I imagine they used a lot of different things," Dad said.

"There must have been a bunch of Indians here at one time as many arrowheads as we see in this field," Rose said.

"Can you just imagine Indians being here and down around the creek about the time Daniel Boone came up Boone trail which is now Highway 421?" Elmer said. "Indians always put their villages close to a good water supply and where there was plenty of game to hunt for their food supply."

"Boy! It sure would have been neat to live in them days, wouldn't it?" Wayne allowed.

"It wouldn't have been so neat if the Injuns were after your scalp, boy," Dad said. "They would have really liked to get a hold of your wavy blond scalp."

Everyone laughed as Wayne reached up to feel of his wavy hair. The first wagon load was ready to go to the corn pile in front of the corncrib. Dad's crew walked over to the house to help unload it as the wagon was a heavy enough load without everyone piling on the wagon. The wagon squeaked and groaned as Old Bill pulled up the hill and into the barnyard.

Dad and Elmer started out with the big scoop shovels unloading the wagon. The big shovels were a lot faster unloading the wagon than the old, smaller shovels used in years past. Soon Wayne and Joe manned the shovels, making quick work of the unloading. It was helpful to have a good work crew that could work together to get the job done.

Back in the field, the conversation turned back to the Indians that used to roam around in years past.

"Dad, is it true that we learned how to raise corn from the Indians?" John asked as he dumped a large handful of good sized ears of corn into the wagon.

"Yeah, I think history has taught us that the Indians did teach us how to grow corn," Dad said. "They also helped us with many other things, too. As time passed, Indians married into the white culture, bringing knowledge of farming with them. The Indian man had it made. The men hunted and the women did all the work in the field. Somewhere along the way, we did not pick up that part of the Indian culture."

Soon wagonload #2 was ready to go to the barnyard. The wagon was unloaded just as Mom called out for dinnertime. One call was enough. Everyone was hungry and headed to the house.

Mom served a good dinner of pinto beans, taters, creamed corn from her canned closet, biscuits, and a good surprise of a sweet potato saunker. Mom was full of surprises. She was cooking for Sunday dinner and decided to make two sweet potato saunkers at the same time. Mom prayed asking God to bless our food and our family.

Joe quickly ate pinto beans and sopped the bean soup with his biscuits. He ate a hardy meal, topped off with the saunker and was ready for an evening in the cornfield.

Rose stayed at the house to help Mom cook and clean to get ready for Sunday.

"Clyde, don't forget that the boys need to get their haircut this evening," Mom said. "Poppa is expecting ya'll about 5:00 p.m."

"I'm glad you reminded me. I'd forgotten about the haircuts," Dad answered.

The conversation in the cornfield stayed with the Indians that were using our land years ago.

"Dad, do you think the Indians used our old spring way back when?" Joe asked. The old spring that Grandpa and Grandma Brown used when they lived over in the cornfield was down at the south end of the cornfield.

"Yeah, it's quite possible that they did. Your Grandpa Brown said that it's been over here as long as he can remember. People tend to build houses around an established water supply, so they won't have to tote water too far," Dad said.

Joe glanced down to the ground in the corn row and found two nice looking arrowheads. He picked them up, examining them and showing them off. Joe and John were always finding arrowheads in the fields on the farm.

"Boy, wouldn't it be something to have to attach this arrowhead to an arrow to shoot and kill food to eat?" Joe asked. "It's so much simpler now to shoot that food with your old 22 rifle, isn't is, Dad?"

"It sure is, Joe. We think we have it rough now and we do in a lot of ways, but we have it easy compared to the real old days," Dad said.

Wagonload #3 was on the way to the corn pile by 2:30 p.m. Dad's crew continued to make good time. Apparently, the Indian history lesson was not slowing up the work crew too much. The corn pile was continuing to grow with each load from the field.

Wagonload #4 was back in the field shortly. The quick working crew would have it full in a little while.

"We do have it a lot better than the Indians as you say, Dad," Elmer said. "They did not use animals to farm like we do. They did most of the work by hand. I guess they pulled their own plows. Of course, they had a more abundant supply of meat to hunt in those days and did not have to use garden food as much as we do. We do not have the game to hunt that they did."

"You're right about that, Elmer. Boy, wouldn't it be good to have all the game to hunt now days!" Dad said as he clucked to Old Bill to move the wagon up to the end of the row. The wagon was filled and running over. The field was about half finished. The rest of the corn would be pulled next Saturday.

The wagon was scoop shovel unloaded in short order and Dad headed the 1950 Plymouth down the road to Grandpa and Grandma Proctor's for their six week haircut. The car was packed full of Browns as Mom and the girls went along for the visit. Mom did not miss an opportunity to go to see her poppa and momma. She did not get to see them very often.

Dad drove out Brown Road to Highway 421 where he turned east to go down past Marler to Asbury Road to Steelman Road to Grandpa's driveway.

"I don't think he's mowed these weeds all summer," Dad said as he drove down the winding, washboard road across three water furrows and turned right to go by the north side of the house and park under the big oak trees.

Grandpa and Grandma heard us drive up and met us at the back door. It was a pretty nice day for mid November, so Grandpa still planned to do his barber work on the screened in back porch.

"How are ya'll doing?" Grandma asked as she made the rounds and gave everyone a hug.

"We're doing good, Grandma. How are you?" Rose said as all the youngins made their way into Grandma's kitchen for their usual treat of them tasty biscuits. Grandma did not even ask. She just opened up the warmer compartment of the stove and got out her biscuits.

"How are they?" Grandma asked.

"They're good, of course. They always are," Joe said as he started on biscuit #2.

Grandpa, who cut hair for about everyone in the community, including the legendary Bones McKinney, Wake Forest basketball coach, started out as usual with Elmer and Wayne. They were more particular with their hair and only wanted a trim. It seemed like the girls wanted to run their hands through the curls and waves or so Joe teased them. Joe was next and got his usual crew cut, as did John. They liked to keep their haircut like most of the baseball players they idolized. Danny was next and wanted his hair cut the same as Joe and John.

"Don't give me one of them Eisenhower haircuts, Grandpa. I want a little of hair left on top," Danny said.

Grandpa laughed. "I won't give you the Ike cut this time, Danny." President-elect Eisenhower was baldheaded. Danny had seen his picture in the newspaper enough to know what kind of haircut he did not want. Dad was last and got his usual crew cut, also. He paid Grandpa the three quarters for the six haircuts and sat back talking to Grandpa as Elmer grabbed the whisk broom and dustpan to clean up the mess.

"Well, we're in for a rough time over the next four years," Dad said. "I wonder how President Eisenhower is going to work out the end to the war. We've heard a lot about it on the radio. Now he's got to show us what he plans to do."

"That sure ought to be interesting," Grandpa said. "I just hope we don't give everything back to the Communists that we fought to win. That would be a shame for all the lost lives of our soldiers."

Soon, Dad had his crew headed back home to do the chores and get their Saturday night baths. This bath was one that Joe looked forward to as the loose hairs were scratching his neck and back something fierce.

Chores were completed in quick fashion with baths and supper to follow. Dad's crew ate quietly and was in bed asleep immediately. It had been a long, hard day.

Sunday was a cool, overcast day. After church and a good Sunday dinner, everyone got a good nap making it a perfect day of rest. It was nice just to lie around and relax. Farm folks did not have many relaxing days.

The Story Teller

After their naps, all the youngins kind of gathered up at Grandpa Brown's house. Grandpa had finished his nap and was sitting on the front porch. It was not warm, but the fresh air felt good. Grandpa had on his lightweight jacket as did the youngins.

"Hey there, youngins!" Grandpa said as he reared back in his chair and put in a big chew of Brown Mule chewing tobacco.

"Hey, Grandpa!" they all sang out. They were soon joined by Uncle Lamar's youngins, Lyman, Jimmy, Lorene, and Avalon. The front porch had filled up quickly. Everyone was ready for Grandpa's stories. All he needed to start his stories was an audience. He had it now and was ready to go. Grandpa began.

"I remember the time when me, Lamar, Clyde, and Guy were working down in the bottom land near the rock. We were clearing land, cutting trees, and getting ready to have a new-ground section that used to be all woods. Clearing land was hard work. We had Old Jack, my horse at the time, down there helping us snake the logs out and pulling stumps out. We had a fire going to clean out some of the brush and undergrowth. It was in a spring of the year, right before tobacco setting time. On this one Saturday, we ran into about every problem you could think of. We uncovered a bed of copperhead snakes. Clyde just walked right into them. They were hissing and trying to bite him on his legs. It's a good thing he had on his work shoes and leggings. I bet we killed 25 copperhead snakes if we killed one. What a bunch of snakes! Then we ran into a big hornet's nest. Boy, did we make them mad! They chased us all the way to the creek. We all jumped in. We had no other choice but to get stung crazy. We all got stung a couple of times, but once we got in the hole at the rock, we were safe. At least we led the pesky varmints away from Old Jack. If they had got to him, they would have stung him to death. We later went back to their nest and soaked them in gasoline and burnt them out. It was late in the day and we were about ready to call it a day."

"All of a sudden, the wind got up and we had a wild fire on our hands," Grandpa continued. "The fire from the hornet's nest blew down through the woods and proceeded to burn till way past dark. It burned a couple of acres. We finally controlled it after the wind died down. Boy, were we tired! Clearing a new ground is hard work, but fighting a fire is the hardest work I've ever done."

"That sounded like a rough day, Grandpa," Elmer said. "That must have been before Dad and Uncle Lamar got married."

"Yeah, it was Elmer. Your dad was probably 15 or 16 years old at the time," Grandpa said.

"Did I ever tell you the story about the boys that were swimming over at the Caudle's mill pond one day when my Grandpa Henry James was a youngin? Grandpa told me about it. There were about 6 or 8 boys there swimming. They could not dive in because there were some stumps in the pond. The water was higher than normal at the time. You could not see the stumps." Grandpa continued, "One of the older boys who was swimming here for the first time was boasting about how good he could dive. Grandpa heard him and warned him of the hidden stumps. The bragger continued to talk big about how he was going to do a big belly flop into the pond. Other boys continued to warn him about the stumps, but he would not listen. He was determined to get himself hurt. He pranced to the big stump that made a perfect diving board."

"He said, 'Watch me do a giant belly flop.' He made a high jump up into the air intending to flop into the deep waters in front of him. He landed on top of one of the sharp pointed stumps. The stump went straight through his belly. He was laid out there on the stump, barely under water drowning while bleeding profusely. He died right there as the other boys could not get him off the stump. Grandpa always talked about what a horrible sight that was. He never forgot it as long as he lived."

"Now that was a sad story," Grandpa said. "I'll tell you a funny one now to quit on. It was right after Molly and me got married. We were attending a baptismal service over at the same mill pond. We had a traveling preacher that was filling in as pastor at Oak Grove. He would be here on the first and third Sunday mornings each month. We had a few people who were waiting for the weather to warm up to be baptized. I guess there were probably about eight people to go under the water that day. It was a hot, dog day in August, the perfect day for a baptizing at the mill pond. We, as usual, had a very big crowd of people that Sunday evening. The choir director led the crowd in a couple of songs," Grandpa continued:

"Shall we gather at the river,
The beautiful, the beautiful river,
Gather with the saints at the river
That flows by the throne of God.

Just a closer walk with Thee,
Grant it, Jesus, is my plea;
Daily walking close to Thee,
Let it be, dear Lord, let it be."

Grandpa went on with the story. "The traveling parson started into the water, feeling his way out to about waist deep water. He motioned to Deacon Cheek to help "Old Lady" Nicks to where the parson was standing. The parson reached out to take the hand of the first baptismal candidate. She grasped the parson's hand as she did not like the idea of being in water this deep. She had already made the statement known that she could not swim a lick. The seven other ladies waiting to be baptized watched nervously as "Old Lady" Hicks was not moving any farther. They were now in water only about halfway between knee deep and waist deep."

"'We've got to go out a little deeper, Mrs. Hicks,' the parson said. 'We don't want to bump your head in the mud on the bottom of the pond.' Holding Old Lady Hicks' hand, the two of them made a big step towards the center of the pond. Then the weirdest thing happened that you could imagine. The both of them stepped into a hole and disappeared totally from sight. Everyone stood around with their mouths wide open. Some of the men and boys snickered. The women were saying, 'Oh, oh, oh.'"

"Deacon Cheek dove into the area where the parson and Old Lady Hicks were last seen and came up in a few seconds with the sputtering woman. The traveling parson also appeared coughing and spewing out water. He stayed in the water while Deacon Cheek helped the woman to dry land here she was determined to stay forever. She never got baptized."

"The traveling parson motioned for the other ladies to come in to be baptized. They wanted no part of it. They backed away from the bank of the pond. The baptismal service was over for the day. It was the first time I had ever gone to a baptismal service and no one was baptized. It was so funny," Grandpa said.

"Boy, I'd like to have seen that!" Lyman declared with a giggle.

It was church time. Stories were over for the day. We all headed down to the house to get ready for church. Wonder if they're going to baptize anyone tonight, Joe thought.

On Monday, Dad pulled all of the popcorn and had it shucked and in the corncrib by the time the school youngins were home.

"We've got a bunch of popcorn for this winter," Elmer told Joe as everyone was finding a seat by the corn pile. Mom, Dad, and Elmer had been shucking corn all day. The shucking would continue all week for Dad's crew before finishing the pile on Friday evening.

"This is a good corn year, Dad, isn't it?" Wayne said. "We don't have many nubbins at all." A nubbin is a runt ear of corn.

"No! It turned out to be a good year," Dad said. "I just hope we can keep dry weather till we get the rest of the corn in and shucked."

The weather was much colder on Saturday as Dad's crew made their way to the cornfield. They seemed to work faster today to stay warm.

It took five loads to finish the field today. That was a very good yield of corn. It would keep Dad's crew in cornbread and milk for the coming year. Who could want anything better to eat?

The corn shucking would continue on Monday. It would be an all week job. The weather was getting raw cold by the week's end. Dad built a fire at the end of the corn pile for all of his hands to warm up. Corn shucking could be rough on knuckles, especially now that it was so cold.

Chapter 4
Grandpa's Last Shucking

"I hope the weather warms up some by Friday for Grandpa's corn shucking," Joe said. This was going to be the last year Grandpa was going to raise a big corn crop. His health was not good and he had slowed down considerably. So this was going to be the finale of Grandpa's corn shuckings. What a sad thing that it has to end, Joe thought. He hoped that the weather would cooperate and Grandpa would have the best corn shucking ever this year.

It did and he did. On Friday, it seemed like everyone in the whole community turned out, especially when they heard this shucking was Grandpa's last one. The weather was clear and about 55 degrees.

The crowd was made up of Grandpa, Grandma, Uncle Lamar's family, Dad's crew, Aunt Daisy's family, Uncle Nelson's family, Annie Sue, Troy, Mary Lee, Allen, Farmer Brown, the Shores, Wiley, Sarah and May Pinnix, Grandpa and Grandma Proctor, Uncle Johnny Brown, Uncle Lonnie Brown, Gene and Jett Groce, Charlie Groce, Walter Groce, Leck and Ida and girls, Pastor Myers, Gurn and Mitt Johnson, Edgar Johnson, and many other folks.

The corn pile was high when Joe saw it on Thursday evening, but by Friday noon, it had decreased considerably. Stories were flying around the corn pile, too. That was the best part of the whole day, Joe thought, even though he loved the food. The stories would go on forever.

Wiley Pinnix was telling the story about the time when the Revenuers came to bust up his still back when he was only 18 years old. Wiley said, "I was just making a batch now and then for medicinal purposes. It was over in behind my house down in the thicket. It was hid real good, I thought. But my downfall was that the brew smelled so good, it was easy to trace. One of the agents named George had a keen nose and found his way to my still and walked right up on us. The other two agents with him were wandering around searching and never did find us. It just so happens that 'hound dog' nose sniffed us out. I was totally surprised when George found us. He was getting ready to fire three shots into the air, a signal for the other two agents to come on in to help him bust up the still."

"I said, 'George, before you break up my work of art, I want you to take a sip with me and tell me how good you think it is. Then you can pow, pow, pow, and bust it up.' I had sipped with George before and knew he liked good old corn liquor. Well, George and me had a sip and a sip and kept on sipping all day long. By then, George was in no shape to pow, pow, pow my still. He said, 'That's the best 'shine I've ever put to my lips. I can't possibly destroy it.' He left and I never had anymore problems with the Revenuers." Wiley reared back his nail keg seat and laughed.

Walter Groce spoke up with one of his tales. "That reminds me of one of my many trips out across the Midwest. I have been thrown off the best of trains. Of course, I hobo everywhere I go. This one time I was headed to Chicago from Indianapolis, Indiana. The railroad agents were hot on my trail. It was a game with me to stay one step ahead of them. I have to sleep occasionally and when I do the agents have their best opportunity to catch me. Well, they tossed me off the train in an un-Christian manner. I landed in the biggest thicket you could ever find. I was stunned from the fall and wandered right into a moonshine still in the western part of Indiana."

"The moon shiners did not receive me with open arms. They thought that I was a Revenuer, pretending to be a hobo. They tied me up and talked all night about what they were going to do with me. I was starving, but they would not give me anything to eat or drink. 'Why should we feed you when we're going to shoot you in the morning?' one of them said."

"I did a lot of fast talking throughout the night to anyone who would hear me. Something I said or did convinced someone that I was not a Revenuer. They were good hard working people and fed me good before letting me go. They apologized to me for treating me unkindly, but they said they had to be careful. They had seen agents in before pretending to be hobos, traveling salesmen, and many other walks of life. I told them I understood and did not have any hard feelings towards them. But I got out of there as soon as I could and caught the next train going west."

Joe loved hearing Uncle Walter's stories. He couldn't get much corn shucked as he seemed to sit there spellbound.

The corn pile was nearly gone as Grandpa rang the supper bell at 5:00 p.m. "I appreciate all of you helping me with my corn shucking this year and all the many years. Some of you have been here with me for 30 years now. This will be my last corn shucking as my health is not as good as it once was. Thanks for your help over the years. Thanks for your friendship. Thanks for all the good food you have brought today. It means so much to me. I'll ask Preacher Myers to say our blessings before we eat."

Pastor Myers prayed, "Heavenly Father, thank you for your many blessings of life. Thank you for this good time of work, fellowship, and food. Thank you for providing. We pray that you'd bless this food in Jesus' name. Amen. Amen."

Amen's rang out all over the yard as the crowd surrounded the makeshift tables filled with about every food you could imagine. Joe hurried to get two ham biscuits, a chicken leg, pinto beans, cornbread, biscuits, and followed that up with chocolate pie, bread pudding, and sweet potato saunker. It was a great end to the many years of Grandpa's corn shucking. In a way, it was sad. All good things certainly must come to an end, whether one likes it or not. Joe did not like the idea that his Grandpa Brown's health was failing and he could not continue to do the many things that he truly loved to do.

The corn pile was finished soon after the supper ended. Grandpa's help carried the corn into the corncrib. Grandpa also had a bountiful year of corn. He would be able to eat all the corn mush that he wanted.

Dad's crew walked down the winding driveway in darkness. It was about 9:00 p.m. They were all saddened by the finality of Grandpa's last corn shucking.

"It's so sad," Jane said as she rode on Elmer's back.

"It sure is," Rose continued.

"We sure do have a lot of good memories that will go on forever," Joe said as he and John walked arm and arm, as was their custom, except when they were fighting.

"Grandpa Brown is a giant among men," Mom said. "He is one of the best men and sweetest man I ever have known. I guess that's why I married and love his son," she continued as she looked at Dad.

"I'm sure glad today is Friday and not bath day," Wayne said happily as he made his way into the house. He was ready for bed as was all of the family.

"Ya'll get a good night's sleep," Dad said. "We'll finish the corn shucking in the morning and then do some more work on the chicken house." Dad had built a good sized chicken house out of blocks and intended to raise chickens to sell. These chickens would be another way to make some much needed money to help make ends meet.

"Happy 19th wedding anniversary Mom and Dad," the youngins rang out at 6:00 a.m. at the breakfast table. It was November 22.

"Thank you, all!" Mom said. "We appreciate you remembering us."

It was an otherwise quiet breakfast for Dad's crew who ate a hardy meal and went back to the corn pile to finish up the shucking. By midmorning, all the corn was shucked and in the corncrib.

The Chicken House

Rose and Jane went to the house to help Mom, while Dad and the boys went to the chicken house to try to get the house ready for a load of baby chicks. The house was coming along. The blocks had been laid and the roof was finished. The front windows had to be completed and the house would be ready as soon as Dad got a couple loads of shavings from the sawmill. Within a week, the baby chicks could be here.

The heaters, feeders, and watering equipment were in the back part of the house. The lights had been hung and would furnish the much needed light to see how to tend to the chicks, even at night.

Dad made a trip to the saw mill and got two loads of shavings delivered after dinner. The house was ready to go. A card in the mail today said 5,000 chickens would be delivered on Monday, November 24.

The chickens were delivered Monday morning while the youngins were at school. Dad and Elmer got the equipment out for the chicks that were kept in one end of the chicken house for the first week as they were so small. Joe hurried home from the bus stop and went straight to the chicken house. All of the other youngins were just as anxious to see the chicks.

"Oh, how cute they are!" Jane said as she picked up one to hold.

"Look at all the different colors, Jane," Rose said.

It would be Rose, Joe, and John's job to feed and water the chicks when they got home from school. Dad and Elmer would tend to them while school was in session. So Rose and Joe were back to toting water. At least it was not all the way up the hill this time. They would tote it from the spigot that Dad put in over near the packhouse.

As long as the chicks were new and did not eat and drink very much, they were a lot of fun. But soon they started to run through a lot of food and water and were quite a chore. Dad's plan was to keep the chicks for 16 weeks and then to sell them back to Holly Farms. Dad then would have one week to clean the chicken house and to start all over again. This job would be a year round job and would help provide much needed funds to help with the expenses of raising a houseful of kids.

In Sunday, November 30, Wayne celebrated his 16th birthday. He was in the 10th grade at school and was quite a lady's man, or so he thought. He took pride each day to make sure his blond waves were combed just right. Was that the reason Georgia Seagraves was so sweet on him?

Basketball

The farmer's winter season started today. It was cold and windy, but not unbearable. At school, Mr. Madison took his class to the gym after dinner to play basketball. Joe loved to play basketball as he pretended to be one of the great Wake Forest players who played with Dickie Hemric in his All-American days there. Jack Williams played on that team and would later come to coach at West Yadkin.

Joe was always a good shooter and quick as a cat. He had a deadly set shot that was the hot shot in those days before the jump shot. Mr. Madison encouraged Joe and worked with him to improve his skills. It would pay off as Joe would get to play more in the gym next year when he was in the 7th grade.

"Keep practicing that set shot and your foul shots," Mr. Madison would say. "You're going to be a good ballplayer if I can get you out of the tobacco field long enough."

Joe listened and kept practicing. He did not have a basketball goal at home. He took an old 5 gallon bucket and knocked the bottom end out of it and nailed it to the old pine tree at the edge of the front yard. This setup helped Joe improve his shooting as the shot had to be perfect to go in the bucket.

Little sister Jane would help Joe by chasing balls and throwing them back to Joe to keep his routine going. It was a lot of fun. Anytime Joe and John had a minute out of the tobacco field, they were playing ball of some sort.

The month of December was a cool, damp month and Mr. Madison would often take his class to the gym to shoot baskets. Some of the class grew tired of it but Joe loved it. Donna Johnson and Joe would like to be paired together to shoot. Both of them loved basketball.

Mr. Madison also loved music. He had a quartet that was made up of students in his class. He was so proud of them and of the way they harmonized together. The quartet was made up of Billy "Bull" Swisher, Sue Wallace, Sylvia Trivette, and Donna Johnson. Mr. Madison worked with this group daily after dinner. He wanted them to have several Christmas songs ready before school let out for Christmas.

The group was pretty good, Joe admits. "Bull" Swisher had a great bass voice and he was only 11 years old. The harmony was best on the old Christmas favorite "Silent Night". This song really flowed for the quartet:

"Silent night! Holy night!
All is calm, all is bright
Round yon virgin mother and Child,
Holy Infant, so tender and mild.
Sleep in heavenly peace,
Sleep in heavenly peace."

They did several other songs, but "Silent Night" was their main event.

Mr. Madison was so proud of this quartet that he even had them sing "Silent Night" for one of his visitors who came to our class in mid February.

"Ya'll sing it real low now so the other classes won't hear us and think we're crazy and just now celebrating Christmas," he laughed.

The visitor was impressed and Mr. Madison was so pleased with his group. Mr. Madison had a way of getting the most out of his students in everything they did. He certainly was an encouragement to Joe. He, like many of Joe's teachers, was instrumental in shaping Joe's life and the values that worked with what he was taught at home and at his church.

Joe did not attend a Christian school. He went to a public school that had Christian teachers who believed God and helped their students have a fear of God and a respect for authority. These teachers and Mr. Wright, our principal, affected many lives for the better in their work at West Yadkin during the tough times of the 1950s.

Only one more week of school until the Christmas break! My, how time has flown this school year! Mr. Madison told the class of the Christmas party planned for next Friday. He gave details to each student what to bring. There would be plenty of cake, cookies, ice cream, candy, and pop. The only problem Joe saw about the party was that it was a long week away. He was ready now.

Each student was told to bring a $1 gift for exchange if they wanted to participate. The gift would be a gift that could be used by either boy or girl. It sure was going to be a fun time.

Meanwhile at church, practice had been going on for several weeks on the Christmas play. Elmer and Wayne had parts in the play while Rose, Joe, John, and Jane had minor parts and verses to memorize. The play was to be presented on Sunday night, December 21. Aubrey and Nell Martin were directing the play. This couple did so much at the church.

Joe loved both of them. Aubrey was the choir director, sang solos, and also sang with his wife, Nell, who had a beautiful alto voice. Mrs. Nell taught Joe and John in training union. Joe nicknamed her Mrs. Quarter. She always gave away 8 or 10 quarters each Sunday night for the youngins that had the quickest draw in the sword drills. Joe won his share of these quarters. That was a big thing for a little country boy that never had very much. He felt rich with three or four quarters in his pocket.

Finally after a cold, wet week of more good quality time playing basketball in the gym, party day arrived. All students brought goodies from home. Donna Johnson's mom, Sonja Royal's mom, and Nancy Reinhardt's mom brought more goodies in with plenty of pop. It was one of the best parties that Joe had attended. Of course, Mom sent her famous peanut butter cookies and chocolate candy. There were enough goodies to make sure everyone got their fill.

When the eating stopped, Mr. Madison showed off his prize quartet again. The parents in attendance had heard of the group, but this was the first time they had heard them sing. The parents were impressed.

"O come, all ye faithful, joyful and triumphant;
Come ye, O come ye to Bethlehem;
Come and behold Him, born the King of angels:
O come, let us adore Him,
O come, let us adore Him,
O come, let us adore Him, Christ, the Lord."

"Joy to the world! The Lord is come!
Let earth receive her King;
Let ev'ry heart prepare Him room
And heav'n and nature sing,
And heav'n and nature sing,
And heav'n, and heav'n and nature sing."

The quartet finished with "Silent Night" and the whole class sang "We Wish You a Merry Christmas" to the parents and to Mr. Wright who had slipped in to enjoy the good singing.

"Boy, your group sure sounds good, Mr. Madison," Mr. Wright said as he was leaving. "We need to get them to sing at our next PTA meeting."

"Thank you, Mr. Wright. We'd be happy to sing anytime you want us to. Just let us know so we can practice," Mr. Madison said happily.

Chapter 5
Christmas 1952

It was time to be dismissed until next year. The next school day would be January 1, 1953.

"You have a good Christmas, Mr. Madison," Joe said as he was leaving.

"Thank you, Joe. I hope you have a nice one. Shoot a few rabbits for me," Mr. Madison said. He knew that Joe loved to rabbit hunt.

"You have a good Christmas, Joe," Mr. Wishon said as Joe went down the hall. Mr. Wishon was the faithful school janitor who loved all students and they loved him in return. Everyone called him "Grandpa."

"I hope you and Mrs. Wishon have a good Christmas, too," Joe said as he went out into the cold, rainy evening.

Once Joe was on old #63, the bus was louder than normal. Everyone was excited to have almost two weeks out of school. Even the cold rain couldn't dampen the spirits today. The chatter continued all the way home.

Later on tonight, the slow rain changed to a fluffy snow. It was beautiful as the large, shapely flakes fell with the porch lights piercing through the cold night air. The snow was a surprise as the WSJS radio Shell oil reporter had not mentioned snow in his 6:00 p.m. forecast.

"I guess the weatherman doesn't know everything after all," Mom said as she stood and watched the artistic artic flakes coming down.

"No, they don't get it right every time, but they do a pretty good job, though. I don't know how us farmers could get along without them," Dad said.

"They have a tough job, don't they?" Elmer asked anyone who was listening.

"Yes, it's a rough job, alright. They can never make all the people happy," Wayne said.

"They'll make me happy if it keeps this up until Christmas," Rose said. "I want a white Christmas."

"A white Christmas would be nice, but I don't want to mess Santa up," Jane joined in.

"Don't you think Santa can make it in snow?" Joe asked.

"Santa can make it through any kind of weather," John said as he looked towards Mom and Dad for their approval of what he said. Mom and Dad smiled and then broke into a laugh as Danny was trying to catch the snowflakes through the window of the front room.

"I like snow. Snow is pretty. I like it," Danny said.

"It's bedtime," Dad spoke as the snow watching was over for the night.

Rabbit Tracks

Saturday morning was cold, but the snow had stopped falling during the night. The accumulation was about four inches. The sky was overcast, but the WSJS weatherman, who could not predict this snow, said it was all over for now. How could he know it was over? He didn't even know it was coming.

Joe got out before breakfast to feed and water the chickens in the chicken house. He noticed fresh rabbit tracks around the barnyard. It sure did look like a good time to track some rabbits.

Maybe Dad was planning to bring it up anyway, but the look on his face when there wasn't any meat for breakfast really did it.

"I think we need to track some cottontails this morning, boys," Dad said. "We could sure use some meat for breakfast until we kill our hogs. We'll kill them next week if it's cold enough."

"Sounds good to me," Joe said. He was always ready to go hunting, whether it was rabbit, squirrel, coon, or possum. He only liked to eat rabbits and squirrel, though. Mom cooked a coon one time and it was tough as shoe leather and tasteless. She said she did not plan to cook another coon as long as she lived. As for possums, Dad's family did not like the sound of possum pie. We'll just let the Beverly Hillbillies have them all.

After breakfast, Dad and the boys headed out in the snow to do some tracking. The sun was trying to break through the gray clouds. It looked like it was going to warm up. It was not very cold now. Dad told Sandy to stay at the house as he would scare away all rabbits if he went along.

Elmer was carrying Dad's 22 rifle. Dad was a dead-eye shot and had the best vision Joe had ever seen. He could sure spot a rabbit sitting in its bed.

Dad already had a set of tracks in his view. After snow, the rabbits would get out and play. You had to pick out a set of tracks and follow them as they left the playing area. Dad tracked this rabbit down by the southwest corner of the chicken house. He spotted the cottontail sitting in a small thicket.

"Let me see the gun, Elmer," Dad said and quickly raised the gun to his shoulder, aimed, and rabbit #1 was shot between his left eye and his right eye. Joe picked up the rabbit and put him in the hemp sack. That was a good start to Sunday breakfast. The hunt went on for about two hours and yielded five rabbits.

The tracking took Dad and his boys down by Hunting Creek, which is the western property line of Dad's farm. As they tracked close to the creek, Dad pointed out two minks as they played in the water around the Rock.

"Boy, I wish I had my traps set there," Dad said. "I could sure use them two pelts on my stretch boards in the corncrib." Dad loved trapping and did not see enough of the expensive mink furs. As soon as the minks detected us watching them, they quickly disappeared under the big Rock.

"I need to go check my traps when we get back to the house. I hope I can get to them today. Maybe I have a mink in one of my traps," Dad said. He did go to check his traps down at the Burgess place as soon as we got back to the house. The sun was out and the snow was melting.

Joe held the rabbits for Elmer to skin. Mom cut them up and salted the meat down immediately. Joe could already taste the rabbit gravy.

Dad did not get that prize mink he was talking about, but he did get three nice muskrats. Joe quickly helped Dad skin them and stretch their pelts out on the boards.

"I saw a lot of good signs down there. I feel sure I'll get that mink soon. I think I'll move some of my traps down at the creek since the minks are moving around the Rock," Dad said as they walked to the house for dinner.

Breakfast was a little more special Sunday morning with the rabbit meat and rabbit gravy. Even without eggs, it was a good meal. The hens did not lay as good in cold weather and many times breakfast was biscuits and gravy.

"This gravy sure is good, Mom," Joe said as he was working on biscuit #5. The tasty rabbit meat was about as good as chicken, though it was smaller portions.

The roads were in decent shape and clear of most of the snow. Tonight was the Christmas play at church. Dad's crew had to be back at church Sunday evening at 4:00 p.m. for the last minute rehearsals for the 6:00 p.m. play. It was always a happy time. Treat bags would be given out after the play to everyone.

The Christmas play "No Room in the Inn" was a stirring reminder of Jesus' birth and how even at birth, the world did not have room for him. The play went well with all the acting and the many verses that were said by the children. As far as Joe could tell, all of Dad's family remembered their parts and places. They were relieved that the play was behind them. Only four days till Christmas.

At Monday morning breakfast, Wayne was all excited. Today was the day that Dad was taking him to Yadkinville to try to get his driver's license. Wayne had turned 16 years old on November 30 and had been hounding Dad ever since to please go with him to get his license. After chores and breakfast, they were on their way to Yadkinville, which is the county seat of Yadkin County.

It didn't take long as Dad and Wayne were back home at 10:00 a.m. Wayne was driving. That must be the signal that the state of North Carolina approved of the way Wayne drove.

"He did real good," Dad said. "The highway patrolman said he parallel parked picture perfect." Wayne was all smiles. Now there were three drivers in Dad's house.

As was the routine, the chickens were fed and watered first thing each morning. The chicks were now four weeks old or about one quarter of the way to the date they would be grown up enough to sell. They really had a good appetite and laid away a lot of feed and drank plenty of water. Rose and Joe were back at their old job of toting water.

Dad's crew spent the rest of the day cutting wood for the wood stove that heated the house.

Dad had been looking at some oil circulators that would provide more balanced heat than the old wood stove. Maybe before another year we would not have to cut wood to heat the house.

Only three more days till Christmas! Danny was getting very excited. He was almost four years old now.

Hog Killing

Tuesday was another overcast, cold day. Dad was talking about killing hogs on Wednesday, Christmas Eve. The weatherman at WSJS said it was going to be plenty cold to kill hogs. Dad made all the preparations by getting everything lined up, the vat, wood for the fire, tables, pulley, and making sure that the smokehouse was cleaned out and ready for the new meat. Only two more days till Christmas, Danny!

It was definitely cold enough. The thermometer read 15 degrees at 6:00 a.m. when Dad's crew was ready to start. Leck Groce was going to help us, and we in turn, would help him with his two hogs in mid January. Grandpa Brown came down even though he did not have any hogs to kill. Grandpa just wanted to do what he could to help.

Dad quickly shot our three hogs and bled them. With all of the help, Leck, Elmer, Wayne, Joe, and John, the three hogs were scalded, gutted, and cut up by 9:00 a.m. Dad was on the way to Martin's Grocery to get a good portion of the hogs ground up into sausage. Mom would can the sausage that would provide the much needed meat for the next year. With all of the top notch crew and with Rose and Jane helping Mom, the hog work was finished by dinnertime, 12:00 noon.

"We sure made good time, didn't we?" Dad said as the last of the meat was put into the smoke-house.

"Sure did!" Leck said. "You've got a good work crew, Clyde. You didn't even need me." Leck laughed.

Of course, Dad had sold all the hams and a half of the shoulders. Selling this meat plus most of the tenderloin brought in some much needed cash for the cold wintertime.

All the boys stayed in the kitchen after dinner to help Mom and the girls in getting all the sausage canned and helping make the liver mush. By mid evening, the kitchen was cleared of all hog meat. Mom appreciated all the help. Now she had to get to work cooking some goodies for tomorrow.

After supper, Dad and his crew wanted to pop some popcorn and also wanted to make some crackerjacks with this year's crop of molasses.

"Boy, these crackerjacks are good, ain't they?" Dad said as he had a mouthful and was making another batch. Joe liked it all, popcorn, crackerjacks, and the "Mom's famous" chocolate candy. All of Dad's crew were about to pop when Dad said it's time for bed.

"Got to get to sleep, youngins. Santa Claus cannot come to see you if you don't get to sleep," Dad said. Danny's eyes lit up when Dad mentioned Santa. Danny really was into Christmas this year. Joe enjoyed seeing Danny's excitement and anticipation of the big day tomorrow. Tomorrow is Christmas.

Even though we never set alarm clocks, Christmas morning at 5:00 a.m. was an automatic get up time.

"It's Christmas! Time to get up!" Joe hollered. The house was immediately alive with the pitter patter of feet hitting the floor and heading into the front room to see what Santa had left. Danny, Jane, and John made a quick check of their shoe boxes to see what they had.

"I got my Barlow knife, Joe," John said as he was checking out the blades. "It looks sharp." Dad would give John some pointers on how to whittle without cutting fingers. Joe got the same instructions two years ago.

"I got my baby doll that cries," Jane said giving the doll a hug. "I love my baby doll."

"I got a fire truck," Danny said as his face lit up happily. He loved anything of trucks and cars. He could play with them for hours.

All of the other youngins got gifts from Mom and Dad. They had learned at an early age to appreciate anything they received at Christmas. Times were always hard. Most of the time, their gifts were clothes. Christmas and tobacco selling time was usually the only time Dad's youngins got new clothes. Most of the other clothes they wore were hand-me-downs.

Soon, Mom was busy in the kitchen getting breakfast ready. Mom happily sang an old Christmas song.

"O come, all ye faithful, joyful and triumphant;
Come ye, O come ye to Bethlehem;
Come and behold Him, born the king of angels:
O come, let us adore Him,
O come let us adore Him,
O come let us adore Him, Christ, the Lord."

You knew Mom was happy when she was singing. Mom had such a sweet voice.

Right on cue, Grandpa Brown knocked on the door. He always came to see us on Christmas Day just about breakfast time.

"Hey, youngins," Grandpa greeted. "How is everyone this cold morning?"

"We're fine, Grandpa. How are you doing?" the youngins chimed.

"I'm okay for an old man," Grandpa said as he pulled up a chair at the kitchen table and enjoyed a cup of American Ace coffee.

"Won't you eat with us, Grandpa?" Mom asked.

"No, I've already eaten. I'll just have my coffee," he said.

Mom prayed, "Heavenly Father, thank you for this good Christmas Day you have given us. Thank you for this food, health, and strength. We pray you'd be with the sick, the shut-ins, the bereaved, and the ones who don't have the loving family like we have. We pray that you'd be with Grandpa. Help him to get to feeling better. Thank you for sending Jesus for us. Help us to be thankful for the many blessings. Thank you in Jesus' name. Amen."

Mom's breakfast was biscuits and gravy, sausage, molasses, and strawberry jam. We always had plenty to eat. We usually ate plain food, nothing real fancy, but just good wholesome food.

Grandpa got up to leave after breakfast. As was tradition, Joe gave Grandpa his box of cigars. Grandpa lit one up and left in a cloud of smoke.

The chickens had to be fed and watered after breakfast. The chicken house was a regular workplace for Rose, Joe, and John. It was a big responsibility for them.

Mom had dinner ready at 12:00 noon and then it was the annual trip to Grandpa and Grandma Proctor's for the Christmas get together. Dad drove the 1950 Plymouth down the road and turned into Grandpa's driveway.

"Still ain't cut these weeds. The weather has beat some of them down, at least," Dad grumbled.

Grandma met us at the door and hugged all of the youngins and Mom and Dad. Grandma led her biscuit eating youngins into the kitchen. It was a never changing routine. We all must have at least two of these biscuits.

"You love my biscuits, don't you?" Grandma asked.

"We sure do!" was the answer from all seven of Dad's crew. It was 2:00 p.m. and gift opening time. The house was full of uncles, aunts, and cousins. A steady flow of chatter and laughter was ever present throughout the house.

"Thank you, Grandma!" Joe said as he got his usual thoughtful gift from her. Joe and John had been getting a baseball from Grandma for the past several years. They loved to play baseball and the two balls would last them until next Christmas.

The evening passed quickly and it was time to get home to do the chores. It was suppertime and then on to bed as it had been a long, busy day. Everyone was worn out.

The day after Christmas was a cold mess, with a mist of rain and sleet. It was just plain dreary, gloomy, and a stay inside day. Saturday was more of the same. It sure wasn't any fit weather to rabbit hunt. That's what Joe wanted to do.

Finally on Sunday, the sun came out even though it was cold and windy. It was to church and back and a good long nap. The year was winding down. 1952 had been a year of action with the election of a new president and lots of hard work on the Little Farm on Brown Road. It was a very productive year with bountiful crops for which we were thankful. We had good health and strength, even though Grandpa's health was slowly failing.

School reopened on Thursday, January 1, 1953, after almost two weeks off for the Christmas vacation. Mr. Madison spent most of the morning talking about Christmas and then all evening reviewing the year of 1952. Most of that time seemed to be about the presidential election.

"We could talk about the election for a long time. There's so many angles to discuss the personalities and the politics of this election. The change of the party in power could be a big change for our country," Mr. Madison said. "We'll keep our eyes on this story for the next few months and continue to discover the progress made by the new president."

Chapter 6
Mr. Shore 1953

January was a cold, wet month. Danny was four years old on the 18th, Joe was twelve on the 21st, and Dad was thirty-nine on the 24th.

February was here and Dad was busy planning his tobacco crop. He had been talking to Mr. Shore about raising his tobacco allotment. Mr. Shore was a hard worker and raised a lot of hay, grain, and beef cattle. He wanted to rent out his sixteen acres of tobacco to Dad and Uncle Nelson. Mr. Shore would help with the crops, but he would not raise any tobacco of his own.

The plans did not work out this year for Uncle Nelson. There would be a one year delay as Uncle Nelson was obligated elsewhere for this year. He would move here next year to raise tobacco and trade work with Dad's crew. Mr. Shore would raise a small crop this year. Dad got the plant beds ready over at Mr. Shore's place in behind Mr. Shore's feed barn in the new ground that had just been grubbed out recently. Dad had a bigger than ever plant bed this year. His crew sowed it on Saturday, February 14. Dad was always glad to get started on a new tobacco season. He so loved working in tobacco.

The February birthdays came for Rose and John on Monday, February 23. Rose was now fourteen years old while John was ten years old. My, how Dad's working crew was growing up! Where has all the time gone? It seems like only yesterday that Rose and Joe were sneaking around playing with matches. Now they are fully productive workers helping Mom and Dad make a go out of farming.

The March winds blew in warm air. It was a welcome sight for the farmer. They were ready to get in the field and turn the land to get it ready for their crops. There was a lot of work to do before the tobacco plants would be ready to set out about May 15.

On Saturday, March 21, the Holly Farm truck came to pick up the 5,000 chickens. The chickens were now sixteen weeks old and ready to become fryers. It was a fun day for Dad and the boys as they got to help catch the chickens and put them in the carrying cages to be loaded on the open back truck. It had been a good house of chickens as the losses were minimal.

Mom kept out twelve of the best looking chickens for future layers or for Sunday dinner if they failed to lay eggs productively.

The chicken truck was loaded and gone by nine o'clock, as they had arrived early and the loading crew was fast.

Dad immediately started on the cleanup of the chicken house. Scoop shovels were working on both ends of the house to empty out all of the chicken manure. Dad would scatter the manure all over the pasture and on the cornfield. We did not use the manure on the tobacco field as it would make the tobacco too green and would cause the tobacco to disease.

The house was clean and ready for the new load of shavings on Monday. The new chicks would arrive on Friday, March 27. Then the whole cycle would repeat itself to run another sixteen weeks. These cycles would continue to run, as it was a good income for Mom and Dad to help throughout the year.

April was here and the frequent showers were helping the plant beds. The tobacco plants were looking good. The weeding was a weekly job as the beds had to be kept clean of weeds and grass or they would bleed off all the fertilizer that the tobacco plants needed. Weeding was a tedious task that was done with care so that the tobacco plants would not be damaged or pulled up.

When the plants were tiny, Dad fixed cushions filled with straw that we sat on as we pulled weeds. You would move around all over the bed until the weeds were cleaned out. Later as the plants grew, the cushions could not be used as they would damage the plants. Plant bed weeding was one of many backbreaking jobs in the farmer's life. Pulling first primings was probably the most trying job, which hurt the back. Whether young or old, the back hurt just the same.

Plant beds needed a lot of water once the weather started to warm up. The warm sun and water would speed up the growth of the tobacco plants. If the beds were not properly attended to, the plants would be late and of an inferior quality.

"The plants are really coming along now," Dad said as his crew had finished weeding. "We need to wet them down again before we quit for the day."

The plant beds had been watered down this morning before the weed pulling started. Now Dad wanted to water again to firm up the plants and to help wet down footprints left by the weeders. The watering would continue until the entire tobacco crop was set out, except on days when we received a good shower of rain.

Meanwhile, Dad was getting the tobacco land ready for the first setting which would be ready in a couple of weeks. Mr. Shore had more modern equipment than Dad had been using in the past. In the past, Dad would have to layoff the tobacco row with a single stalk plow, fertilize it by hand, and then make up the ridge for the tobacco plant by running the single stalk twice, one time on each side of the fertilized row.

Mr. Shore had a fertilizing machine that the horse would pull which not only fertilized the row, but it also made up the ridge. This machine saved a tremendous amount of time. Dad was like a youngin with a new toy.

"Boy, I like this machine!" Dad said as he was filling it with fertilizer at the end of the row. "They sure hadn't done anything to ease the burden of handling these 200# bags of Agrico fertilizer yet, though."

It would be a couple more years before Joe could handle a bag of Agrico by himself. He and John together could move a bag but they could not do much with it. It was like a bag of lead.

"These bags are too heavy for us, John, but we'll get to where we can handle them in three or four more years, won't we?" Joe said.

"Sure will!" John said. "We've got a few more pinto beans to eat first."

Joe was cooling his feet into the fresh plowed soil, waiting for Dad to make the turn with his tobacco row machine. Yesterday was May 1, barefoot day. Now it was legal to go barefoot. Joe would not wear shoes except for school and church until the end of September. He so loved going barefoot.

Joe always laughed and joked about going barefoot so much that he would wear out his Sunday shoes from the inside out. His feet were so tough by summertime that he could walk on gravel without even noticing any pain.

Dad and his crew stopped for a water break about 3:00 p.m. They walked up the hill from the Shore's hill field and got water at Grandpa Brown's well.

Grandpa's Old Sayings

"Hey there, youngins. How are you doing?" Grandpa said as they stopped to talk a minute. Distant thunder was rattling over in the western sky.

"Do you hear them corn wagons a rolling over to the west of us?" Grandpa asked. That's what he used to call thunder, especially in its initial stages. It was an old timey saying. Grandpa had a lot of old sayings.

Grandpa would also say, "The sun sets behind the bank on Monday, it'll rain before Wednesday, or on Wednesday, it'll rain before Friday." These sayings were common for Grandpa. They meant that if the sun set when it was behind clouds, we were looking for rain soon.

Grandpa seemed like he knew about everything, at least to most of his grandchildren. Joe thought Grandpa was the smartest man in the whole world.

We would always go to Grandpa with warts on our hands. He said we got warts by handling "hoppy toads." Grandpa would cure anyone who came to him with warts. He would take a gum tree stick and rub the wart several times and then tell the youngin with the wart to go and bury the stick without anyone else knowing where it was buried.

"When the stick rots, the warts will disappear," Grandpa said. It seemed to work.

"Ya'll come up this evening if you get through in time and I'll tell ya'll some stories," Grandpa said.

"We will if we can, Grandpa. If we can't this evening, we will tomorrow after preaching," Joe said as they made their way through the front yard over the hedge and back down the hill to the hill field. The hill field was eight acres of the twelve acres that Dad was tending for Mr. Shore. Joe would have many good memories of this large tobacco field and the barn down at the lower end at the bottom of the Shore's hill.

"We'd better quit and get to the house, boys. We have chores to do and baths to take before supper," Dad said as he looked at his pocket watch, which he always kept in his Big Mac overalls watch pocket. It was 5:00 p.m.

Joe and John fed and watered the chicken house chickens and then gathered eggs from all the loose chickens. Dad, Elmer, and Wayne milked the cows and fed them and Old Bill, our horse. Sandy, our good old dog, followed along with Joe's every move. He was getting old and had slowed down some, but was still the best dog around.

After a hard day in the tobacco field, Mom's cornbread and milk was just what Joe needed to get his energy back up. Mom could really make a cake of cornbread. The supper Joe never grew tired of was always filling. Cold sweet milk poured over hot cornbread was so good.

"This sure is good cornbread, Mom!" Joe said as he was on his second big bowl. Like Dad, Joe ate his cornbread in a big bowl with a big spoon.

"Thank you, Joe. I'm glad you like it," Mom said as she slowly ate her supper. Mom always ate slowly. Elmer was another slow eater, but he could eat forever. Dad and the others were all fast eaters.

"Let's hurry and clean up the dishes so we can all go hear Grandpa's stories," Elmer said.

Everyone pitched in and cleaned up the kitchen in just a little while. All the youngins, except Danny, were off to Grandpa's. Danny was off to bed.

"Don't ya'll run and get sweaty now after your baths, youngins," Mom said as they left.

Grandpa and Grandma were sitting on the front porch when we got up there. Grandpa had a big chew of Brown Mule chewing tobacco in his jaws. He would have won the long spit contest at the county fair if they had one. He was quite a spitter.

Soon, Uncle Lamar's youngins joined in on the fun. Lyman, Jimmy, Lorene, and Avalon were all sitting around the feet of Grandpa with Elmer, Wayne, Rose, Joe, John, and Jane. They were all waiting for a story. Grandpa would not keep them waiting long. He was always a story waiting to happen.

"Do you know how Hunting Creek got its name?" Grandpa began. Hunting Creek was the creek on the west border of Dad's land. "My Grandpa Henry James tells the story of Indians that used to live down there when he was a little boy of six or seven years old. That would make it about 1818. There was just a small bunch of them that stayed around for awhile when the other Indians moved westward."

"The land around the creek was so plentiful with all kinds of game that the Indians gave the creek the name of Hunting Creek. The Braves would spend all their time hunting while the womenfolk would do the gardening to raise corn to eat with all the meat they brought in."

"It seems like there had been some trouble with the Indians back when Great-Grandpa James Brown was little. Grandpa Henry James did not know too much about it, but he had heard it mentioned. It sure would be good if each of these ancestors had kept records about these happenings, wouldn't it?" Grandpa said.

"That's why there are so many arrowheads over on that hill, Grandpa," Elmer said. "We're always finding them when we're working on that field."

"That's right. Who knows? That could have been a great battlefield for the Indians. It could also have been a burying ground. I guess we will never know. I know one thing, though. It's past our bedtime. We'll be snoozing through church tomorrow if we don't get our sleep," Grandpa said. It was about 8:00 p.m. That was kind of late for Grandpa Brown, as he always "went to bed with the chickens."

For non-country folks, chickens always get to their roosting place before dark and the old rooster will wake you up with the country alarm clock, his crowing long before dawn.

Youngins told Grandpa bye and headed home. We told Lyman, Jimmy, Lorene, and Avalon bye as they headed down Brown Road. and up to their house on the curve. In just a few minutes we were in the house and asleep instantly. Joe was dreaming about his Indian neighbors.

White Thunder

Joe had made friends with Little Thunder who was the twelve year old son of Chief Big Thunder of the Cherokee tribe of Hunting Creek. Little Thunder had a fast young mustang named Blackie. Joe and Little Thunder played all over the hills around Hunting Creek. The boys would go hunting together. Little Thunder was an excellent shot with the bow. He taught Joe how to track game and how to shoot the bow.

In return for Little Thunder's kindness, Joe taught him how to read. The two boys were the best of friends and became blood brothers. Some of the elders of the tribe and some of the young Bucks did not like Joe teaching Little Thunder the white man's ways, but Chief Big Thunder approved of the help Joe gave his son. Chief Big Thunder called Joe "White Thunder," so it looked like Joe was an adopted son of the chief.

One day, Joe and Little Thunder were hunting down around Hunting Creek. Joe had learned so much about hunting the Indian's way that he could move quickly through the woods without making a sound.

On this cold winter evening, Joe and Little Thunder were tracking a deer. They had tracked the deer from the big maple tree towards the creek.

"He go to creek for water," Little Thunder said in his broken English Joe had taught him. "I go north of big rock and you go south. We get deer."

"I'll see you there, Little Thunder," Joe said as he checked his bow and arrows to be ready. As Joe went around the south side of the gigantic rock, he saw Little Thunder lying prone on the rock watching the eight point buck drinking water.

Behind Little Thunder in a tree, was a full grown panther perched and ready to pounce on Joe's friend. Quick as a cat, Joe readied his bow for a shot. He must save his friend from death by this vicious animal. Joe drew back the arrow with all his might and let go. The arrow found its mark right in the neck of the panther. It was a perfect shot. The panther fell to the big rock below and landed next to the startled Little Thunder who had no idea of the danger he had faced.

Joe let a yell of gladness even though the deer escaped them. Joe's friend was okay. That was the most important thing. The boys smiled as they looked over the panther lying on the big rock. They had not been hunting a panther, but they sure got one.

Joe and Little Thunder ran to Chief Big Thunder's teepee to tell their story.

Little Thunder said, "Father, White Thunder saved my life. He kill big panther." Little Thunder went on to explain in their language what had happened. Chief Big Thunder rode down to the rock and got the massive panther and brought it back to the village. The panther would be on display outside the Chief's teepee for a long time.

Chief Big Thunder had a big celebration to honor Joe for saving his son's life. He made Joe an honorary Cherokee Brave to show his thanks for the heroic act. Joe was now like one of the family.

"Thank you, Chief. Thank you," Joe was saying happily.

Elmer shook Joe. "Joe, you're having another one of your dreams. Wake up! Wake up, Joe!"

Joe woke up for a few minutes and then went back to sleep. In the morning, he would tell his family about his dream.

"Boy, you dream more than anyone I've ever seen!" Dad said.

"Clyde, remember what his name is. Joseph, the dreamer, was in Genesis 37," Mom said. "He was a very wise man and quite a dreamer."

Mother's Day

Today was Mother's Day, May 10, 1953. Joe remembers many Mother's Days. He had made a Mother's Day card at school to show his love and appreciation to Mom.

Pastor Myers preached on "The Godly Mother" from Proverbs 31. His messages were always stirring, especially on Mother's Day and Father's Day. After the invitation, Pastor Myers asked that all the children make their way to their mother and give her a hug and tell her how much you love her. The aisles looked like a school hallway and youngins were all over looking for their mom. One by one,

Elmer, Wayne, Rose, Joe, John, Jane, and Danny gave Mom a big hug and told her how much she was loved.

Mom was a sentimental, soft hearted lady and had tears dropping all over. Rose and Jane were teary eyed too, but the boys managed to keep their composure, even though they loved Mom as much as the girls did.

"Isn't this a beautiful sight?" Pastor Myers said. "Thank God for our mothers. Let's sing one verse of "Faith of Our Mothers." That's page 183 in your hymn book if you need the book. It's the same words as "Faith of Our Fathers," just substitute mother for father."

Brother Aubrey Martin led the congregation as they sang:

"Faith of our mothers, living still
In spite of dungeon, fire and sword.
O how our hearts beat high with joy
When-e'er we hear that glorious word!
Faith of our mothers, holy faith,
We will be true to thee till death!"

Pastor Myers closed the teary eyed congregation in prayer.

"Heavenly Father, thank you for our godly mothers. Help each person here today to be thankful for their mother. Help each mother to set the right example for their children. Thank you, Lord, for the sweet spirit here today. We pray you'd bless each person here today in Jesus' precious name I pray. Amen. Amen."

After the usual scrumptious Sunday dinner, Mom and Dad headed down the road to see Grandpa and Grandma Proctor.

"Still hasn't cut these weeds," Dad said as he drove down the winding driveway to a bigger than normal Mother's Day crowd. Most of Mom's brothers and sisters came home to see their mom.

In addition to Mom, others at home for Mom's day were Uncle Claude, Uncle Paul, Uncle Porter, Uncle Zeno, Uncle Harold, Aunt Dorothy, Aunt Hazel, Aunt Dee Ette, and Aunt Jane. Of course, the house was full of spouses and youngins. Uncle Troy was not here as he lived in Texas.

Grandma still greeted us and gave us all some of her choice biscuits from the warmer at the top of the stove. As always, the biscuits were out of sight.

It was so good to see Mom with her family. She missed seeing them, as she only saw most of them two to three times a year. The house was buzzing with chatter and laughter. Though the family was spread out in all directions, they still were a close knit family and really enjoyed being together.

Most of the men folk sat outside in the yard chairs. They would keep a continuous conversation going on all evening.

"How's your plant beds looking, Clyde?" Grandpa asked.

"Looking real good now. I plan to start setting tobacco by the end of next week," Dad said. "How's your crop looking?"

"Pretty good. I should be ready to set by the middle of the week," Grandpa said.

"How many acres are you raising this year, Clyde?" Uncle Porter asked.

"Looks like fourteen acres," Dad answered. "How about your crop?"

"I'll raise the same four acres. That's about all we can handle with me working as much as I do with McNess," Uncle Porter said. He sold flavoring, peppers, spices, and other household cooking products all over Yadkin County for McNess Products. He had been on this job for years.

"Joe, run tell your mom we need to be going. It's about chore time," Dad said as he stood up getting ready to go. Joe went inside and came out in a few minutes with Mom and the rest of the youngins.

"Bye, youngins," Grandma said. "Ya'll hurry back."

"Bye, Grandma. We'll be back soon," they answered as they loaded up the 1950 Plymouth and were on their way home.

"It sure was good to see my family. Mom sure enjoyed seeing everybody," Mom said. "I sure wish Troy could get home once in a while. We miss him."

"Let's stop by Mom's for a few minutes, Gladys," Dad said.

"Yes, you need to see her today, Clyde. I know she will be glad to see you," Mom said.

Grandpa and Grandma were in their usual chairs on the front porch. They loved to sit there and complain about all the many people who drove by all evening wasting gas.

"Hey, Mom. Happy Mother's Day! How are you doing today?" Dad asked as he sat down beside Grandma.

More Country Sayings

"Hey there, youngins," Grandpa said as he chewed away on his Brown Mule chewing tobacco.

"Hey, Grandpa," they answered. "How are you doing today?"

"Oh, I'm just tolerable," Grandpa said. That meant he wasn't feeling great, but he was okay. Joe loved some of the old sayings. When someone was "peert," that meant they felt pretty good.

What did he "allow" meant what did he have to say. I "hope" him in tobacco today meant I helped him. Hand me that "poke" meant to hand me that paper sack.

Mom had a favorite when we asked her to wait. "Wait is what broke the wagon down," she'd say. What teacher did you "go to" meant who was your teacher. When you took a "fancy" to someone that meant you liked them. "Courting" meant to date someone. When you took a "hankering" to do something that meant you decided to do a certain thing. To "go to bed with the chickens" meant to go to bed very early. Sometimes older folks would go to bed before dark and get up before 4:00 a.m.

Another of Mom's favorite sayings was, "Your eyes were bigger than your belly," meaning that you got more food on your plate than you could eat.

After a short visit, it was time to do the chores and get to church. Mom and Dad taught their family to be faithful to their church. Many times they were tired and worn out, but they still took us to church. Thank God for a good Christian home!

It was Monday morning and Dad talked about watering the plant beds today.

"We'll have to water them everyday this week if it doesn't rain," Dad said. "Then we need to get the rest of the tobacco rows made up. Looks like that'll take us the biggest part of the week. You youngins, come on over when you get home from school. Me and Elmer need all the help we can get."

"We sure do! It makes a big difference when we don't have all of our help," Elmer said.

Old #63 was coming to a stop as the youngins hurried to the bus stop. The school year was winding down. It had been a good year. Joe learned a lot from Mr. Madison. Three more weeks and the 6th grade would be history.

"We're going to have a picnic on Wednesday, May 27, over at my house. We'll leave school at about 10:00 a.m. and spend the rest of the day hiking, playing games, and enjoying a picnic lunch. There's a nice lake over behind my house," Mr. Madison said. "We'll have a lot of fun. You don't have to bring anything. Just come prepared to have a good time."

When Joe got home from school, he told Mom and Dad about the picnic. He wanted to make sure they were aware of the plans, just in case that might be a stay-at-home tobacco setting day.

"I hope I'll be able to go, Dad," Joe pleaded.

"You can go, son. We'll work out the schedule. We know that this day will be a special fun day for you," Dad said.

Chapter 7
Tobacco Setting 1953

On Friday, May 15, Dad and his crew started setting tobacco in the two acre spring field. Dad kept Wayne, Joe, and John home from school to help. He let the girls, Rose and Jane, go on to school today.

"We can handle it today without you girls, but when we get to setting Mr. Shore's field, we'll probably have to keep ya'll out, too," Dad said.

Dad's crew was in the plant beds at 6:00 a.m. pulling plants for today's setting. Dad watered the beds first, pulled a truckload of plants, and then moved to the spring field.

Mom dropped for Dad while Joe dropped for Elmer and John dropped for Wayne. When the girls got home from school, Rose would drop for Elmer and Jane would drop for Joe. John kept up with the water and plants. Dad's work crew was becoming more productive each year. Four rows at clip would really add up.

By the time the girls got home from school, Dad's crew had finished the spring field and had set about an acre in Mr. Shore's hill field.

"Boy, ya'll are really going to town setting today," Jane said as she started to drop for Joe. Soon the click-clack of four tobacco setters were playing the music Dad liked to hear. Dad was all smiles now and also later at the supper table when he bragged on his work crew.

"We set about four acres today, youngins. That's real good. At this rate, we'll finish setting in three more days. We'll set tomorrow and then let the plant beds grow for a couple of days," Dad said as he ate his cornbread and milk.

On Saturday morning at 6:00 a.m., Dad's crew was in the plant beds pulling plants for the day. The whole family was at it bright and early. Mom would help until dinnertime and then she would go to the house to cook for the rest of the day.

Four crews were setting again today. Mr. Shore came by about midmorning and bragged on Dad's crew.

"Clyde, you sure have a good work crew here. At this rate, you'll finish setting over here in a couple of days," Mr. Shore said.

"Thank you, Mr. Shore. Our crew does pretty good, if I must say so," Dad said with a smile. He and Mom always loved to hear people brag on their workers.

The setting went good again today. The hill field was over half way finished by the end of the day. Mom had stayed at the house this evening to cook. Rose dropped for Dad, Joe dropped for Elmer, and Jane dropped for Wayne this evening. John would keep water and plants to all setting teams. At quitting time, five of the eight acres in the hill field was set. Setting would resume next week with three more acres in the hill field and the four acres in the middle field. The middle field was located next to Mr. Shore's second tobacco barn. His third tobacco barn was over across the little branch in the woods.

Chores were done. Joe and John fed and watered the chickens in the block chicken house. Baths were taken and supper was on the table.

"Did we smell a surprise for supper?' Joe and John asked each other as they came into the kitchen. Sure enough, a still hot strawberry saunker was on the stove.

Mom prayed, "Heavenly Father, thank you for this good day. We thank you for our health and strength. Be with the sick, the shut-in, and the bereaved. Bless them. Thank you for our food. Bless it to the nourishment of our body. We pray in Jesus' name. Amen. Amen."

Mom poured sweet milk all around to the hungry youngins who had filled their bowls with crumbled cornbread. It was quiet while they were eating cornbread and milk, but after all the cornbread was gone, Dad's tired crew let Mom know how they felt about her strawberry saunker.

"This saunker is so good, Mom," Elmer said.

"It's the best ever," Wayne said.

Strawberry saunker is my second favorite," Rose said.

"Mine, too! Sweet potato is #1," Jane said.

"Umm. Umm," Joe said as he pigged out.

"It's good, but even better with a touch of milk in it," John said.

"Good!" Danny said.

"All I can say is its kind of musty," Dad said. "I must have more."

"Thank you all. I appreciate the good grades you gave my saunker. There's more for Sunday dinner tomorrow," Mom said as she was just now getting to taste her saunker.

"Grandpa Brown wants some of ya'll to help him pick strawberries on Monday," Dad said. "Elmer and me are going to finish laying off the last of the tobacco rows. All of you can help before and after school. Joe, you and John can stay out and help. He really needs to get them picked."

Joe and John were in the field Monday morning at 6:00 a.m. They picked all day until about 5:00 p.m. All the strawberries were picked over. Grandpa had a big load of over 200 quarts to take to the market early Tuesday morning. Joe picked 50 quarts while John picked 25 quarts. Both of the boys felt rich.

"Thank you boys for staying out of school to help me today," Grandpa said. "I could not have finished by myself."

Joe always enjoyed working with Grandpa Brown. Joe considered the time with Grandpa as quality time. If you stayed with Grandpa and watched, listened, and worked, you would learn valuable lessons about life.

Joe was back in school on Tuesday, Wednesday, and Thursday. Dad decided to put off the rest of the setting to Friday and Saturday. That way the school youngins would only have to miss one day, Friday.

At 6:00 a.m. Friday morning, Dad's crew was back in the plant beds. Dad wanted to finish the hill field today and also set at least an acre of the middle field.

Four setters started setting at 9:00 a.m. in the hill field. Mom dropped for Dad and Rose dropped for Elmer. John dropped for Wayne and Jane dropped for Joe. The click-clack of the tobacco setters echoed down towards the tobacco barn at the bottom of the hill of Brown Road. The barn was near the curve of the road as it headed out past Mr. Shore's new house.

At about 10:00 a.m., Mr. Shore paid Dad's crew a surprise and brought everyone a bottle of Pepsi and a pack of nabs to eat. What a treat this was, as Dad's family did not have pop to drink unless it was a special occasion.

"I thought ya'll might need a break," Mr. Shore said.

"It sure is nice of you to bring us this snack. We sure do appreciate it," Mom said.

The snacks didn't last long, but they were definitely enjoyed by all of Dad's crew.

"Thank you, Mr. Shore," they all said.

"You're plumb welcome, youngins. I'm just so glad to have a good, dependable work crew to tend my tobacco this year," Mr. Shore said.

After a short dinner break, Dad's crew finished the hill field at 3:00 p.m. They were making even better progress than Dad had figured.

Wayne hopped into the old pickup truck and headed the work crew over to the middle field. Soon the click-clack echo was moving across Grandpa Brown's back acres and over towards Aunt Lucy Pardue's place.

By 6:00 p.m. when Dad's crew ran out of tobacco plants, Dad figured they had about three acres left to set out on Saturday. Dad made a quick trip back to the plant beds to water the plants down good for tomorrow morning's pullings. Dad always planned ahead and did little things to help out tomorrow's schedule.

On Saturday, Dad's crew made quick work of the three acres. It was finished at 4:00 p.m. Dad's crew certainly was productive this year more than ever. Dad and his workers looked forward to working with Mr. Shore this year. They liked his equipment, which was more modern than what they had used in the past. Also, his tobacco barns were big, airtight, and all were cured by oil. Good productive work crews can only get better with better equipment.

Mr. Shore had finished setting his small patch of two acres. He had so many other things to do with all of his cattle and grain that he wanted to get out of the tobacco completely. But, of course, come priming time, Mr. Shore would always be there to help. Mr. Shore and Dad were the two hardest workers Joe had ever seen. They both simply loved to work out in the hot sun.

On Monday, Dad had his work crew planting corn, working in the garden, and starting to plow and hoe tobacco at the spring field. Corn planting was simpler now. Dad borrowed Mr. Shore's corn planter and made quick work of fertilizing and planting corn. What used to take about three days now only took one day. Imagine a machine for Old Bill to pull that both fertilized, planted, and covered the corn. What do you think they'll come up with next?

"Boy, this sure beats the old way, doesn't it, Joe?" Dad said as they loaded the machine up with fertilizer and corn.

"It sure does, Dad. I remember helping you when it would take us three days to plant corn," Joe said.

Joe helped Dad in the cornfield on Monday after school while Elmer and Wayne plowed tobacco and Rose, John, and Jane were planting the rest of the garden. It was nice to have a large work crew that was dependable enough to split up and work in three different places.

Hoeing Tobacco

On Tuesday, Dad's full crew was in the spring field hoeing the freshly plowed tobacco. Dad had a crew of three working their way across the field during school and then eight after school. Eight rows at a clip will eat up two acres quickly. By 4:00 p.m., Dad left to start plowing the eight acre hill field.

Mr. Shore had a fancy two horse riding cultivator that Dad simply loved. This cultivator would plow one row at a time whereas the regular one horse cultivator would have to make two passes to complete one row. Dad would plow with Old Maude and Old Kate, Mr. Shore's large horses.

By the time that Elmer got our work crew to the hill field, Dad was far enough ahead that the hoeing crew would not catch up. It was 5:00 p.m. and this field would keep Dad's crew busy for the next three or four days. After this last week of school, Dad's crew would be a dominating work force.

As was the custom, Elmer helped Jane on her row as she was the youngest of the hoers and could not keep up on her own. She was now 7 ½ years old.

The Picnic

"Dad, you remember that I'll be home late tomorrow, don't you?" Joe asked at supper. "We'll be going to our picnic over at Mr. Madison's house."

"Yes, I remember, Joe. You go and have a good time. We'll save some work for you," Dad said.

Joe was at the bus stop early Wednesday morning. He was excited about the class picnic and also glad that there were only two more days of school this year. He was ready for the summer break.

The bus to Mr. Madison's house left West Yadkin at 9:00 a.m. It would be a trip of about thirty minutes to get to the Windsors Crossroads area. Mr. Madison had a real nice place out in the middle of the country. Immediately the whole class, including Mr. Madison, started playing baseball in the big field in back of the house.

Mr. Joe Pinnix, who was student teaching, had one team while Mr. Madison had the other team. Girls played on both sides and some of them did fairly well. Donna Johnson could play any sport and was fun to be around. Somehow, Joe got on the team with Mr. Madison, Bull Swisher, James Allen Shore, and Donna. This team could not be beaten and promptly routed the Pinnix team 21-6.

It was certainly more fun to win than it was to lose. Joe never did get used to losing. He liked to win and would sometimes get an attitude if he lost.

The rest of the morning went fast with a variety of games. Soon it was time to eat. Mrs. Madison and three mothers of classmates, Mrs. Johnson, Mrs. Royal, and Mrs. Allen, had a nice meal of hot dogs and all the trimmings, potato salad, fried chicken, cookies, cake, and plenty of pop to drink. Joe ate himself plumb full. It was certainly the highlight day to an already good year.

After eating, Mr. Madison and Mr. Pinnix led the class on a long hike down through the woods and around the huge picturesque lake. It looked like a postcard picture. It was so peaceful and quiet.

"This place is where I come to do some quiet thinking," Mr. Madison said. "There's something about nature that will help you think."

"Boy, I wish we had a lake like this!" Joe said. "It looks like a good place to go for a swim. The water looks so cool."

After the hike, which ended as a lazy walk, Mr. Madison gathered the class up behind the house for more games. The sack race was one of the favorites. It seems like everyone took a spill in the clumsy race. Relay races and individual races followed. As usual, Joe was the winner "hands down" in the individual race. Joe was proud of his speed. He loved to run.

"Well, class, it has been fun. I wish we could stay longer, but we've got to get the bus back to school," Mr. Madison said. "Some of you are leaving with your parents from here. Some will go back to school and some we'll drop off on the way back. I'm glad all of you were able to be here today."

"Thank you, Mr. Madison and Mrs. Madison for a nice time today!" the class said in near perfect unison as the bus loaded up and left down Windsor Road over towards Pea Ridge and onto Highway 421 towards West Yadkin.

Mr. Pinnix was driving the bus. He made several stops on the way to let students off close to their houses. The bus stopped at Paul Dobbins' store to let Joe off. The walk of about one mile would not take long as Joe was excited about the fun day. He got home about 5:00 p.m. and hurriedly changed clothes to go to the hill field to hoe tobacco for a little while.

"How was the picnic, Joe?" Dad asked.

"It was a lot of fun!" Joe said and he put the hoe to work chopping crabgrass and pulling the fresh soil around the tender tobacco plants.

"I ate four hotdogs and a whole bunch of sweets," Joe said. "Just two more days of school and we'll be home for the summer."

"That's good," Elmer said. "It'll be nice to have all of this help everyday."

Chapter 8
School's Out

School dismissed Friday at 12:00 noon. Joe was glad to be out for the summer, but he would miss Mr. Madison, one of Joe's best teachers.

"I've enjoyed learning in your class, Mr. Madison. It's been fun. Thank you for helping me in basketball, too," Joe said.

"You're a good student, Joe. You come from a good family and that usually makes good students. I hope you have a good summer," Mr. Madison said.

Wayne was promoted to the 11th grade while Rose was moving to 9th grade. Joe was promoted to the 7th grade and John to the 5th grade. Jane was promoted to the 2nd grade. My, how Mom and Dad's youngins were growing up! There were no babies anymore. Even Danny was 4 ½ years old.

"Bye, Wayne, you sweet thing! Come to see me now," Georgia Seagraves told Wayne as she got off the bus for the final time this year.

Joe waved bye to her brother Tommy who was in Joe's class this year as well as about every year.

"See you in September, Tommy," Joe said.

"Come over sometime and go swimming with me, Joe," Tommy said. His dad had a nice fish-swimming pond.

On Saturday morning, Dad's full work force moved into the hill field to finish up the hoeing. Dad left at 9:00 to start plowing with his dream, riding plow in the middle field. He would have a good head start by the time the hoeing crew would be there after dinner.

After an always good, healthy dinner of pinto beans, taters, and plenty of biscuits, Dad's crew was back in the field by 1:00 p.m. The four acre middle field was going to take at least 1 ½ days to hoe. Dad hoped to finish hoeing on Monday if all went according to plans.

By late evening, the gathering clouds back in the west looked like they might alter plans. Dad quickly sheltered the plow and let Elmer and Wayne take the horses to the barn. With a full two hours left in the work day, the thunder and lightning rolled in and the heavens opened up raining "cats and dogs." It was 5:00 p.m. when Dad's crew ran for cover under the middle tobacco barn shelter. Elmer and Wayne got back in time to quit.

"It looks like this rain is going to last awhile," Dad said as his crew snuggled together under the tin roof shelter of the tobacco barn. "This is not a very good place to spend a thunderstorm. We'll draw all the lightning to us under all this tin."

After about thirty minutes, the thunder and lightning eased up, but the rain continued to pour. For sure, hoeing was over for the day and maybe the first part of next week.

"Let's head home, youngins!" Dad said at 6:00 p.m. Dad, Rose, Jane, and John piled into the truck cab while Elmer, Wayne, and Joe braved it and rode in the back of the truck with all the hoes.

The rain would slow down somewhat, but continued a "set in" type rain all night. Chores were done and chickens were tended to as these were jobs that must be done rain or shine.

"Looks like we'll be out of the field for a few days," Dad said at supper. "The ground is already good and wet now and it looks like it's going to rain all weekend." Dad had been listening to the WSJS Shell oil weatherman.

Everyone was in bed right after supper as the work crew was worn out. The pitter-patter of the rain helped serenade the deep sleep in the Brown house.

On Sunday morning, May 31, 1953, Memorial Day dawned with the same "set in" rain of last night. The ground was soaked by now. Tobacco hoeing would have to wait awhile.

Gabriel Heater was reporting the news about truce talks that were still going on in Korea. President Eisenhower was constantly working to keep his campaign promise to end the war. Today's Memorial Day paid tribute to all of our soldiers who had paid the price with their life. Certainly, Americans should be grateful to all these soldiers. Freedom is never free.

The sun broke through the clouds and the rain stopped late Sunday evening.

"We needed the rain, but it's good to see the sun again," Dad said as we drove to church for the night services. "It'll probably be Wednesday or Thursday before we can get back into the field again."

It was Thursday and Dad's crew used the three wet days to do work around the barn, corncrib, and chicken house. There was always plenty of work to do. Dad saw to it that his workers did not have idle time. He was the best work inventor Joe had ever seen.

June was here. The country summer had begun. Dad got back on his riding plow and started back up plowing the middle field. His work crew started back hoeing. A long daylight to dark day finished the middle field. Dad's crew would start the hoeing all over again on Friday at the spring field. The cycle of farm work continues at the Little Farm on Brown Road.

The hoeing would continue through June when all the tobacco and corn was laid by. Laid by means the tobacco or corn was getting too tall to plow. The last plowing would be done with larger plow points to pull more fresh soil up around the plants to help them grow.

July roared in hot and dry. The garden was yielding many canning items for Mom. She would soon fill up the canning closet for the winter season. She canned green beans, corn, tomatoes, sauerkraut, and made jellies and jams from the abundant crop of blackberries the youngins picked. Mom stayed so busy and worked harder than ever for her family. Happy birthday, Mom, on July 16.

The tobacco was topped out, and then suckered and sprayed for worms. Priming time was drawing near. Dad's crew repaired the six sleds at the house tobacco barn and the eight sleds at Mr. Shore's tobacco barn.

On July 27, 1953, a truce was signed in Korea to end all fighting. President Eisenhower had delivered on his main campaign promise. People were happy as they expected all American soldiers would be home immediately. It was a slow process with many concessions made to the Communist. Joe did not like the sound of it all. U.S. troops would continue to be in Korea for many years to come.

Chapter 9
Tobacco Priming

July was gone. On Saturday, August 1, Dad's crew pulled first primings at the spring field. The two acres were only a small trial run for the big fields of next week. Dad, Wayne, Joe, and John primed while Elmer tied at the barn with Mom, Rose, and Jane handing up. It was a smooth day as the sparsely filled barn was ready to cure our first of many barns this summer. Dad's work crew would be up to the task, however, as they were a working machine.

On Monday morning at 6:00 a.m. after a hardy breakfast, Dad's work crew hit the hill field to begin a long and busy day. Dad and Mr. Shore were planning to put five acres of the hill field in the "road" barn. Their plan was to follow up on Tuesday with the remaining three acres of the hill field plus Mr. Shore's two acres in the "middle" barn and the middle field four acres in the "woods" barn on Wednesday.

"Boy, it sure wooks wike a wet one this morning," Mr. Shore said as the priming crew was ready to jump in and get wet. Mr. Shore had a speech problem and could not pronounce L's as they always came out W's. He helped us prime all year long and we helped him in his two acres. In later years, he helped even though he did not have a crop of his own. He was one fine man.

"It'll be about like jumping in the creek," Dad said.

Dad, Mr. Shore, Elmer, Wayne, Joe, and John all helped prime the first sled. Then Elmer went to the barn to tie with Rose, Jane, and John handing up. When Mom got to the barn at about 7:00 a.m.,

Mr. Shore went to the barn so Rose could start the second tie horse with John and Jane handing up to her. Mr. Shore and Mom handed up to Elmer. The barn crew, though behind at the start because of one hour with only one tie horse going, caught up and stayed up with the three primers all day.

Mr. Shore came back to the field to prime when Mom went to the house at 11:00 a.m. to finish dinner. Danny, who was now 4 ½ years old, helped some but usually played in the sand over in the shade near the barn.

Dad brought the primers in at 11:30 a.m. to hang the tobacco before going to dinner. Everyone got wet again as the tobacco which had been packed in the shade was still wet. Dad hung the tobacco on the bottom 4 tier poles while Elmer worked the top 4 tier poles. Hanging tobacco was the hottest job as the tin roof barns would build up heat to 100 to 110 degrees on the hottest days. The stifling hot air would really bring out the sweat.

"Boy, it's right up here today, Dad!" Elmer said after a few minutes. "It don't take long to work up a sweat."

"I know," Dad said. "I don't know which is getting me wetter, the tobacco or you sweating on me."

Dad's crew made short work of the hanging as everyone toted the heavy sticks of tobacco to Mr. Shore who handed them up to Dad who would hand Elmer 4 sticks to hang before hanging the bottom 4 tiers. This process was repeated until a little over two rooms were hanged.

Elmer and Wayne rode Old Maude and Old Kate to the feed barn to feed them before returning them to work. Horses were a valuable helper in tobacco and must be fed and watered morning, noon, and night.

Dinner was Joe's favorite time of the day, though he was also fond of supper. It wasn't hard to figure out what was for dinner at our house. We had pinto beans and taters one day and then taters and pinto beans the next day. Today we also had corn on the cob, green beans, fried squash, and, of course, a big pan of hot biscuits. On a tough first priming day like this hot August day, Joe would eat a minimum of six biscuits for dinner.

You didn't have to worry about getting fat when you worked for my dad. He would keep you lean and mean. You'd better eat all you can before you hit the tobacco field.

Mom was always full of surprises when it came to having a dessert to top off an already delicious meal. Today, she pulled a peach saunker out of the stove. Boy, was it tasty!

"This saunker is really good, Mom," Joe said as soon as he tasted the perfect dessert. "If you keep up this all star cooking, you're never going to lose any of your youngins. We'll just stay on with you. No one else can cook like you do."

"Thanks, Joe. I'm glad you enjoy my cooking," Mom said.

Meanwhile, back out in the tobacco field in the hot sun, the tobacco plants drooped under the scorching heat. The steamy, humid evening, along with the backbreaking job of pulling first primings, would really zap the energy out of even the younger primers.

We stopped often and walked to Uncle Nelson's well and drank long from the dipper that hung from a nail under the shelter that covered the well.

"Boy, this water sure hits the spot!" Dad said.

"It is really cool, isn't it?" Joe said.

"I like well water and spring water best of all," Wayne said. "I mean water that does not have to go through them old copper pipes."

Joe remembers drinking water often from the old spring down near the cornfield. Dad usually kept an old pork'n bean can down there to get a drink. When the can was missing Joe would lie flat on his belly and drink like a horse with his lips down in the water and slurping up the water. Now that's the way to get a country drink of water.

The evening priming would go on until about 6:00 p.m. Five acres was a lot of tobacco to pull in one day. By the time the last sled was tied up and all the tobacco was hung, it was about 7:00 p.m. The barn was closed up to get it ready to turn on the heat and start curing in the morning.

Chores still had to be done. Chickens had to be fed and watered. The chicks were now a little over a week old as chicken house crop #2 had been picked up two weeks earlier.

Supper was always good when you worked so hard with first primings. Dad's crew gathered in the back corner of the kitchen with Mom and Dad out front, Elmer and Wayne on the ends of the table, and Rose, Joe, John, Jane, and Danny on the homemade bench in back.

Mom prayed, "Dear Heavenly Father, thank you for this good day. Thank you for health and strength, for this food, and for our family. Bless the sick, the shut-in, and the bereaved. Help us to be a blessing to others. Thank you in Jesus' name. Amen. Amen."

Cornbread and milk never tasted better. Joe ate two large bowls and then had a leftover biscuit with peanut butter on it. Everyone was tired and ate quietly, but did manage to clean out the cornbread.

Giggling at the Table

Joe remembers many times when the youngins on the back bench would get tickled and start giggling. Mom and Dad would not permit giggling at the table. The guilty parties, usually two or three youngins, would have to crawl out under the table and go outside until they could come back to the table and eat without giggling. Once outside, nothing was funny to the youngins. They were hungry and not too many things are funny when you are hungry but you can't eat.

The "giggled out" youngins would go back inside and crawl back under the table to their seats on the bench.

"Make sure you're through giggling before you go back to the bench," Mom said.

"It's not funny outside, Mom," Rose said.

"Why is it so funny in here and not the least bit funny outside, Mom?" John asked.

"That's just the way it is. It's easy to giggle, but harder to giggle when you're hungry and your family is eating," Mom said.

When supper was finished, everyone pitched in to help Mom clean up the kitchen and then it was off to bed for the entire work crew. 5:00 a.m. would come all too soon for this tired bunch of farmers. After a day of first primings, no one wanted to stay up late.

Day #2 of Dad's plan for this week began again at 6:00 a.m. in the wet lower three acres of the hill field.

"It's even wetter this morning than it was yesterday," Joe said as he was soaked to the bone in the first ten minutes.

"It's wet alright," Dad said as he moved Old Kate along with the sled. A veteran horse like Old Kate knew her job and did not require much attention. A simple cluck to get her started and a "whoa" to stop her would do the job. Sometimes if we forgot to "whoa" her, she would stop anyway. A lesser-experienced horse or a hardheaded mule would go on to the end of the row if you didn't "whoa" them.

Runaway Mule

Joe remembers the many experiences with Riley Ashburn's mules the past three years. Those two mules, John and Kate, were so touchy that even the least thing touching their belly would spook them. One time when we were priming tobacco, we had a sled about half full. Somehow an old tobacco stalk got under the sled and it got pushed up under Kate's belly where it poked her. She immediately let out a bray and headed to the end of the tobacco row wide open. The faster she ran and the farther she ran, the more she was spooked.

Dad and Wayne ran after the terrified mule, which was pulling the heavy tobacco sled half full of tobacco like she was at Darlington Motor Speedway. The sled was destroying the tobacco on both sides as the panicked mule kept up her speed until she had reached the end of the row. The run had started at the beginning of the row and made a full row with tobacco stalks slapping the sled.

Finally, Old Kate gave out and stopped. She was soaking wet with sweat and would not be any good for the rest of the day. We had to get Old John to relieve Old Kate. Funny thing about the whole ordeal was the sled stayed upright. Normally, the sled would have turned over.

Today was another smooth day. The hill field was finished at 12:00 noon. Dad decided to finish priming this field before dinner and wait to hang the morning's work after dinner.

Dad's crew and Mr. Shore were back at the barn at 1:00 p.m. to hang all the tied tobacco. All of the workers worked together to get the tobacco hung in the barn before we started on Mr. Shore's field. At 1:45 p.m., the primers were ready to go back to the field while the barn crew started to tie the last Brown sled.

The dog days of August made for another hot day of 95 degrees. It was hard to get your breath down on the ground pulling the ground leaves. It seemed like the heat made the first priming back-aches worse.

Dad's crew took water breaks again today about every two rows.

"Boy, this water is good," Joe said as he took a long drink from the dipper and then poured a small amount on his head and neck. "That sure is re-freshing," he said.

At 5:00 p.m., the primers finished Mr. Shore's two acres. The last sled was tied and on the way into the barn to hang by 5:30 p.m. Dad made sure his last sled was hung first and then put a marker of empty sticks between the Brown's tobacco and the Shore's tobacco.

Barn #2 of this week was finished about 6:15 p.m. The barn was closed and ready for the curing to start at daybreak on Wednesday.

Day #3 of Dad's plan started just like the pre-vious two days, early and wet. The cold dew at 6:00 a.m. was as cool, as the midday sun was hot. The primers moved to the middle field of four acres while the barn crew was all the way over to the "woods" barn. The sleds would have to be pulled a longer distance today.

Mr. Shore would keep the sleds moving as both horses were used. Mr. Shore would be waiting at the end of the rows with an empty sled each time Dad's crew had one full. This organized plan helped the primers as they did not have to wait for the sleds to come back to the field. The barn crew got behind as they missed Mr. Shore helping them all the time.

The priming was finished early today at 3:00 p.m. By the time all the tobacco was tied up and hanged, it was about 4:30 p.m. It sure was nice to get through early. Joe was hoping for a break with maybe a little while to toss the baseball with John, but Dad had other plans as the suckers were growing in all fields.

Dad's crew, minus Mom who went to fix supper, started in the spring field at 5:00 p.m. and would get to work for about an hour before chores and cleaning up for prayer meeting at church tonight.

Thursday and Friday were spent in the tobacco field pulling suckers and worms. The spring field was finished in no time and the hill field was next. This field would take a while as Dad's crew worked Thursday and Friday and were only about a half of the way through.

Chapter 10
The Dentist

Saturday morning dawned with a steady rain. Joe loved these kinds of days during tobacco season. These days were few and far between. Of course, there was always plenty of work to do on the Little Farm on Brown Road. Dad seemed to invent work to do. Joe and John worked most of the day in the chicken house feeding, watering, and doing some general cleaning work.

Dad, Elmer, and Wayne worked in the feed barn getting the old hay situated for the new crop, which was ready to cut when the weather cleared up.

Since it was raining, Elmer drove Mom into Elkin after dinner. Mom took Joe with her to see the dreaded dentist.

"Joe, we've got to get that rotten tooth pulled out before the pain gets so bad you can't stand it," Mom said.

"I can wait a while longer, Mom," Joe said as he did not like any dentist, even though the toothache was getting worse by the day. Nothing hurts worse than a throbbing toothache.

"You need to go on and get it pulled, Joe," Dad said. "We can't stand for you to be out of work when the weather is good."

Elmer drove the 1950 Plymouth to Dr. Schebel's office on Main Street just past the Reeves Theater. Of course, the movie theater was off limits for Mom and Dad's crew. The theater was a sinful place as was dancing. Television was just now becoming popular, but we did not have a TV as they also were on the sin list and we could not afford a TV anyway.

Mom took Joe by the hand and headed into the office of the dreaded dentist. Elmer stayed in the car and watched traffic go by.

"My boy's got a toothache. I need to get the dentist to pull it out. How long do you think we'll have to wait?" Mom asked the slender, pretty young lady behind the desk who greeted us with a smile.

"Yes! You smile at us to trick us to get into the dentist chair and let Dr. Schebel pull all of our teeth," Joe thought to himself. Joe saw right through the scheming plan.

"It will not be very long, ma'am. Probably less than fifteen minutes. Have you been here before? What is your name and your son's name?" asked Miss Evans.

Joe had noticed the nametag the nurse had pinned to her uniform.

"I'm Gladys Brown and this is Joe Brown. We haven't been here before. We used to go to Dr. Smith who was on Bridge Street until he retired," Mom said.

All of a sudden, Joe did not like the rainy day in August. He would rather be suckering tobacco than sitting in a dentist's chair. There was not much Joe could do now. The dreaded dentist walked into the room. He sure did look mean and ornery.

"Who's next, Miss Evans?" Dr. Schebel asked.

"This young man has a bad tooth, Doctor. His name is Joe," Miss Evans answered. She was a nice lady for a dentist office, Joe thought as she led him into the teeth pulling room.

"Which one hurts, young man?" Dr. Schebel asked.

"This one down here in the back," Joe said as he pointed out the sore spot and sat down in the teeth pulling chair.

"It looks like it would be sore. It's infected. How long has it been hurting you?" Dr. Schebel asked.

"It's been hurting for about a week, but gradually getting worse," Joe said.

Dr. Schebel probed around the sore tooth for a few minutes before he made an observation.

"The tooth has to go, young man. There's not enough left to try to save it," Dr. Schebel said. "Let me give you a shot to numb the area around the tooth."

The shot was not that bad. Soon the tooth was not aching anymore. Maybe I can go now, Joe thought.

Dr. Schebel had other ideas. He and Nurse Evans were lining up their tooth pulling instruments to start to work on Joe's soon to be gone tooth. By now, Joe's face and lips felt about the size of a basketball.

Dr. Schebel checked Joe's mouth to see if it was numb.

"Do you feel this?" he said as pinched Joe's gums around the sore tooth.

"I can't feel anything except oversized lips," Joe answered. The tooth extraction was ready to begin.

"Open wide!" Dr. Schebel said as he tilted Joe's head back and began to pull the tooth. He gripped the tooth with what looked like a big set of wire pliers and started to twist the tooth out. The tooth, being a jaw tooth, was embedded in to stay as it was a permanent tooth. Slowly the tooth began to give way and suddenly it was out.

"See what I have here," Dr. Schebel said as he held up the tooth for Joe to see. Joe wished that the dentist would do something about all the blood that was filling his mouth. Joe knew he could not swallow blood or it would make him sick. There was no way to help it as some of the gushing blood had been swallowed.

Joe was feeling very poorly. He always had a weak stomach and could not stand the sight of blood. Dr. Schebel and Nurse Evans were finally packing Joe's mouth with gauze and told Joe to clamp down on the gauze to help stop the bleeding. Joe tried to follow their instructions but he was now sick on his stomach. He felt like he was going to pass out.

"Put your head down between your knees, Joe," Miss Evans said as she put a cold cloth on Joe's neck. She was so kind.

"I told you not to swallow that blood," Dr. Schebel said in a hateful tone. "I told you that it would make you sick."

Mom Lectures Dentist

Mom had been watching all of this from a chair in the corner of the room. She had heard about as much from this hateful dentist that she was going to take. Mom had that look on her face.

"He could not help swallowing blood, Dr. Schebel. His mouth was full of blood," Mom said in an agitated voice. "Quit fussing at my boy and do something to help him."

Dr. Schebel saw that Mom was serious and helped Nurse Evans with Joe. Dr. Schebel put some smelling ammonia to Joe's nose, which perked Joe up. Soon, Joe was okay and ready to get out of this man's torture factory.

Nurse Evans gave Mom instructions. "You need to change the gauze every two hours for the rest of today and tonight, Mrs. Brown. Start gently rinsing his mouth out with warm salt water tomorrow if the bleeding has stopped. I'm sorry Joe got sick, but it's not unusual for that to happen. It just bothers some people more than others."

"Thank you, Nurse. You've been very nice to us and we appreciate it. I do not like the dentist and his attitude, but that's not your fault. How much do I owe you?" Mom asked as she reached into her pocketbook.

"That'll be $5.00, Mrs. Brown," Nurse Evans said. "I don't blame you for the way you feel about Dr. Schebel. A lot of people feel that way."

Mom paid the bill and led Joe out into the fresh air and the steady rain.

"This feels better, Mom," Joe said as he tried to talk without moving his jaws. He wanted to keep the pressure on the hole where the tooth used to be. It was quite an experience for Joe. He would not go back to the dentist for about five years because of Dr. Schebel. Joe would make one trip to the dentist in the next twelve years, which led to rapid deterioration of Joe's teeth.

"Are you alright, Joe?" Elmer asked when they got into the car to head home. Elmer watched Joe's puffed up jaw with all the gauze stuffed in where the tooth used to be.

"He's okay now, Elmer, but I thought I was going to have to whip me a dentist," Mom said. "Dr. Schebel was hateful to Joe when he got sick."

"Why didn't you come and get me, Mom?" Elmer asked. "Maybe I could have helped you," Elmer giggled. "We'd show that old dentist not to mess with a Brown."

Joe would never forget that visit to the dentist and how Mom was so riled. Mom did not take any more of her youngins to Dr. Schebel. He was on Mom's bad list.

After quite a lot of bleeding until about midnight Saturday night, Joe's tooth problem improved Sunday morning. Mom stayed at home from church with Joe both Sunday morning and Sunday night to help him use plenty of salt water to rinse and soothe the sore area.

Joe laid around and took it easy all day Sunday. The rain had stopped early Sunday morning, which meant that Monday probably would be too wet to get into the tobacco field. Dad did not like to work in the field when workers would mire up. So Monday would be another maintenance day around the barnyard and in the chicken house.

On Monday morning, our home barn was ready to empty. Dad's crew took the first curing of the year and packed it up in the packhouse.

On Tuesday morning, the road barn was ready to empty and pack in Mr. Shore's packhouse down behind his big two story house. So far, two straight barns had cured exceptionally well for first primings. The rest of the day was spent suckering in the hill field.

The rainfall over the weekend would delay second primings for a few days. Barn #3, the middle barn, would be emptied out on Wednesday morning. Again the tobacco had cured well. Dad's crew worked the rest of the day suckering the hill field. It was finished at 6:00 p.m. The middle field was next in the suckering parade.

On Thursday morning, the woods barn was emptied. All barns had yielded good quality first primings and all barns were empty and ready for the second primings, which were due to start up on Friday.

On Friday, August 14, Dad's crew would start the long push to go through fourteen acres of tobacco, four days a week until all of the crop was pulled.

Dad's home spring field was first of the second primings. The road barn was filled with second primings from the top hill field on Saturday. The middle barn followed on Monday, August 17, with second primings from the lower hill field and Mr. Shore's field. The seconds were completed with the woods barn on Tuesday from the middle field.

School – Mr. Phillips

This four day a week schedule would continue till all the money crop was pulled and safely in the barn just over two weeks after school had started back up on Monday, September 14.

School would operate for half days the first week. The half days would be a big help to the tobacco farmer. All farmers depended on their youngins who were their work force. Dad's work crew would have to miss eight days in September to work priming tobacco. Mom and Dad did not like for their youngins to miss school but it could not be helped. Tobacco must be pulled when it was ready or the crop would be lost.

Dad's crew got to go to school on day #3 after priming tobacco on the first two days. Joe was ready for school. He welcomed the break from the tobacco field. Joe was in Mr. Phillip's room. He was a new teacher at West Yadkin. The seventh grades were in an old building straight across from the third grade basement classes.

The "chicken house," as we referred to the old building, was a stand alone building and was built between the elementary school building and the playgrounds. Again, like the third grade classes which were isolated, Joe liked the seventh grade building out in the open all by itself. The class was heated by a large pot belly stove in the middle of the room. In cold weather, the stove would be "red hot."

Joe liked Mr. Phillips who must have been talking to Mr. Madison about Joe's basketball game.

Mr. Phillip's class was always playing Mr. Pinnix's class in basketball. Joe was Mr. Phillip's star player. It would be a fun year. Joe would get to know Archie King a little better this year. Joe and Archie would be very good friends for the rest of their school years. They would later play football and basketball together in high school.

Mr. George Holmes was new at school this year. He was the physical education teacher. Joe liked Mr. Holmes who used to take the seventh grade to P.E. everyday after dinner. Joe loved playing "tag" football with Mr. Holmes playing quarterback for both teams. Mr. Holmes threw the best catchable long passes that Joe would run down and catch for long touchdowns.

Joe would later play high school basketball for Mr. Holmes, who later left teaching to go into a family insurance business. This business would lead him into a successful career as a member of the N.C. General Assembly for many years.

On Friday, September 25, Dad's crew started pulling tips at the spring field, followed by the upper hill field on Saturday. The lower hill field and Mr. Shore's field were tipped on Monday, followed by the middle field on Tuesday, September 29. It was a big relief to finish this year's crop well ahead of Jack Frost.

"Yeeeess! Yee! Woo, Woo, Woo," came the cry from the field as the last tips were pulled. An echo was heard from the barn crew. It was always a joyous time to complete the hard work of priming so many acres. There was a good feeling of having accomplished something by working hard as a team.

Chapter 11
Packhouse

"Now we can get you youngins back to school," Dad said as the last sled of the year was on its way to the woods barn. There was still much work to do, but the emphasis would now shift to the packhouse to get the tobacco ready for the market. That work would start on Wednesday as Dad's crew filled the basement at their packhouse with first and second primings to get the tobacco in case.

Tobacco would dry out after being stacked in a hot packhouse for two months. It could not be worked dry. All packhouses would have basements with a damp place to hang dry tobacco to get in case before grading and tying the tobacco for the market.

After working in the packhouse on Wednesday, Thursday, Friday, and Saturday, Dad's crew had a load ready for Gurn Johnson to take to Cook's Warehouse to sell. It was always good to get that first sale over with as early as possible.

On Sunday, October 4, we had the James Henry Brown Reunion at Grandpa Brown's house. It was always a fun time for family and friends to get together for a time of good food and fellowship.

Dad's family got to the reunion at about 12:45 p.m. after going to church first. Ralph Winters again came with Joe and John. He liked the good eating reunions. The large turnout included Dad's family, Uncle Lamar's family, some of Aunt Daisy's, Uncle Nelson, Aunt Jo, Cousin Gray who was now about 5 years old, Cousin Fay who was 2 ½ years old, Aunt Annie Sue, Uncle Troy, Cousin Terry, Aunt Mary Lee, Uncle Allen, Cousin Betty Jo, Cousin

Nickey, Uncle Johnny, Uncle Lonnie, Aunt Stella, Uncle Charlie Moore, Aunt Sally, Leck and Ida Groce and girls, Aunt Lucy Pardue, Gurn and Mitt Johnson, and a whole bunch of Statesville cousins who Joe did not know. Of course, Farmer Brown was with us, too.

Preacher Myers was invited again this year and said the blessings for the food, which was in abundance, as always, when the Browns got together. Joe spied his target of fried chicken and country ham biscuits. He also got a good helping of Mom's pinto beans and biscuits for starters. Ralph and John followed closely, also getting a full plate of good eating. They found a shady seat underneath the old apple tree and quickly laid away the food.

Next, Joe, John, and Ralph made their way to the dessert table, which was crammed full of good looking sweets. Joe got a piece of chocolate pie, a piece of coconut cake, and a good helping of Mom's cherry saunker. Soon, Joe was so full he could not possibly eat another bite. He wanted to find a place to lie down and take a nap.

There would not be naps this evening though as the old baseball was soon being flung all over the front yard. It was a fun evening of baseball with cousins. This year was blessed with beautiful weather for the annual reunion. It was such a fun time.

On Monday when Joe got home from school, Gurn Johnson was backed up to Dad's packhouse loading tobacco for the Tuesday sale. Dad and Gurn would leave out Tuesday morning at 3:00 a.m. to take the load to market. Joe could already taste that good coconut candy. It was always such a treat.

Dad and Gurn got back early Tuesday evening. Mom had supper on the table when Dad got home.

"Come on in and eat with us, Gurn," Mom urged as Gurn had come to the door to speak to Mom and the youngins.

"No. I thank you, but I'd better get home. Mitt will be looking for me," Gurn said. "Joe, your dad got some extra candy for you to take to your girl-friend at school tomorrow," Gurn said with a chuckle.

"I told you I don't have a girlfriend, Gurn. Dad keeps me too busy to even think about a girl," Joe said. However, Joe was beginning to notice girls more now as he was getting older. He had a crush on a cute classmate named Gail Swaim, but Joe was too shy to talk to her or any girl. Joe was becoming more popular now that he was being noticed as the best basketball player on Mr. Phillip's team.

Joe sure wasn't going to let Gurn Johnson know how he felt, though. Gurn would never let up on his kidding if he knew how Joe felt. Those feelings would have to be Joe's secret.

At supper on Wednesday night, October 7, we sang "Happy Birthday" to Jane on her eighth birthday:

"Happy birthday to you.
Happy birthday to you.
Happy birthday to Jane.
Happy birthday to you.

Jane was now in the second grade. John was in the fifth grade. Rose was in the ninth grade, high school already, and Wayne was now a junior with only one more year to go. The ladies man with the wavy blonde hair was hard to guard.

The tobacco tying was moving along nicely as Dad kept Gurn Johnson going to Winston at least one time and sometimes two times a week. The target date of being finished with the tobacco by the first of November looked reachable, even with a few days out of the packhouse to make molasses.

Grandpa's Last Molasses

This year would be the last year Grandpa would have a cane crop and make molasses. Next year the cane mill would be moved over on the hill at Uncle Lamar's to cook the sweet 'lasses. Dad would continue to grow cane.

So there was another note of sadness this year. Last year it was the last corn shucking and this year the last of the cane production at Grandpa Brown's.

On Tuesday, October 13, Grandpa, Dad, and Elmer started cutting cane. The fodder stripping was followed by the whole crew when the school youngins were home. The stripping and juicing of the cane lasted Wednesday and Thursday with the final cane stalks being fed into the cane mill on Friday morning after the cooking had already started. The cooking would last all day, all night, and all day on Saturday to have the sweet juice finished.

All week, Dad's crew was spending the night hours in the packhouse steadily getting the tobacco ready. Dad, Elmer, Wayne, Joe, and John took off long enough Friday night to help Grandpa with his cooking. Joe, John, and Wayne helped Grandpa until midnight when the second shift of Dad, Uncle Nelson, and Elmer would take over the graveyard shift.

Grandpa Brown got into his storytelling tonight as Wayne, Joe, and John urged him to tell us some of the old stories.

Grandpa began, "I remember a few years back when an old man in the community died after a long illness. The man had a severe back problem.

His back was so humpback that he could not stand straight or lay down flat. His back formed into an "L" shape or as the form of his body sitting in a straight chair."

"When the man died, the funeral home strapped the man down tightly in the casket with straps around his feet and also around him up just under the arms. Otherwise, the man would have been sitting up in his casket. In those old days as now, people would sit up all night with his body on the night before the funeral."

"The funeral home would deliver the body to the house and turn it over to the friends and neighbors of the community. The house would be packed with people until about midnight when the majority of the neighbors would go home. They would have eaten their fill of the good food brought in by the best cooks in the community."

"The shift from midnight to 6:00 a.m. would be desolate with only three or four people at the most around for what has been called the graveyard shift. One of the newest of the neighbors, who had not sat up with a body before, was sitting next to the coffin, which was placed next to an open window."

"This neighbor had boasted he would sit all night with the body by himself. The general opinion was deep down this neighbor was scared to death."

"Well, about 2:00 a.m., the neighbor was dozing a little when the strap under the body's arms broke. All of a sudden, the body sat straight up in the coffin. The boastful neighbor was totally spooked. He reached over to the windowsill and picked up a hammer and promptly hit the sit up body in the head while declaring, 'If you're gonna be dead, be dead!' He took off running and did not return to sit with the body. That is a true story, mind you. I've heard many other stories about strange "goings on" at the sit up nights."

Grandpa checked the fire and skimmed off the foam from the molasses and was ready for another story. Joe's eyes were getting heavy but he would not go to sleep as long as Grandpa was telling his stories.

Grandpa went on with another story. "These two men had been fishing all night up on the Yadkin River. They had managed to accumulate a large string of good sized fish and one really big catfish. They finally called it quits about 3:00 a.m. and headed up through Elkin towards their houses. As was convenient to them, they stopped at the town graveyard to divide their fish. They dropped the large catfish at the gate beside of the big marble tombstone of one of the town fathers. They went on into the graveyard to get into the moonlight to have better light to divide the fish."

"Unknown to the two fishermen, a grave robber had heard them coming and hid on the other side of the large tombstone, the opposite side of the big catfish. The grave robber clutched his bag of valuables that he had stolen from graves tonight. He was afraid that he had been caught. He nervously waited in hiding."

"The fish dividing was taking place a few feet away under the full moon. The grave robber could not bear to look. He was petrified. He just sat there and listened. 'One for you and one for me' went on and on. 'One for you and one for me. One for you and one for me.' The dividing was about finished. 'One for you and one for me.'"

"One of the fishermen, remembering the big catfish, asked loudly, 'How about that one up by the front gate?' The grave robber took off running and was never seen again. He was scared to death. He left his bag of valuables at the gate.

The fishermen found them and turned them over to the local law officers. The graveyard never had another problem with grave robbers. I wonder if he is still running." Grandpa reared back and laughed at his own story.

It was midnight and shift change time. Dad, Uncle Nelson, and Elmer took over the molasses cooking.

Wayne, Joe, and John hurried home and to bed to get about five hours of sleep. Dad would be rearing to go in the packhouse by 6:00 a.m.

Dad's crew worked in the packhouse until noon and then went up to Grandpa Brown's for the evening of fun as the molasses was finishing up. As usual, family and neighbors were all over the place to enjoy the event and to buy some of Grandpa's molasses. It was a good day. Joe could not believe that this was the last cane week for Grandpa. Why couldn't things stay the same? Joe so enjoyed spending time with his Grandpa.

Dad loaded his share of the 'lasses on the old truck and put them in the canned goods room. It was a good sight for the upcoming winter to see the room full of food. It paid to be prepared for the months ahead. Mom would fix food from this room for the next year. Of course, the hog killings would add meat to this diverse food supply in December.

The next two weeks would wrap up the packhouse work. Most of this work was in Mr. Shore's packhouse down on the road to Little Hunting Creek. The packhouse was in behind Mr. Shore's house.

On Wednesday, October 28, Dad's crew finished getting the 1953 crop of tobacco ready for the market. We had kept Gurn Johnson busy for the past month and today, he would load up the last load to go to the market on Thursday morning.

What a long season! Joe was glad to see the last of the golden brown tobacco ready to sell.

The tobacco had brought a good price all this season. Mom and Dad made their trip to town to stock up on supplies for the next year. They bought 100 pounds of pinto beans, 100 pounds of sugar, 50 pounds of white beans, and 4 gallon cans of American Ace coffee.

Mom and Dad also bought new clothes and shoes for all of their youngins. Joe finally got blue jeans to wear instead of the old overalls he had to wear in prior years. Dad had stopped by Paul Dobbins' store to pay off the fertilizer bill and also the bill for food items charged since last fall.

November came in with a heavy frost. The corn crop was pulled and shucked. It was another good year for corn. The popcorn was bigger and better than ever.

"I sure do miss Grandpa's corn shucking this year," Joe said as Dad's crew sat around the corn pile. "It just doesn't seem right."

"Speak of Grandpa and here he comes," Mom said with a smile.

"Hey there, youngins! Thought I'd come down and help ya'll with your corn," Grandpa said as he pulled up a nail keg and sat down.

"We miss your corn shucking this year, Grandpa," Wayne said.

"We sure do!" everyone echoed.

"I miss seeing all the people and the good fellowship," Grandpa said. "I saw the same bunch of people every year for so long it'll just take a while to get over it."

On Friday, November 13, the Holly Farms truck came to get chickens as they had fattened up nicely after sixteen weeks of eating day and night. The chicken house was empty when Joe got home from school. Now the job of getting the house ready again for new chicks was under way. The new chicks would arrive on November 20.

The chickens brought a good price, but losses were higher in this house. Losses were usually higher in July and August when the weather was so hot and humid.

Wayne turned seventeen on November 30.

"Happy birthday to you.
Happy birthday to you.
Happy birthday to Wayne.
Happy birthday to you."

Wintertime

November was gone and wintertime was here. Joe enjoyed almost everyday in the gym during P.E. Mr. Phillip's room was giving Mr. Pinnix's room a good trouncing in basketball about every time they played. Joe and Archie King worked together to do most of the scoring. Both of them had a good set shot and were quick with the ball.

On Tuesday, December 8, when Joe walked into the classroom before school, Mr. Phillips and Mr. Pinnix were discussing yesterday's rare loss by Joe's team, 8-6.

"My star player had an off day. He couldn't get it going. I guess he was due a down game. He's played so well all this season," Mr. Phillips said.

"We were fortunate to win," Mr. Pinnix said. "You have all the best players. That's for sure."

Joe checked the pot belly stove and added some coal to the fire. It was a cold morning and the fire had not really got going good. When the weather got real cold, the stove would be totally red hot. All the students would huddle around the stove before school to get warm before moving to their seats.

The classroom was not very airtight and the back of the room would get cold even when the pot belly stove was red hot. On the coldest days, Mr. Phillips would let the students in the rear come up often to warm their cold hands.

Chapter 12
Christmas 1953

December was moving along, cold and damp, with threats of snow every few days, but only flurries would fall. School was scheduled to shut down for the Christmas holiday on Tuesday, December 22. Joe was hoping for a party and they had a nice one. Monday had been very cold with temperatures about twenty degrees for the high. Today was even colder. The artic weather made for a brisk walk to the bus when school dismissed.

"Merry Christmas, Joe! Hope you have a good two weeks off," Mr. Phillips said. School would be out until January 4, 1954.

"I hope you have a nice vacation, too, Mr. Phillips," Joe said.

Dad didn't wait any longer for the hog killing. He didn't want to miss this streak of cold weather. At first light on Wednesday morning, the hog killing began. Dad had three huge hogs to kill and Grandpa Brown had one.

Dad, Elmer, Wayne, Joe, and John got to work. Grandpa Brown helped, too, but he did not get involved in any of the heavy work. He sure enjoyed being a part of the hog killing, though.

By 11:00 a.m., Dad's crew had finished their three hogs and also Grandpa's. Elmer and Wayne were on the way to Martin's Grocery on Swan Creek Road to get the sausage ground up. As usual, Dad sold the hams, half of the shoulders, and most of the tenderloin to Mr. Martin. This sale sure did help out with much needed cash for the Christmas gifts.

The smokehouse was filled to the top again while Mom's canned goods room was overflowing with all the jars of sausage. Dad was ready for the long, cold winter now as we had plenty of food to eat.

To celebrate a good hog day, Dad's crew had popcorn, crackerjacks, and Mom's famous chocolate candy after supper while sitting around the fire.

"This sure is good, Dad," Joe said as he tried to eat all three of the snacks. Dad had popped six bowls of popcorn as he needed a bunch for this large and hungry family.

"It is good, Joe," Dad said as he was trying to hold Jane in his lap and eat at the same time.

Mom was helping Danny who soon would be five years old. Danny's favorite was the chocolate candy. Mom's candy was a favorite of all of her family, though.

"It's bedtime!" Mom said as it was about 9:30 p.m. The youngins could stay up a little later now that school was out. "Tomorrow is Christmas Eve," she added.

Joe woke up Thursday morning to the smell of sausage cooking. What a good smell! Mom had a way of waking everyone up cooking breakfast. This morning's breakfast was complete with the sausage, scrambled eggs, and those tasty biscuits. Joe could eat all day with this kind of food. He ate six biscuits or was it seven? It's hard to tell when they're smothered with Mom's good gravy.

The outside chores were done quickly as the cold wind was quite brisk. It felt like snow with the north wind blowing in our faces.

The work in the chicken house was not at all bad today. It was warm inside as the heaters were going full blast. The chickens were now almost five weeks old and eating more every day.

"It feels good in here, John," Joe said as they toted water from the outside spigot, which had to be thawed out by Dad earlier.

"I don't mind working in here on these cold days," John said. "These chickens have it made, don't they? All they do is eat, drink, and sleep."

"No, they don't have it made," Joe said. "After they eat and drink and get fat, they die."

After supper, John, Jane, and Danny put out their shoe boxes for Santa's visit. Mom always saved the shoe boxes for this occasion. She did not have stockings to spare as most people used to hang up. It wasn't a bad deal as the shoe box could hold more than a stocking.

At precisely 5:00 a.m. on December 25, the feet hit the floor and the house came alive.

"It's Christmas!" John said as he ran to check out how he had done with Santa. "Wow! Look at my ball glove, Joe." John picked up his first store bought baseball glove. "It's a Jimmy Piersall glove, Joe."

Joe's mind was working overtime. He figured that he also would have a ball glove in his gift under the tree. Joe and John always got the same gifts.

Joe would have to wait a few minutes as he watched Jane and Danny enjoying their Santa Claus. Jane was excited over her "Little Red Riding Hood" doll. She was showing the doll to everyone who would look at it.

"That's a nice looking doll, Jane," Joe said as he looked it over.

"Look at my tractors, Joe," Danny said showing off the three farm tractors Santa brought. Santa also left fruit, nuts, and candy, but that would have to wait. The toys were getting all of the attention now.

Finally, it was gift opening time for the nor Santa youngins. Joe excitedly opened his gift, throwing paper everywhere. Sure enough, he had his first store bought baseball glove, too.

"Look, John! I got a Phil Rizutto glove. It is so nice and soft. Smells good, too," Joe said as he worked on the pocket of the glove with his fist to break it in.

Mom was fixing breakfast, which was a real treat today. We had sausage again and also tenderloin, Joe's all-time favorite breakfast meat. It was so good.

Breakfast was on and right on cue, Grandpa Brown knocked on the door.

"Merry Christmas, youngins!" Grandpa said as he came in blowing fog from the artic air. "It's North Pole cold today. I need a cup of that American Ace coffee to warm me up," Grandpa said.

"Here's your coffee, Grandpa," Mom said as she put the coffee on the table between Dad and her. Grandpa sat down as Mom prayed, "Heavenly Father, thank you for this day and for what it means to us. Thank you for sending Jesus to give us salvation. Bless the sick and shut in. Be with the bereaved. Bless this food now in Jesus' name. Amen. Amen."

"Grandpa, you need to eat some of this tenderloin," Joe said. "It is the best ever."

"I'll make me a tenderloin biscuit to go with my coffee," Grandpa said. "Boy, it is good. You make the best biscuits in the world, Gladys."

"Thank you, Grandpa," Mom said with a smile.

After breakfast, Grandpa was ready to go. He seemed restless this morning. He wasn't feeling well, but he still managed a smile as he lit up one of the cigars we gave him for Christmas. He talked to Trixie and Sandy as they barked at him as he slowly walked up the winding driveway to his house. It hurt Joe to see Grandpa not feeling well and slowing down more day by day.

After dinner, as tradition was with our family, Dad drove down to Mom's family's Christmas at Grandpa and Grandma Proctor's house.

"He hasn't mowed these weeds down in six months," Dad said as he turned the car into the driveway. "I guess he'll wait till springtime now."

Cars were everywhere around the house and in the yard. It certainly looked like a good turnout today.

"Come in, youngins!" Grandma Proctor said as she hurried to the kitchen to hand out her biscuits. Hands were reaching out from all directions. Joe had three of the most perfect biscuits he could possibly want. The other youngins all had two or three.

"Time to give out presents!" Grandma said as everyone headed to the front room. All of Mom's brothers and sisters were here today except Uncle Troy from Texas.

Aunt Jane, Aunt De Ette, and Aunt Dorothy were giving out the gifts. The chatter was nonstop as the kinfolk were making up for lost time. Some of these people would only see each other two times a year.

Joe appreciated all of his gifts, that is, except the one he got from a cousin who thought Joe was five or six years old. He got Joe a coloring book and crayons. Joe, who would be thirteen years old in January, gave the coloring book to Danny when they got home.

The gift of the day at the Proctor's was always from Grandma. Joe was hoping for the same traditional gift, a baseball. He was not disappointed as he and John both got one.

"Thank you, Grandma!" Joe said as he gave her a hug.

"Thank you, Grandma!" John said.

"You're welcome, boys. I hope you don't get tired of baseballs each year. That's what your mom says you want," Grandma said with a sweet smile.

"No, we don't get tired of them. We will use them up as usual before next Christmas," Joe said.

The evening passed quickly. Darkness was lingering as the skies were still gray.

"We need to go," Dad said as he headed to the car. Goodbyes were said and Dad's crew was on their way back to Cycle to the Little Farm on Brown Road.

Chores were done. Cows were milked. Chickens were watered and fed while Mom got supper ready. She sang an old Christmas song quietly as she stood by the stove:

"It came upon a midnight clear,
That glorious song of old..."

The song faded into a hum with Rose and Jane joining in to help Mom. Soon, Danny came into the kitchen and he and Jane started singing:

"Jingle Bells, Jingle Bells.
Jingle all the way.
Oh, what fun it is to ride
In a one horse open sleigh..."

Supper was over. Christmas was gone for another year. Everyone was exhausted and headed to bed to get warm under all of them quilts. The cold wind was howling. Snow was falling lightly as Joe fell asleep listening to the wind.

The Cold Night

Joe was dreaming immediately. He was rabbit hunting with Grandpa Brown in the snow. They had tracked and shot four good sized cottontails. Suddenly, the weather turned bad. The cloudy skies became a furious blizzard. In just a few minutes, the blizzard was so bad, Grandpa and Joe sought refuge in the small cave underneath on one of the big rocks at the Rock. They had to feel their way into the cave. Then they could look out at the blinding snow.

Grandpa built a fire as they sat and waited for the big storm to lift. The storm did not let up. Grandpa had a concerned look on his face. A glance at his pocket watch told him it was almost 5:00 p.m. It would be nightfall soon and would be even darker. As it was now, there was not a chance of heading to the house. It would be safer to stay in this shelter until the storm broke.

It was now dark. Joe would have been scared except that he was with Grandpa Brown his hero. He knew he would be okay in any kind of weather with Grandpa Brown.

"The storm is not going to let up, Joe," Grandpa said. "We'll stay here in our little cave until the weather improves. We cannot make it back home in this mess. I'll cook us a rabbit and we can eat some snow."

Snow was piled up everywhere around the little cave. The night had a stillness about it with the exception of the howling wind. Joe just hoped Grandpa's bear friends did not also need a shelter tonight. A bear sure would crowd this little cave.

"Ain't this where you and Wiley Pinnix got run off by the great big bear, Grandpa?" Joe asked as he ate hungrily on a rabbit leg.

"It sure is! Right here where we're sitting," Grandpa said with a chuckle.

Joe knew that Mom, Dad, and the other youngins would be worried about them. Grandma Brown would be a basket case by now and would already have Grandpa and Joe as good as dead. Grandpa and Joe snuggled together near the fire and dozed off to sleep about midnight with the blizzard still going strong.

Joe awoke first at daybreak and quickly rubbed his eyes and tried to figure out where he was.

"Oh, that's cold!" Joe said as snow fell on his neck. "Oh! It's cold!"

Joe awoke from his dream. Elmer was putting snow on his neck to wake him up.

"Stop! Stop! That's cold!" Joe said as he realized he had been dreaming. "Boy, what a dream I had!"

Joe told about his dream while eating sausage, eggs, and gravy with Mom's biscuits. He shivered as he thought about the storm.

"Your dreams are amazing, Joe," Mom said as she sipped her American Ace coffee. "We need to make a book of your dreams. They would be fun for your grandchildren to read some day."

The snow lingered around for three or four days. With the cold temperatures, there was not much to do except stay by the fire. Dad was in a popcorn popping mood about every night. It was always fun when we had the treat of popcorn, crackerjacks, and Mom's chocolate candy. It was no wonder Dad put on the weight during the wintertime. He could eat some popcorn, crackerjacks, and candy.

1953 was about gone. Time sure was going fast for Joe and his family.

"Can we stay up tonight to bring in 1954, Dad?" Joe asked knowing what the answer would be.

"No! It's bedtime. We've got a lot or work to do tomorrow," Dad said. It was off to bed for everyone as "Happy New Year" would have to wait till morning.

Chapter 13
New Neighbors

January 1, 1954, came in cold as you would expect for January. Dad got everyone up early as usual to do chores and get ready for a big day. Uncle Nelson and Aunt Jo were moving into Mr. Shore's old house down on the road to Paul Caudle's Mill on Shore Road. Uncle Nelson was Dad's youngest brother who would now be renting tobacco from Mr. Shore. We would spend the next several years together in the tobacco fields.

Dad and Uncle Nelson always seemed to get along so good. They were both hard workers who loved to be out in the tobacco field.

"Nelson is moving today," Dad reminded us at breakfast. "Elmer, Wayne, and me will go down to help him load up and then the rest of you can come over to help us unload. Joe, you and John get the chickens watered and fed while we're gone."

Joe could tell right away that today was going to be a cold day. The sun was up but it definitely was wintertime, about fifteen degrees. Joe ran to the chicken house pretending to be playing halfback for his favorite football team, the Cleveland Browns, of course. He made quick moves left and right and broke into the clear and scored again.

Joe repeated his running with the imaginary football under his arm as he returned to the house. He would run off and leave John behind. John was not a speedy runner.

Back at the house, Joe had to wait until 10:00 a.m. to go over to help Dad and Uncle Nelson. Dad thought they would be over with the first load about midmorning.

Joe and John bundled up and headed out across the field past the thicket to Shore Road. The thicket was the hiding place for rabbits.

"How many rabbits do you think are in there in their warm beds, John?" Joe asked.

"Probably hundreds of them. I don't blame them this morning. It's too cold to be out and about," John said.

Just as Joe and John got to Shore Road, Uncle Nelson and Aunt Jo came by in their borrowed pickup truck followed by Dad, Elmer, and Wayne in the old 1950 Plymouth. Dad stopped to give Joe and John a ride.

"Get in out of the cold, boys," Dad said. "It's hog killing weather today."

Dad pulled up into the driveway behind Mr. Shore's car. Uncle Nelson had backed up to the front door of the big old country house. Joe was amazed at how big this house was. Was it really that big or did it just seem to be so big because our house is small?

Mr. Shore had bought the house and farm from Walt Chipman a few years back.

Mr. Chipman was Joe's Uncle Bill's dad. Bill had married Dad's oldest sister Daisy. Mr. Shore had recently built a new brick house on Brown Road just past the curve at the road tobacco barn. Joe wondered what it would be like to have a nice, new brick house. It looked so fancy.

Unloading a pickup truck of furniture did not take long with all the help that was around. Soon, Uncle Nelson headed back to get another load. He was anxious to get the moving done. They had wanted to move back to the old home place for years now.

Two years earlier, Dad helped Uncle Nelson start a house on Brown Road across from Grandpa Brown's. The basement was dug and blocks were laid but times were so hard that no more work had been done except the well was dug. This well was used by Dad's work crew when they worked Mr. Shore's hill field.

By the end of the day, the move had been completed. As always with a move, it takes time to get the house in order. Mom invited our new neighbors to supper tonight.

It was a good meal and was appreciated by Uncle Nelson, Aunt Jo, and cousins Gray and Fay. Gray was 5 years old and Fay was 2 ½ years old.

"We sure do appreciate this good meal, Gladys," Aunt Jo said. "I'll get all my cooking utensils and dishes unpacked tomorrow."

"Moving is a big job, isn't it?" Mom said.

"It sure is!" Uncle Nelson said as he ate his cornbread and milk after first wiping out a big plate full of pinto beans. Uncle Nelson was a big eater who had eaten dinner on the run today.

After supper, our new neighbors left quickly as they were worn out from the long, hard day. The two youngins were ready for bed in their new house.

School was back in session on Monday, January 4. Joe was glad to see some of his classmates again. It was back to the old gym today as the weather did not allow for outside play. Most of January's P.E. time was spent in the gym.

On January 18, Danny had his fifth birthday followed by Joe's thirteenth birthday on January 21. Joe was now a teenager. My, how does time go so fast? Dad celebrated his fortieth birthday on January 24. January is a busy time in the Brown family.

February came in with continued cold weather. The old groundhog saw his shadow on Tuesday, February 2, which meant that there would be six more weeks of bad weather. Some people believe in the groundhog and some people scoff at him, but this year he was right. The weather was a mess until about mid March.

Dad managed to sneak in some work on the plant beds and his crew got them sown on Saturday, February 13. Immediately we got snow on and off for the next two weeks. This weather suited Dad perfectly. The snow was the steady, but slow moisture the tobacco plants needed.

Dad sowed plant beds again this year for fourteen acres, two acres at home and twelve acres at Mr. Shore's farm. Uncle Nelson was tending four acres at Mr. Shore's farm and two acres at his spread. Dad and Uncle Nelson would start a working relationship between their families that would last for many years.

Dad and Uncle Nelson would help each other throughout the year, but the swap work between the families would be in the tobacco priming. Between the two families, they would produce twenty acres of tobacco this year and for the next six years that Joe was on the farm. On February 23, Rose had her fifteenth birthday while John was now eleven.

March came in windy and getting warmer. The farmer's spring had arrived. There still would be some cold weather but the air felt like springtime.

Catching

Basketball season was over at school and Mr. Holmes had his P.E. class playing baseball. As usual, Joe was catching. In old days, catching was called "hind catcher." Joe was quick, mobile, and determined enough to catch whoever pitched. He would later turn to playing the outfield where he could use his speed. The older Joe got, the less he wanted to squat down so close to the baseball bat of a reckless batter.

No masks were available for catching to wear in P.E. Joe had a good memory of how it felt to be hit with a baseball bat. Back when Joe was in the sixth grade, he was just standing around waiting for his turn to bat when he was hit flush in the forehead by Lonzo Brown, no kin, who was recklessly swinging his baseball bat. Joe was knocked down and dazed for a while and later would have vomiting spells from the possible concussion he had received.

This experience was the beginning of the end of Joe's catching career. He would now concentrate on chasing down fly balls in the outfield.

April was here with warmer weather and a lot of plowing being done in the tobacco fields, getting them turned and ready to lay off tobacco rows soon.

Dad had a new house full of chickens, which were now two weeks old. The old house of chickens had been picked up on March 12.

Setting Time

The tobacco plants were coming along and looked like they would be ready the first week of May. Dad was throwing a lot of water on the plants to make sure they would be ready.

May 1 came and the celebrated barefoot day. It sure was good to get out of them brogans and get your feet in the freshly plowed soil.

On Friday, May 7, Dad's crew set the two acre spring field. Dad only kept Wayne out of school today and still got the two acres finished before dark with help from the school youngins.

"We'll get a good start on the hill field tomorrow," Dad said at supper. "Then we'll have to miss some school next week to get the rest of the tobacco set out at Mr. Shore's farm."

The hill field was set out on Saturday and then finished on Monday with the full school crew staying home. Dad had four crews operating the old hand setters in rapid style. The click clack sound echoed all over the hill field and down into the woods behind the road barn.

Mom dropped for Dad while Rose dropped for Elmer. John dropped for Wayne while 8 ½ year old Jane dropped for Joe. Jane was turning into a good dropper as Joe was patient with her. Joe and Jane were always close and worked good together.

After a few days for the plant beds to recover, Dad's crew finished the tobacco setting for the year on Thursday, May 13. The four acre middle field was set out in rapid production fashion. The crew Dad now had was his best ever. This year would be the last year for this crew as this year would be Elmer's final year on the farm. After working two additional years past graduation, Elmer was looking to go to a public job after this year's tobacco harvesting was completed.

The next two weeks were filled with a lot of hoeing work and corn planting.

Every day after school, Dad's crew would work until dark chopping crabgrass and hoeing the important money crop. This repetitive work would keep going until Dad would lay by the tobacco in late June.

On Friday, May 25, at 12:00 noon, the school year was over. Joe had really enjoyed this year in the seventh grade "chicken house." He continued to learn a lot about basketball from Mr. Phillips and the P.E. teacher, Mr. Holmes.

Wayne was promoted to grade 12. He was now a senior. He primped more than ever with those wavy locks of blonde hair. Rose was promoted to grade 10 while Joe was going to grade 8. John would now be in the sixth grade. "Baby Jane" as she was known as not long ago, was now promoted to grade 3. Where does time go?

Jane loved school. Joe remembers how she so wanted to start to school. In 1952 when we were working in tobacco at Riley Ashburn's farm, Jane was talking about school to Mr. Ashburn.

"What grade will you be in this year, Jane?" Mr. Ashburn asked as Jane was handing up tobacco.

"I'll be in the oneth grade, Mr. Ashburn," Jane answered proudly. She was ready to start to school in the oneth grade.

June was here. The weather was getting hotter. The hay crop was good this year and the creek felt so good after the two days of getting up hay. The pour-over waters were cool, but it was bearable, blue lips and all.

The garden was starting to come in with lots of early peas, which were so tasty as they blended in with the pinto beans and taters.

After three and a half years at Mineral Springs, Pastor Myers left at the end of June. He had done a great job and would be sorely missed. Pastor Hankins was our new pastor.

July was hot and dry as Dad took his crew back to the mountains to again pick cherries at West Jefferson. This day was always a welcomed break from the day in and day out tobacco field routine.

Blackberries were plentiful. Mom's canned goods room was beginning to fill up again. Most of last year's canning was gone with the exception of some sausage and molasses. The garden yield was excellent this year. Mom was so busy preparing food for next winter. Mom just kept on going. She was amazing. We wished her a happy birthday on Friday, July 16.

Chapter 14
New Team

On Friday, July 30, Dad's crew and Uncle Nelson and Aunt Jo began their tobacco priming swap. The spring field was pulled first and then Uncle Nelson's two acres were pulled. Both two acre fields were combined in Dad's barn. It was a full barn but it worked good together.

The new swap worked good as Dad, Uncle Nelson, Wayne, Joe, and John primed while Elmer tied with Mom and Jane handing up to him. Rose also tied with Aunt Jo, Danny, and Gray handing up to her. Danny and Gray were now over 5 ½ years old and were excited to be learning how to hand up tobacco. Youngins learned to work at an early age on the Little Farm on Brown Road.

Aunt Jo's other children, Fay, who was three years old, played nearby and baby Debbie, "Debbie Dean" who was only 2 ½ months old, slept in the playpen set up in the shade under the shelter. "Debbie Dean" got an early indoctrination into the tobacco work. She immediately became a favorite of Dad's work crew.

First primings were continued on Saturday with plans to pull about three fourths of the hill field to put into the road barn. The balance of the hill field and the middle field would be pulled on Tuesday to go into the middle barn. Uncle Nelson's woods field would be pulled on Wednesday and would be cured in the woods barn. Later on in the priming season, our barn space would be tight and we would use Grandpa Brown's old barn.

In the hill field, Dad's work crew got a new challenge. This day's primings would be the most we had ever primed. With our new help and with

Mr. Shore to help, the challenge was met. Mr. Shore loved to work and he also loved his new renters. This year was Dad's second year and Uncle Nelson's first year on Mr. Shore's farm. They worked as a good team to get the job done. Again, Mr. Shore worked without charge to his renters.

The priming crew was the same today as yesterday with Dad, Uncle Nelson, Wayne, Joe, and John. Elmer and Mr. Shore helped prime the first sled but then moved to the barn to help them keep up.

Uncle Nelson was excited about working with Dad's crew. All of Dad's youngins loved Uncle Nelson and Aunt Jo. We would become very close over the next five or six years. "Clyde, I believe we could tend thirty acres of tobacco with this crew, don't you?" Uncle Nelson said as we reached the end of the row.

"I think we could, too," Dad answered. "But remember, we're going to lose Elmer after this year and probably Wayne, too. He's talking about going to public work where Elmer goes."

"I forgot about that," Uncle Nelson said. "We'll still be good, but we'll definitely miss them."

Saturday was a long work day as six acres of the hill field was finished and in the road barn. It was late, about 7:00 p.m., when the work ended.

Sunday was a welcome day of rest for Dad's work crew. Two straight days of first primings would make you appreciate a Sunday. Pallets were spread all over the front yard under the shade trees. The after church naps were about to begin. It was too hot in the house to sleep.

Cow Pasture Ball

As hot as it was, it wasn't too hot to play baseball. Joe and John met Jimmy and Avalon down in

Uncle Lamar's pasture for the evening of fun. Sweating profusely, the youngins would play ball until the time for church, about 5:00 p.m., when we would hear Dad's whistle. Joe and John would rather play on the same team and beat their cousins from up on the hill from the spring. It was never a contest that way, though, as Joe and John would always beat Jimmy, who was fifteen years old and Avalon, who was the runt and nine years old.

Many times the cousins, who were best friends, would get into a fight after their games. So, usually, the teams had to split up and play with Jimmy and John against Joe and Avalon. Joe was stuck with the runt. Avalon had not yet learned to play the game. He, like most nine year olds, was wild with their throws and could not hit.

Joe and Avalon would usually lose. Joe hated to lose in anything and anytime. Joe was never a good loser. To help balance things out, Joe and Jimmy, the two older youngins, would bat left handed instead of right handed. The fence behind right field would be a homerun as well as the trees in centerfield.

With only two players on a team, it would be necessary for the defensive team to throw the ball back and forth when the other team got both runners on base. Most of the time, the throwing would not take long as Avalon could not catch the ball or throw it very good.

Such times could be trying, but Joe and John loved to play baseball and would sacrifice not being able to play on the same team. Joe and John would toss the baseball back and forth in the barnyard endless hours after a long day of work in the tobacco field. They would pretend to be their favorite hero. Joe was always Mickey Mantle and

John was Rocky Colavito of his favorite team, the Cleveland Indians. My, what good dreams we had!

On Monday morning, bright and early at 4:00 a.m., Dad woke up all the youngins. He wanted to be in the field by 5:30 a.m. to beat some of the dog day's heat. It would be another long, hard, hot day.

Mom had her award winning breakfast ready at 4:30 a.m. She had scrambled eggs, fried sausage, gravy, and, of course, her "blue ribbon" biscuits. A breakfast like this was worth getting up at 4:00 a.m. to eat.

Mom prayed, "Dear Heavenly Father, thank you for this good day you've given us. Thank you for health and strength, this food, and the many blessings of life. Bless this food to the nourishment of our body. Be with the sick, shut in, and the bereaved. Help us through this day. We pray in Jesus' name. Amen. Amen."

With a breakfast like we have and our praying Mom, who could possibly fall short in their work efforts for today? Mom with her preparation and Dad with his supervision kept all of us youngins on the go.

The hill field first primings were finished and the middle field four acres were also pulled today. The middle barn was packed full and ready to cure at 6:00 p.m. So far this priming season, we were making good progress. It was more fun this year, too, with Uncle Nelson. He was always fun to work with. He loved to pick and play around. Many times at the end of the tobacco row, Joe and John would wrestle with Uncle Nelson. They loved to pin him and then harass him about it.

On Tuesday, Dad's crew finished the last of the first primings at Uncle Nelson's four acre field over next to the wood's barn. Mr. Shore had a watermelon patch over near this field and, as tradition was, every morning about 9:30 to 10:00, all the primers would go to the barn to pig out on good, cold, juicy watermelons that had been put in the little branch between the tobacco field and the barn.

Watermelons

Watermelon tasted so much better when you could eat them and not worry about getting the juice on your clothes. You could wipe your mouth on your shirt sleeve and keep on eating. Watermelon seeds would be spit in all different directions. It was just a plain, old, carefree watermelon feast.

All them watermelons did make it mighty hard for us to bend back over to pull first primings, though. It wasn't long before we were going at full blast again and would be ready for Mom's dinner. The watermelon break, being all water, did not keep our energy level up for very long.

Uncle Nelson's four acres were finished at 4:00 p.m. It was early to finish as most barns would not be completed until close to dark. Uncle Nelson was excited like a little youngin with his tobacco crop. He continued to work hard and be happy about this crop, his first crop at Mr. Shore's farm.

The rest of the week was spent in the tobacco field suckering tobacco. It was hot, humid, and dry. We really needed some rain. The swim at the pour-over each day felt mighty refreshing, even though the walk back to the house would really dry you out again.

Finally, we got some rain on Thursday, which cooled things off a little. Dad and Uncle Nelson delayed their second primings until Monday because of the rain showers we had received. Not priming tobacco, however, did not mean we didn't work in tobacco. We stayed in the field pulling suckers except in major downpours and thunderstorms.

Chicken Thief

On Saturday evening, we all gathered up at Grandpa's for fun and stories. It was mid evening and Dad had let us off work a little early. We looked at him kind of funny. Was Dad sick letting us off so early on Saturday?

We enjoyed playing with Lyman, Jimmy, Lorene, and Avalon for awhile, but what we really wanted was to hear Grandpa's stories. With his chew of Brown Mule tobacco in his jaw and his cigar ready to be lit, we knew the stories were about ready to start.

Grandpa began, "Back when Annie Sue was a baby, we had a big chicken lot full of laying hens. They were really laying us a bunch of eggs. We were selling eggs all over the community. The egg money really helped as it was in the Great Depression. Well, something was getting our hens. Two or more would disappear each night. We thought an old weasel was sneaking in or maybe a fox. It was definitely happening at night so it could not be chicken hawks."

"I decided to stay up one night to watch after I had lost hens for four straight nights. I had lost a total of ten hens. Well, I got me a good chew of Brown Mule tobacco and loaded both barrels of my old 12 gage shotgun with scattershot. I set my easy chair out in the corner of the yard out of sight but where I could watch the henhouse and fenced in lot."

"It was a clear night with a full moon. I didn't hear anything for hours and had dozed off when at about 1:00 a.m., the hens started cackling. I raised up my shotgun to take aim and saw a two legged varmint, a chicken thieving man, going over my fence with two hens in each hand."

"I let go with both barrels and watched the scoundrel get hit in the seat of his pants as he was almost over the fence. He let the chickens go, screamed, and ran down towards the road where he had someone waiting for him in a car. They sped off before I could get down there to get another shot at him."

"I saw Dr. Bell a few days later and asked him if he had any patients lately with buckshot in the rear. Dr. Bell looked at me in amazement and said, 'I sure did one day last week. I picked buckshot out of his rear for an hour.'"

"That was my chicken thief, Doctor. I wish I could have got a hold of him. I would have fixed him where he would not steal anymore chickens. But at least I left my mark on him," Grandpa laughed.

"That's a good one, Grandpa," Rose said as she moved closer to him. Grandpa didn't hear very good anymore.

Soon everyone headed to the creek to swim and to get their Saturday evening bath. The bath always seemed to last longer at the creek. The soap would be passed around until everyone was somewhat clean.

Tent Revival

Tonight after supper, Mom and Dad headed us down the road towards Marler to a tent revival. Preacher Johnny Luffman had just put up his big tent in a field on the right side of Highway 421 just past the Marler Store. Mom and Dad would travel all over the county to go to revivals and tent meetings. This tent revival would last for about two weeks. We would attend every night except Sunday night. Preacher Luffman would not open the tent on Sunday. He didn't want to conflict with the local churches.

Wayne had recently met Preacher Luffman's daughter, Elvie, and they seemed to be sweet on each other. When an eighteen year old boy and a seventeen year old girl sit around and giggle a lot, that means they like each other. Wayne and Elvie were together every night of the tent revival. It looked serious to Joe.

Tent revivals would attract a lot of good country people who liked good preaching. The tent would be put up and, like our chicken house, shavings would be put down on the ground. Benches or folding chairs would be lined up to accommodate a good turnout. Sometimes, Preacher Luffman would have special singing.

Tonight, Mom's brother, Uncle Porter (Curly), was the special singing. Uncle Porter would play the guitar and sing with his trio. Sometimes his wife Aunt Nancy would sing with them. A particular song caught Joe's attention as they sang:

"Precious memories, how they linger,
How they ever flood my soul;
In the stillness of the midnight,
Precious, sacred scenes unfold."

They also sang Joe's favorite song:

"Amazing grace how sweet the sound
That saved a wretch like me!
I once was lost, but now I'm found,
Was blind, but now I see."

"When we've been there ten thousand years,
Bright shining as the sun;
We've no less days to sing God's praise,

Than when we first begun."

Preacher Luffman then preached a "Hell hot" and "Heaven sweet" message with plenty of amens from all over. The message stirred up the faithful who had come out even after a hard day of work in the tobacco field.

Joe would become friends of Preacher Luffman's son, Nelson. They would spend time together playing baseball as Wayne and Elvie became a steady couple.

On Monday morning, Dad's crew started to work on their round of second primings. The spring field and Nelson's home field was knocked out fairly easily by the machinelike crew. The four acres were in the barn by 3:00 p.m. even though Dad and Uncle Nelson had to hang the tobacco closer in the barn. Second priming leaves are larger than first priming leaves making for a fuller barn of tobacco.

Dad could see problems later on this summer of having more than a barn for these four acres. That was a good problem to have, as it would mean bigger and heavier tobacco, which would weigh more and sell for more money.

Dad took his crew to the hill field to sucker tobacco for about four hours before chores and supper. There was never an idle minute in Dad's schedule. His tobacco schedule brain kept us too busy to even think that we would have slack time.

The rest of this week finished second primings at the hill, middle, and woods field. The weekly schedule would be tough as ever as most barns would mean a 3:00 a.m. to at least 8:00 p.m. day. It definitely was "prime" priming time.

Chapter 15
The Ocean

The dog days of August passed into September. The tobacco harvesting was moving very productively. Dad and Uncle Nelson decided to tie up a bunch of their first primings and send them to the eastern part of the state at Fairmont to sell. Mr. Shore had a friend, Roy Hunter, who was hauling a load down to Fairmont and he had room for our tobacco.

Uncle Nelson decided to drive down to the market also and followed Roy's truck. Uncle Nelson told Dad to let Elmer, Wayne, and Joe go with him.

"That'll be alright, I guess. You're going to leave after we prime your woods field on Thursday, aren't you?" Dad asked.

"Yep, that's the plan," Uncle Nelson said.

Joe was so excited. He had never been anywhere before and now he was going to the tobacco market and then on to see the ocean at Myrtle Beach after the tobacco was unloaded in Fairmont.

"Tomorrow is the day," Joe said at supper. "I don't think I'll be able to sleep at all tonight. I am so excited."

"Will you bring me a seashell, Joe?" Jane asked.

"I sure will if I can find any," Joe said. He did not know how plentiful seashells were at the ocean. He'd never been there before. He was so thrilled about the trip.

Joe was up before Dad made his wake up rounds at 4:00 a.m. Joe was geared up to go. He packed a little poke to carry his bathing suit, which was cutoff jeans and a couple of other things.

In the field today, Joe was ahead of everyone all day. He was wired. The day seemed to last forever. Finally, the barn was full and Roy Hunter came to load up the tobacco. At 5:00 p.m. sharp, the trip to the tobacco market and ocean was under way. It was a long drive and seemed to take forever to get to Fairmont. We arrived at about 10:30 p.m.

The tobacco was unloaded and lined up for sale on Friday. Uncle Nelson then headed his car towards Myrtle Beach, South Carolina. Elmer, Wayne, Joe, and Roy Hunter were along for the ride. It would be the first trip ever to the ocean for Elmer, Wayne, and Joe. Needless to say, they were excited.

The long trip to the ocean lasted until about 1:00 a.m. when Uncle Nelson pulled his car in and parked near the oceanfront. Joe was dumbfounded by the appearance of the wall of water. To Joe, it looked like a mountain of water.

"Just imagine how much water is in there," Joe said. "It is awesome! I will never forget this trip as long as I live!"

Soon, Uncle Nelson, Elmer, Wayne, and Joe changed into their cutoff jeans and hit the water. Roy Hunter just watched and laughed at us. We played for a couple of hours in the waves before we grew tired and quit. Everybody lay down on the sand of the beach for the night. They were all sleeping soundly when they were rudely awakened by the beach patrol at about 4:00 a.m.

"You cannot sleep on the beach," the patrolman told us. "It is against the law. You have to move on now!"

We sleepily moved on to the car and made our way back to Fairmont for the tobacco sale. Joe was careful to get a handful of seashells with a special one for Jane. He wanted to keep his promise to his baby sister.

Uncle Nelson drove the car into the tobacco warehouse parking lot at 6:30 a.m. They were all dead tired, but were still excited about seeing the ocean.

"Let's go in here and get some breakfast, boys," Uncle Nelson said as he led the way across the street to the tobacco café. "It looks like a good place to eat."

It was a good place. Uncle Nelson and the boys ate a hardy meal and were then ready to see the tobacco sell and then head back home.

"Boy, the gnats are terrible here, ain't they?" Joe asked.

"They are really bad," Wayne said.

"I've never seen such swarms of gnats," Elmer said.

"Wonder why they don't spray to get rid of them?" Uncle Nelson asked. "People down here probably don't even notice them."

The tobacco sold at 11:00 sharp. Within the hour, Roy Hunter and Uncle Nelson headed their vehicles back towards Yadkin County. Joe slept a good part of the trip back home as he was totally worn out. They got back home at 4:30 p.m. They made good time on the return trip. Everyone was tired.

"Thank you, Uncle Nelson, for taking me to the ocean," Joe said. "I really appreciate it. It's a trip I will never forget."

"You're welcome, son. I'm glad you were able to go," Uncle Nelson said.

"Thanks!" Elmer said.

"Thanks!" Wayne said.

It had been a fast but fun trip for three boys who had visited the ocean for the first time. Now they had to settle back down to earth.

Joe gave Jane her special seashell and also gave one to Mom, Rose, John, and Danny. He put the last one up to save as a memento of his first ocean trip.

It was back to the real world on Saturday for the oceangoing youngins.

"Welcome back to the sucker field," Rose said as the day's work began. Joe would rather do anything else in the world but sucker tobacco. Today, however, there was not an option. It was sucker pulling day.

On Monday it was time to move on with the sixth primings. Dad's crew was moving up the stalk. No longer would Joe have to stoop down to prime. He loved it when he could prime standing up. Also that meant that they were getting closer each week to pulling the last leaves or tips as they were called.

Happy birthday #20 was sung to Elmer on Friday, September 10. Elmer is appreciated by all.

Joe in Eighth Grade

On Monday, September 13, school started back up with the first week being half days. Since Dad was pulling the spring field and Uncle Nelson's home field, he let all the youngins go to school on the first half day. They would have to miss the next three days and also three days next week. The barn was finished at 8:00 p.m. even with the youngins in school for half days.

Joe was in Mr. Todd's class this year. Mr. Todd had a split class with half seventh graders and half eighth graders. Joe had never been in a class like this before. He liked it. While the teacher was teaching the seventh grade, Joe could get all of his homework done.

Mr. Todd was an "old school" teacher in that he was strict, but fair. Joe never had any problem with Mr. Todd. The room was right next to the principal's office and on the other side was Mr. Madison's room. You had to be on your best behavior when your class is between the principal and the assistant principal.

Joe got his assignments for the rest of the week as he knew he would not be back until Friday.

Dad and Uncle Nelson decided to go ahead and pull their tips on Saturday, two days early and put them in Grandpa Brown's barn. The tips were ripe and ready to pull so they decided to pull while the youngins were home.

It was a fast, good day. It was always good to pull tips and to see the naked tobacco stalks standing so alone in the field.

After a day back in school on Monday, Dad's youngins would miss Tuesday, Wednesday, and Thursday as the tipping continued. The last of Dad's crop was tipped on Wednesday, September 22. Uncle Nelson's crop was finished with the tipping being on Thursday, September 23. A long year of tobacco harvesting was finished. It had been a long, hard, but productive year.

The Wienie Roast

Plans were made immediately for the end of tobacco priming wienie roast. Dad had not held a wienie roast for the last few years, but we were starting the tradition all over now with Uncle Nelson's family and Mr. Shore. It would be a fun occasion. The wienie roast was planned for Saturday, September 25.

Mr. Shore insisted that he pay for the wienie roast. "I appreciate the way you take care of my tobacco and my equipment. The least I can do is to give ya'll a wienie roast."

He did and we sure did have a great time. In attendance were Mr. and Mrs. Shore, Grandpa Brown, Dad, Mom, Elmer, Wayne, Rose, Joe, John, Jane, Danny, Uncle Nelson, Aunt Jo, Gray, Fay, and Little "Debbie Dean."

Uncle Nelson and Elmer ran a close contest to see who could eat the most hotdogs. It seems like Uncle Nelson won by eating ten hotdogs. Joe managed to eat five hotdogs. Everyone got their fill and had a fun time around the fire.

It was with a touch of sadness, though, as we knew that Dad's work crew was going to change as Elmer and Wayne would not be with us next year this time. It seems like we all should be ten to twelve years old and here we go losing two workers to public work within the next year.

On Monday, Dad returned to the packhouse as getting the tobacco ready for market had begun the day after tips were pulled. Dad set his sights on getting all of the tobacco to market by November 1. That was a tall order with all of the fourteen acres we had to get ready, but Dad's crew usually met his deadline.

Soon, Gurn Johnson was hauling a load of tobacco a week for Dad.

"How many hundred acres of tobacco did you raise, Clyde?" Gurn said. "Those poor youngins don't ever get to do anything except work in tobacco, do they? You have the best work crew in the whole county."

"They work hard, alright, Gurn. They work just the way that I was taught to work. That's the only way we can halfway make ends meet," Dad said.

Happy birthday was wished to Jane on her ninth birthday on October 7. We love Jane.

Almost halfway through the tobacco tying, Uncle Lamar wanted to make molasses the week of October 11. Dad had put out a smaller crop this year since Grandpa was not raising any cane. The cane was cut, stripped, and hauled over to the north side of Uncle Lamar's house where Grandpa's mill was set up.

It was a fun time but it was not the same as before at Grandpa's. We enjoyed being with our cousins, Lyman, Jimmy, Lorene, Avalon, Elaine, and little Tim who was now three years old. We all sopped molasses to our fill. We also had fun with the horseshoes. Uncle Lamar had a good set of horseshoe stobs set up. We always loved trying to toss ringers. Lyman and Elmer were the best horseshoe throwers. Joe was just learning as the older youngins did not give him a chance to throw.

The molasses was finished on Saturday evening and Dad and Uncle Lamar divided the sweet juices as they were dipped from the vat and put in gallon mason jars. Dad got all the molasses we needed but it probably was about a half of last year's crop.

How about Dusty Rhodes and the New York Giants who swept the best team in baseball, the Cleveland Indians, in the World Series? Sometimes a team that gets breaks can beat a better team.

It was back to the packhouse for the last two weeks of getting the tobacco ready for market. Dad's crew spent every night except church nights in the packhouse to meet Dad's target date for finishing the tobacco.

The deadline date was met as Dad's crew finished the tobacco on Saturday, October 30. Gurn was loading it up immediately and would be ready to head to Winston on Monday morning at 3:00 p.m., November 1. Dad would go with Gurn to see the last load of 1954 crop sell.

Joe continued to play basketball at the gym at school during P.E. time. Joe didn't know it but he was getting good training from Mr. Holmes for next year when he would be in high school. Joe continued to improve on his game. His set shot was deadly but still he continued to practice every chance he got at home. Jane would always practice with Joe chasing balls for him.

Another house of chickens sold on Friday, November 5. It was a good sale. Dad's crew immediately started the cleanup for the one week turn around before new chicks would be here. The chicken house was always cleaned out and ready to go.

A good, but not great, corn crop was pulled on Saturday, November 6 and November 13. The corn pile was shucked over the next two weeks. The popcorn crop was as good as ever. Dad always had his popcorn. As usual, Grandpa Brown came down to visit us as we shucked corn. Grandpa missed his corn shuckings.

November was passing and the weather was getting nippy at night.

Chapter 16
Elmer Leaves Farm

On Thursday, November 25, Elmer left for Greensboro to work at Cone Mills. He worked with Jimmy Vestal from Mineral Springs Baptist Church. Jimmy got Elmer the job and let him ride back and forth to and from Greensboro on weekends. It was so sad to see Elmer go. He had been so dependable over the years on the Little Farm on Brown Road. He could not see much of a future on the farms.

On Tuesday, November 30, we all wished Wayne happy birthday #18. He was a handsome young man with blonde wavy hair. He took pride in his hair and he spent a lot of time caring for those blonde waves. This birthday would be the last one at home for Wayne.

December blew in with the cold north winds as it generally does. It was plumb cold.

"The air today is from the North Pole," Dad said as he came in from milking. "It feels like snow."

It did not snow yet, but it felt like it all week long.

"I think we're going to have a rough, snowy winter this year," Mr. Todd told the class today. "I can feel it in my bones."

Outside playing was over for awhile. All P.E. for the next three months would be in the gym. Joe got in more practice on his basketball game. Joe always loved basketball as he did all sports.

Joe Sees First Game

Joe remembers in February of last year when Mr. Shore took him to see the Yadkin County boys' championship game in Yadkinville. Joe had never been to a game before. The game was between West Yadkin and archrival Jonesville. What a battle the game was! It was nip and tuck all the way with West Yadkin leading all the way. Joe was quietly taking in the game.

"Joe! Who are you pulling for?" Mr. Shore asked at halftime of the close game.

"I'm for West Yadkin, of course," Joe replied.

"You need to make some racket and let them know then. You are too quiet," Mr. Shore said with a smile. He was such a good man. He didn't have to take Joe to the game, but he decided to be nice to a little, old country boy who would really appreciate it.

Joe made some racket and the second half continued to be close. It went down to the wire with the West Yadkin Golden Eagles winning the county championship by two points over the dreaded Jonesville Blue Jays. It was a big moment for West Yadkin and for Joe. He was so thankful to Mr. Shore.

"Thank you for taking me to the game, Mr. Shore. I sure did have a good time," Joe said as he got out of the car and went inside.

It was Tuesday, December 21, the last day of school before Christmas vacation. Joe always enjoyed this day at school. There used to be a lot of partying and not much schoolwork. Now there was a small party with goodies to eat, but not like old times.

With the cold weather that had been around since the first of the month, Dad decided today was the day to kill our three hogs. They were big enough alright. They had to be 300 pounds each. Dad, Wayne, Joe, and John were busy with the task at first light. Dad's youngins were old pros at this job now. They would miss Elmer, but they could certainly handle the job.

Grandpa Brown came down to enjoy the fun of being around the fire and being reminded of the good old days when he used to help kill hogs.

"I believe these hogs are the biggest you've had yet, Clyde," Grandpa said as he watched them scald the hogs and scale off the hair.

"If they're not the biggest, they're certainly close," Dad said.

By 11:00 a.m., Wayne and Joe were on the way to Martin's Grocery Store on Swan Creek Road to get much of the meat ground up into sausage. Mr. Martin had been grinding Dad's sausage for years.

Joe had recently been noticing Mr. Martin's daughter, Jerry, who was about two years younger than Joe was. She was pretty and Joe, who was going to be fourteen years old next month, was starting to notice the girls. He still was too shy to talk to them, but he sure could look. Unfortunately, Joe never did get up enough nerve to ask Jerry for a date. He wanted to, but he just was too shy. Joe really did regret it.

The hog killing work took most of the day. Even though the outside work was done before noon, Mom and the girls had plenty of work to do all day long. The sausage was canned and liver mush, a family favorite, was made. The whole kitchen smelled like hog meat. It was good eating, but the smell kind of lingered for days.

The canned goods room was really packed full now with sausage stacked on the floor.

"Looks like we're ready for the long, rough winter now," Mom said. "The old timers are talking about a bad winter. I think we'll have the food for it."

"I think so, too, Mom," Rose said as she was tired of seeing hog meat. She had worked all day in the kitchen.

If the December weather was any indication, it did look like a rough winter. All the month so far was cold. Snow was being forecast by the WSJS Shell Oil man for today and tonight. Chores were done quickly as the cold wind cut to the bone.

Joe and John moved on to the chicken house where it was nice and warm for the six week old chicks. They took their time feeding the chickens, but they moved faster when they had to go outside to tote water.

Just before nightfall, it began to snow. At first there were snow flurries, but soon it became a beautiful assortment of flakes of all sizes, small, medium, and large.

"It is so beautiful," Jane said as she watched with the porch light illuminating the dancing snow-flakes. The ground was now white as Mom called everyone to supper. A good supper of cornbread and milk was soon followed by a favorite winter-time snack of popcorn, crackerjacks, and Mom's chocolate candy.

Everyone made periodical trips to the front porch to make sure it was still snowing. It seemed to be snowing even harder as the night passed.

"It might snow twelve inches the way it looks now," Dad said as the snack was finished and everyone hurried to bed. Joe could hear the wind softly blowing and occasional sleet hitting the windows of the bedroom. Soon, he was in deep sleep dreaming about playing basketball for West Yadkin High School.

Chapter 17
The Perfect Dream

It was the big game against archrival Jonesville for the county championship. Joe was the starter at guard. His friend Archie King was playing forward. Joe and Archie were the two stars on the team. They repeatedly scored one basket after another to give West Yadkin a big lead in the first quarter.

Jonesville made a little run in the second quarter, but Joe hit two long set shots right before half to give West Yadkin a ten point lead at halftime. It looked like a safe lead at the time.

However, Jonesville made another run and Archie got into foul trouble and had to miss most of the third quarter. With only thirty seconds left in the quarter, the score suddenly was tied at 40-40. Joe quickly hit a long set shot and then stole the inbounds pass to score a lay up that gave West Yadkin a 44-40 lead after three quarters.

The fourth quarter was back and forth until Joe and Archie both got hot in the last two minutes and hit the needed shots and played tough defense to lead the Golden Eagles to a convincing 56-46 win. It was bedlam at center court as the victorious team celebrated. Joe was so happy to beat the dreaded Blue Jays, but was even happier when Jerry Martin, Mr. Martin's daughter and Blue Jay cheerleader, tapped him on the arm and congratulated him over playing a great game.

"You were great, Joe. You deserve to win. I didn't know you were such a good basketball player," Jerry said.

"I just do the best I can," Joe said modestly. "I love to play." Then Joe got a bold idea. "Do you have plans, Jerry? Could I drive you home and maybe we could go to the Minute Grill for a snack?" Joe asked.

"Sounds good to me, Joe. I'll go tell Mom and Dad. Come over and speak to them. They'd like to see you, I'm sure," Jerry said.

"Hello, Joe! Great game!" Mr. Martin said and Mrs. Martin nodded her agreement. "You sure did our team in tonight."

"Mom, Dad, is it okay if Joe drives me home? He asked me if he could. We'll be on later. I think we're going to get something to eat," Jerry said.

"That sound like fun. You kids take your time and have fun," Mrs. Martin said. "We'll stay here with you while Joe gets changed."

Joe hurried and took his fastest shower ever. He couldn't believe it. He had a date with Jerry Martin. She was the most beautiful girl in the world. Why hadn't he asked her for date before now?

Soon, Joe was driving Dad's 1950 Plymouth up Highway 601 to Highway 67 at Boonville and on up to the teenage hangout, the drive-in Minute Grill in Jonesville. They ordered their hamburgers and ate as they talked and listened to the music on the speaker outside the car. Joe couldn't believe how easy it was to talk to Jerry.

"I didn't think you knew I was in the world, Joe," Jerry said. "You always spoke to me, but you didn't ever talk to me."

"I've always been so shy, but I'm glad we got to talk tonight. I promise we'll do a lot of talking from now on if you want to," Joe said.

"I do want to," Jerry said as Joe thought his heart was going to beat its way out of his chest. He hoped she couldn't hear his heart thumping. It was so loud.

Time flew by. It was getting late. Joe drove down Swan Creek Road to the Martin house next to the grocery store. He walked around and opened the car door and walked Jerry to the door.

"Can we go out Saturday night, Jerry?" Joe asked quickly.

"We sure can!" Jerry said. "Then you can go to church with me on Sunday night, okay?"

"Okay with me," Joe said. "It has been a great night. The best part is getting to know you."

"Thanks, Joe! You're so sweet," Jerry said as she reached up and gave Joe a quick but firm kiss.

"Goodnight, Joe!" Jerry said.

"Goodnight, Jerry," Joe said as he floated back to the car. I must be dreaming, Joe thought to himself. This is simply too good to be true.

Sadly, he was and it was. Joe woke up very disappointed that he had been dreaming.

White Christmas

It was Christmas Eve and there was about six inches of fluffy snow. The trees were covered. It definitely was winter wonderland now. It was a cold twenty degrees. The whole family was excited about the white Christmas they were about to have.

Joe enjoyed the snow, but he was very perplexed about his dream. Usually he would just write off his dreams, but this dream would linger on for a long time. Joe didn't mention this dream at the breakfast table as he often did. He kept it all to himself and never told anyone the full dream. He did tell Archie about dreaming that they won the county championship.

After breakfast, Dad, Elmer, Joe, and John went rabbit hunting in the snow. This hunt was a favorite of Joe's. Elmer had come home from

Greensboro for Christmas. He slipped in sometime during the night and just got into bed without waking anyone up. This trick of his would become his trademark as he did the same thing many times later when he came home on leave from the Air Force.

The rabbit hunt in the snow yielded four good sized cottontails. Fried rabbit and rabbit gravy for Christmas breakfast sounded real good to Joe as he skinned the rabbits with Jane holding them for him. Dad had given Joe the skinning job along with other chores since Elmer was no longer living at home. Joe and Wayne were now responsible for milking the cows each night. Dad would milk them in the morning on school days.

After supper tonight, Jane and Danny put out their shoe boxes for Santa. They were the only two left young enough to do the Santa thing. It just was not as exciting anymore. It would be exciting tomorrow, though, seeing the younger two happy with their gifts and then with the opening of the gifts by the older youngins.

At precisely 5:00 a.m., everyone was up. Jane was happy with her new doll. Danny had a new Radio Flyer red wagon. He was so excited. Joe was busily opening a large box from Mom and Dad. He couldn't figure out what it was. It was not very heavy and by the size of the box, it could be a derby hat. Joe finally got it open.

"Just what I need, a basketball," Joe said as he bounced it on the floor. "Thanks Mom and Dad. My old one was about gone. Now I can keep practicing."

"Can I still play with you, Joe?" Jane asked.

"You know you can. You're my official helper," Joe said as he gave Jane a big hug.

"Here's something for you, Joe," Elmer said with a smile. He handed Joe a small box.

"My very first watch! Thanks, Elmer. I appreciate it a bunch," Joe said. "A Bulova watch is the best from what I hear."

The whole family was happy with their gifts and with their family all at home together. In future years, there would be several Christmas's that the whole family could not be together.

Mom was busy with breakfast when Grandpa knocked on the door.

"Come in, Grandpa," Joe said as he opened the door.

"Merry Christmas, youngins!" Grandpa said as he took off his heavy coat and cap. "It's wintertime, ain't it? What do you think about this white Christmas?"

"We like it, Grandpa," Elmer said.

"When did you get home, boy?" Grandpa asked.

"Night before last. I came in with the snow," Elmer laughed.

"Breakfast is on," Mom said. "Come and get it! Come on in and eat some rabbit with us, Grandpa."

"I believe I will," Grandpa said. "I didn't eat breakfast at the house. I wasn't hungry then, but rabbit gravy is just what I want."

Mom prayed, "Heavenly Father, thank you for this good day you've given us. Thanks for the food, health, and strength. Be with the sick, shut in, and bereaved. Thank you for allowing Elmer to be home with us. Thank you for Grandpa. We pray you'd strengthen him and bless him. Bless this food to the nourishment of our body. We pray in Jesus' name. Amen. Amen."

Everybody dug in. There was rabbit, rabbit gravy, eggs, biscuits, molasses, jelly, jam, milk, American Ace coffee, and fresh butter. It was a breakfast fit for a king.

"This rabbit gravy is the best I've ever sopped, Gladys. It is just tops," Grandpa said as he reached for seconds.

Joe was now working on biscuit #6, sopping the gravy. He would later eat #7 with strawberry jam on it. He had to quit as he was about ready to pop.

"This breakfast is the most I've eaten in weeks," Grandpa said as he pushed away from the table. "I'm glad I got to eat with ya'll. I sure do love ya'll," Grandpa added with a slight tear in his eyes.

"We love you, too, Grandpa," everyone said together and then gave Grandpa a big hug. Grandpa Brown was a hero to all of our family. In our eyes, he could do no wrong.

"Here's your box of cigars, Grandpa," Wayne said as he got a match from the mantle and lit Grandpa's cigar. "Now you can keep warm while you walk," Wayne added with a smile.

"Thank ya'll! See you later," Grandpa said. He moved slowly but happily through the snow as he talked to the two dogs, Trixie and Sandy. The dogs also moved slowly as they were getting old, too.

Joe suddenly remembered back a few years when Sandy was just a puppy. It was fun teaching him to bring the cows and Old Bill up to the barn. It was a blast to see Sandy jump high to pull the old rag from the tree limb. Joe just kept moving the rag higher and Sandy would still jump and get it. He had certainly been a fun, smart dog. He was going to be missed when he was gone. He was just like a member of our family.

After dinner, Dad loaded up the car for the Christmas get together at Grandpa and Grandma Proctor's house.

"I can't believe he hasn't mowed these weeds. They're so tall the snow didn't even cover them,"

Dad said as he turned in the driveway. The temperature today was moderating and some of the snow was melting. That was good as, otherwise, many of the family members would not have been able to get home for Christmas.

Grandma met us at the door as she always did. She had hugs for everyone.

"How is your new work, Elmer?" Grandma asked. "What do you do?"

"It is fine, Grandma. It's a decent job in the cotton mill," said Elmer. "I hope to get a better job later. I'm thinking about going into the Air Force."

"I hope you don't do that, Elmer. You'd be gone for a long time, wouldn't you?" Grandma asked as she had the group of youngins into the kitchen for her "cookie biscuit" treat. Everyone got their fill of the tasty biscuits before moving on into the crowded front room where the company was gathered.

In attendance were Grandpa, Grandma, Mom and Dad's family, Uncle Claude, Aunt Cora, cousins Larry, Lee, and Bruce, Uncle Paul, Aunt Lena, Cousin Lola Jean, Uncle Porter, Aunt Nancy, cousins Judy and Benny, Uncle Parks, Aunt Dorothy, Uncle Brice, Aunt Hazel, Uncle Raymond, Aunt De Ette, Uncle Phillip, Aunt Jane, cousin Pam, Uncle Harold, and probably other cousins from High Point that Joe did not know when he saw them. Mom knew them all well, though, and made the rounds talking to all of them.

Again this year, Joe was happy with the baseball from Grandma Proctor. She kept Joe and John's baseball game going from year to year.

"Thank you, Grandma," Joe said. "I really appreciate the baseball you give me each year."

"You're welcome, Joe. Keep up the baseball playing. Maybe you'll be playing in front of your

Grandpa one of these days over at Lee Wood's field," Grandma said.

By 4:00 p.m., people began leaving as they were concerned about the condition of the roads as nightfall approached. Dad was ready to go and we left at 4:30. By the time chores were finished and the chickens were fed and watered, it was dark and supper was on the table.

Hot cornbread soaked in sweet milk with a touch of salt sprinkled in the big bowl was good eating with the big spoon like Dad used. Joe would love this meal for the rest of his life, even though he had it every night for supper when he was on the Little Farm on Brown Road.

Soon after supper, the whole family was in bed. Everyone was beat. It had been a long day. It was officially 8:15 p.m. on Joe's new Bulova watch.

"Thank you for my watch, Elmer. I sure do like it," Joe said.

"You're welcome, little brother. I'm glad that you like it," Elmer said as the lights went out.

Elmer left to go back to Greensboro after church Sunday morning. Jimmy Vestal was ready to go right after preaching.

"See ya'll next Saturday," Elmer said as they left.

"Bye, Elmer," the whole carload of Browns answered.

Monday morning's weather continued to moderate with the temperature in the high forties. It was a short lived three day moderation as a cold front moved in tonight with a low of fifteen degrees. So much for the heat wave!

The rest of the week was cold, cloudy, and with threatening skies. By Friday night, New Year's Eve, it was snowing again.

"Can we please stay up until the new year comes in, Dad?" Joe asked. "We don't have to get up early tomorrow. Please?"

"I guess it'll be okay," Dad said as Mom nodded her approval.

Joe could not believe what he had heard. Dad had never let them stay up before. They all settled around the fire and waited for 1955 to arrive. The snack of popcorn and crackerjacks was good. Eyes were getting heavy, but Wayne, Rose, Joe, and John were determined to stay awake.

Jane and Danny were asleep early along with Mom and Dad. Snow continued to fall all night. At the magic midnight hour the ground was a powdery white.

"Happy New Year to you all," Wayne said.

"Happy New Year to you, big brother," Rose, Joe, and John said. It was Saturday morning, January 1, 1955. Where in the world did time go?

Mom cooked the special New Year's Day dinner of black-eyed peas, collard greens, and, of course, biscuits. It was good eating no matter when you were eating it.

In church on Sunday morning, Pastor Hankins preached on making a commitment to the Lord, not just a New Year's resolution. It was a good message that stirred up the faithful members of the little church.

"That was a good message this morning," Mom said as Dad drove home.

"It sure was," Dad said as he slowly made his way down Swan Creek Road. There was still snow on the road and there were slippery spots. Elmer did not get home this weekend because of all the snow.

We missed Elmer a lot in the month plus that he had been gone. It wasn't the same anymore. Our family was changing.

As always, Joe looked towards the Martin house as Dad drove by. Joe could not get over the dream that he had and how real it had seemed.

The roads were clear enough to go back to school on Monday, January 3, 1955. A new year was here. So many things would change this year. Mom and Dad's family would continue to change.

School went well for Joe. He was being prepared for the ninth grade, high school next school year, which would be in September.

The January birthdays came quickly. Danny was six years old on January 18. He would start to school in September. Joe was fourteen on January 21 and Dad turned forty-one on January 24. School was snowed out for five days from January 21 to January 28. These lost days were bad news for the tobacco farmers as it meant school would get out late or go on Saturdays or both, depending on how many other days would be lost.

Joe loved to be out on snow days, but he did not like the idea of the school year being extended into his summertime. The school board approved Saturday school to start immediately on Saturday, January 29, so at least one of the five days was made up.

"I don't like Saturday school," Joe said at suppertime.

"It's better than having to go in June, Joe, when we need you in the tobacco field," Dad said.

"Yes, I know it is," Joe said.

February came in cool, but with clear skies. Maybe the bad weather was over. The groundhog said otherwise as he saw his shadow on Wednesday, February 2, meaning six more weeks of winter weather.

"I hope that old hog is wrong," Mom said. "I'm ready for springtime."

Springtime would have to wait. On Thursday morning, the ground was covered with snow and it was still falling. School was out again for Thursday, Friday, and Saturday. So much for the make-up schedule that the school board set up!

To make matters worse, Sunday morning dawned with more fresh snow, which lasted all day. Dad's family missed both church services as it snowed all day with an overall accumulation of twelve inches of snow.

School would be out until Wednesday when the weather moderated and the roads were cleared. The weather stayed clear, windy, and dry for the next week. Dad got to work on the plant beds on Saturday, February 12. Thanks to the March like winds that had been blowing all week.

All the plant bed work was done in one day including the sowing for the first time ever that Joe could remember. Dad had a hunch about the weather getting ready to break bad again.

"I'm glad we got the plant beds sowed today. I think the old groundhog is about ready to bite again," Dad said at the supper table tonight.

Dad was a smart man. He went by his feelings and he was usually right. On Sunday night, a silent snowfall of four inches fell. School was out again for Monday and Tuesday. Joe was losing track of how many days were lost so far.

"It must be up to ten days by now," Wayne said as he was anxious to get this year, his senior year over with.

School opened again on Wednesday, February 16. It was hard to concentrate on school work with so many missed days and with little time to go over homework. The rest of the school year would be a disruptive attempt to catch up on the missed work.

The rest of February was free of snow with every Saturday being a makeup day.

March blew in with warmer weather. The chickens were sold on March 4 and a new bunch of chicks came on March 11. The cycle continues at Cycle.

Just when we thought winter was gone, a new snowstorm blew in on Saturday, March 12. It snowed six inches of wet snow, which was gone by Monday morning. School ran Monday after missing the make-up day on Saturday. The temperature was suddenly in the sixties all week long. The snow was gone and flowers and trees were starting to bloom. At long last, the rough winter was over.

School was in session every Saturday for the rest of the school year to make up for lost days.

Chapter 18
Elmer Joins Air Force

April came with showers and flowers. The plant beds were flourishing due to all the moisture from the snowfalls. Dad was getting the land ready for tobacco, plowing and harrowing it towards the end of the month.

Elmer left to join the Air Force this month. He would be gone for four long years. He was now in San Antonio, Texas, where he would have basic training and then advanced training at Lackland Air Force Base. We miss Elmer.

May 1, barefoot day, came nice and warm, but we couldn't go to church barefoot. We went barefoot on Monday, though, as we helped Dad lay off tobacco rows. Soon it would be setting time again. We had a bunch of land to get ready over the next two weeks.

Dad planned to really test his work crew this year with the same fourteen acres as the past two years, even though we would be missing Elmer and then Wayne come graduation day for Wayne. It sure sounded like a rough summer on the horizon.

On Friday, May 13, we started the season out by setting the spring field of two acres. Dad let all the youngins go to school, but he came to pick all of them up at noontime. Dad had pulled all needed plants and his crew could easily set the two acre field in the evening.

With Elmer being gone, Dad's setting crews changed. Mom dropped for Dad while Rose dropped for Wayne. Jane again dropped for Joe while first year dropper Danny dropped for John.

"Be patient with Danny, John," Dad said as we were beginning. "He'll be slow to begin with." John was not usually a patient person.

It was good to hear the click clack sound of the four tobacco setting crews moving across the hilly, red clay soil of the upper spring field. Dad's crew made excellent time this bright, sunny evening. The two acre field was finished by 5:00 p.m. Dad was happy to see the good progress his rearranged crew had made.

It was on to the chores for Rose and Joe who milked the two cows while John and Danny fed and watered the chickens. Chore assignments were changing as Dad's work force was being reduced by school graduations.

Wayne had a date tonight to go with his steady to her Dad's tent revival. So the milking team of Rose and Joe got a feel for what chores would be like when Wayne moved out in two weeks on graduation day.

Rose's Favorite Cow

Rose was not happy with her milking assignment. She had to milk the young, stubborn heifer that would not hold still and constantly beat Rose on the head with her "cuckle burr" loaded tail. A cow could drive you crazy with her tail, which she used to try to keep the pesky flies away.

Rose had about all she could stand from this stubborn heifer. One more swat on her head from the loaded tail was it. Rose had just started milking and only had about a quart of milk in the bucket. She grabbed the bucket up off the ground and went around to the front of the heifer and poured the milk on the heifer's head.

"You can have your stinking milk, you hateful heifer!" Rose said as she marched toward the corncrib where Dad was working and told him about her problem.

"You can't let that heifer get the best of you, Rose. Go on to the house and help your mom with supper. I'll milk the heifer," Dad said.

Joe took note of the happenings. Now if I had done that and wasted milk, Dad would have given me a whipping, Joe thought as he milked Old Bess. Milking wasn't easy. It was sometimes a pain, especially with a heifer, which is a young cow. They had to be broken just like a wild horse.

Joe remembers the heifer that he butted heads with one time. He really did. Joe had given the heifer feed to eat as was the procedure when you took their milk, you gave them food. The cows would be tied up to a tree or post so they would not run off during milking. Evidently, Joe did not tie this heifer tightly enough and she kept moving around. Joe went around to correct the situation and the heifer gave him a head butt to the top of his head as he was leaning down. Joe was knocked over backwards.

Joe retied the heifer leaving no room to move around. The heifer then behaved. You had to show the heifer who was the boss.

Milking sometimes could be fun. All the cats would line up for their free warm milk. Joe would squirt milk all over the cat's face to see how much they could catch. It was funny seeing milk faced cats lined up.

Sometimes the milk cow would get out of the pasture and eat wild onion or honeysuckles. When this happened, the milk would taste exactly like what the cow ate. Wild onion milk was not fit to drink. Honeysuckle milk was drinkable, but was not a favorite with Joe.

Other times a cow would get out of the pasture and straddle the barb wire fence. The barb wire would tear up the cow's bag making it hard to milk. The cow had to be milked as her bag was full, but the milk would be contaminated with blood from the cow's bag and the milker's hands. This situation was not too much fun.

A cow with diarrhea was not any fun to milk, either. The cows did not take a shower before milking. They would come to the milker just like they were, messy or not. Such was milking a cow on the Little Farm on Brown Road.

Dad would soon let John start milking with Joe. John took Old Bess, the old steady cow that didn't even need tying. Joe would get the heifer, which he gradually broke in, to become an okay cow to milk.

On Saturday, May 14, Dad's crew was ready for day #2 of tobacco setting. Mom, of course, put on a winning breakfast first. She had scrambled eggs, sausage, milk gravy, biscuits, molasses, jelly, jam, and good, cold, sweet milk to drink. Not wanting to pass out in the tobacco field, Joe proceeded to eat seven of those biscuits with the eggs, sausage, and gravy.

Seven biscuits might sound like a lot, but Mom's biscuits were on the small side. They were not the large "cathead" biscuits that some people make. Mom's biscuits were perfectly shaped and truly a work of art. Was it seven or was it eight biscuits? Joe had to eat enough to keep his energy level up for the hard morning's work.

Today, Dad's crew tackled the hill field after first pulling plants for about three hours. The click clack sound of the setters was started up at 9:15 a.m. The echo down through the field and the hollow behind the road barn was Dad's music playing again.

As yesterday, Mom dropped for Dad and Rose dropped for Wayne who was helping set out his last tobacco crop. Jane dropped for Joe while Danny dropped for John as the newest setting team for Dad.

"Remember, John, patience!" Dad reminded John again.

Jane was becoming a pro at dropping for Joe even though she was only 9 ½ years old. Their team was becoming about as fast as Mom and Dad. They had passed "fireball" Wayne last year. Wayne was never a real fast worker. He was steady, but not fast. Wayne took a lot of kidding.

Wayne was a fast rock thrower, though. Joe had the scars to prove that fact. Now, was this scar on Joe's head from one of Wayne's rocks or was it from the time John had hit him with the homemade tobacco stalk knife? This weapon was a machete looking knife, which was used to hack down tobacco stalks at the end of the season.

Either situation was scary and painful. Brotherly love was expressed in many different ways on the Little Farm on Brown Road.

The setting of the hill field went very well today. Half of the eight acre field was finished at 6:00 p.m. The field would be finished on Monday with all youngins being kept out of school for the day.

Dad hurried his work crew to do their chores while he took care of Old Kate, Mr. Shore's horse, who faithfully pulled our wagon loaded with water and plants.

Joe and John hurried home to get their milking done in hopes of having some daylight left to toss the baseball around in the barnyard.

Rose, Jane, and Danny took care of the chickens and then moved on to gather the eggs from the barnyard hens.

Soon all the youngins were running and playing before Mom called supper. As usual, Joe did his

Mickey Mantle imitation catching and hitting the ball while John pretended to be Rocky Colavito.

Jane and Danny were playing with Sandy, our faithful dog, who was old but still wanted to play with the youngins.

After supper, it was bath time for everyone. Rose had been asking Dad about an indoor bathroom and tub.

"When do you think we'll have our bathroom, Dad?" Rose asked as she was letting her blonde hair dry out.

"It won't be long now, Rose," Dad said. "I'd say within the next year. How does that sound?"

"I'm ready now. I can't wait to lay in the tub and soak in a bubble bath," Rose said.

"Me, too!" Jane said.

"I want a shower!" Joe added.

"We'll probably have a shower and a tub together," Dad said as he let everyone know it was bedtime. That is everyone except Wayne who had left earlier to go "courting" again. He was very serious with this preacher's daughter.

On Monday morning, Dad's full crew got another early start on a long, hard day. They were in the plant beds at 6:00 a.m. pulling tobacco plants for the last four acres of the hill field. It was a productive day with the big field being finished at about 5:30 p.m. Now we had only one more field to set and this year's crop would be finished.

Dad decided that the plant beds needed a couple of days to recover from the heavy pulling of the last few days. The middle field would wait until Thursday. In the meantime, Dad's crew threw the water to the plant beds to make sure that they would be ready on Thursday.

All youngins were back in school on Tuesday and Wednesday. The school year was winding down. Joe couldn't believe that he soon would be in high school. Time never stopped. It was flying by.

On Thursday, Dad's full crew set out the last four acres, the middle field. It was another productive day as Wayne's last tobacco setting was finished at about 5:00 p.m. Joe had a little ceremony at the end and awarded Wayne a leftover tobacco plant. "In appreciation of your hard work, we award you this one memory of your 18 ½ years on the tobacco farm. We wish you the best in your future job. We'll miss you," Joe said as the full crew clapped their hands and laughed.

Wayne Graduates

It was May 27, 1955. School was out at 12:00 noon. Joe and the other youngins got out early for Wayne's graduation at 11:00 a.m. Wayne was officially out of school now. Dad's work crew now had lost two workers in the past six months.

Wayne was happy as was his girlfriend, Elvie. Wayne would go to Greensboro with Elmer on Sunday to go to work at Cone Mills. Both of Joe's older brothers were now out of the hot sun and working in the cotton mill. They were going to be missed.

Joe was promoted to grade #9, high school. John would be in grade #7 while Jane was going into grade #4 in Mrs. Paris' class, one of Joe's all-time favorite teachers. And, of course, Danny, the baby of the family, would start to school in September. The family certainly was changing and growing up.

June came as summer was here. It was hot. Tobacco hoeing seemed to take up all the time these days. We missed those two hoes that were missing from last year. With Mom, Dad, Rose, Joe, John, Jane, and Danny hoeing, we still took quite a swipe across the field. Dad would hoe half of

Danny's row as the youngest of Dad's workers was learning.

The Lard – The Whipping

The hoeing would continue through June until Dad would lay the tobacco by at the end of the month. That meant the tobacco was getting too big to plow and hoe. Joe was glad.

Joe remembers when Dad was laying the hill field by and for some reason did not leave instructions for Joe and John. Dad would always leave word with Mom for the boy's work. They fed and watered the chickens and Mom then sent them to Paul Dobbins' store to get her some lard as she was out.

Joe and John went down the Shore hill carefully to stay behind the bank and out of Dad's sight. They didn't want Dad to put them to work. They timed it perfectly, they thought, and ran down around the curve and past Mr. Shore's new house. Dad could not see them now. They continued to the store where Joe asked Paul Dobbins for a bucket of lard.

"Would you please put that on our account?" Joe asked.

"I sure will, Joe," Paul answered. Joe always dreaded asking for something to be charged to Dad's account. He was ashamed and thought it showed that we were poor. Well, we definitely were poor.

"How would you boys like a Pepsi?" Paul asked as they were getting ready to leave.

"No thank you, sir! We don't have the money," Joe said.

"These drinks are on the house, boys. They are at no charge to you. Sit down and drink them so you can leave the bottles," Paul continued.

"Thank you, sir!" Joe said.

"Thank you, sir!" John said.

What a special treat the Pepsis were! They did not have Pepsis at home. They were always for special occasions.

Joe and John finished their treat and left for home wondering how they were going to get back by Dad without being seen. They felt sure they had passed by unnoticed on the way out. As they approached the hill field, they sneakingly got in the east side ditch of the road. It seemed to be working as they moved on up the ditch past the barn and all the way up the hill.

"We made it, John," Joe said as they ran the rest of the way to the house.

"Did your Dad see you and tell you to come to work?" Mom asked as she took the bucket of lard and put it up on the counter.

"No! He didn't see us," Joe said. "We had the lard with us."

They laughed about it, but the laugh did not last long. Dad came through the kitchen door "madder than a wet hen." He was armed with a long, heavy duty switch, which he stole from a peach tree in our little orchard beside the house. Dad would wonder why we never had peaches. It was simple. Peaches need limbs to grow on.

"Why didn't you two come on up to the field to help me this morning?" Dad asked as he began switching Joe and John. He moved them outside where he could get a better swing of the switch. He gave them both a good flailing.

"We didn't know we were supposed to come to the field, Dad," Joe said. "I thought we were through hoeing."

"You need to go behind the plow and uncover the leaves," Dad said as he headed them up to the field in a hurry. The boys had whelps all over their arms and legs. They were not very happy with their Dad who they thought seemed to enjoy whipping them.

Joe and John worked quietly all morning. They remained quiet during dinner and the rest of the day. When they were upset, they stayed to themselves and stayed quiet.

Mom gave Joe and John a hug before they went back to the tobacco field for the evening. She felt partly responsible for them getting a whipping.

"I'm sorry, boys. I should have sent you to the field this morning," Mom said.

We felt like Mom thought Dad whipped us too much and too hard at times, but she did not mention it to Dad, at least not in our presence. We preferred switching from Mom as she was tender-hearted and would not hurt us like Dad did.

The only switching Joe got from Mom that really hurt was the time that Joe heard a bad word at school when he was in the sixth grade. Joe came home and called Rose that name in front of Mom and the whipping was on.

July was here. Another house of chickens was sold on July 1. A new batch of chicks arrived on July 8 after Dad, Joe, and John got the house clean and ready. The chickens had turned into steady income for Dad. It was needed for necessary purchases throughout the year. There really wasn't too much work involved with the chickens. It was just a steady job that had to be done.

Wayne Marries

On Saturday evening, July 9, 1955, Dad's crew got to quit work early. Wayne and Elvie got married. It was not a surprise as they had been courting steadily for a year now. They would live in Greensboro where Wayne worked at Cone Mills.

Joe would later enjoy visiting Wayne over the Christmas holidays at their small apartment on East Bragg St. These visits were a big treat for Joe who had never been anywhere.

The blackberries were plentiful as was the garden. Mom, Rose, and Jane stayed busy canning for the winter season. The cycle to survive continued year in and year out. It was a struggle.

On July 16, it was Mom's birthday. At supper we sang to her:

"Happy birthday to you.
Happy birthday to you.
Happy birthday to Mom.
Happy birthday to you."

"Thank ya'll. I appreciate it," Mom said as she poured milk for everyone.

Joe and John were busy this summer trading baseball cards with cousins Jimmy and Avalon. Our cousins pulled for the Brooklyn Dodgers, a team that the Yankees usually killed every year in the World Series. Joe pulled for the Yankees while John was a Cleveland Indians fan.

When Joe and John picked and sold blackberries, they bought a handful of baseball cards. Joe tried to get all the Yankees. He would trade with John for Yankees and also would trade his cousins Dodgers for Yankees. At one time, Joe had a full stack of later valuable Mickey Mantle cards. These cards would mysteriously disappear after Joe left home and would never be seen again.

Joe figures he would have been wealthy if he still had all the prized cards. No one knew or no one said whatever did happen to the cards.

1955 would turn out to be the year of the Dodgers. They had an amazing comeback team this year. Joe could remember hearing many of their improbable comebacks on the radio while relaxing on the pallet in the shade on Sunday evening. He would never forget the rusty voice of the Dodger's announcer, Nat Albright. This voice was a one of a kind voice.

There would be many arguments between these cousins about who was the best team and the best player. Jimmy always liked Dodger centerfielder, Duke Snider. He was always compared to Yankee phenom, Mickey Mantle. When playing cow pasture ball, Joe, Jimmy, John, and Avalon would pretend to be their heroes.

Chapter 19
Dad's Crew Minus Two

Tobacco was topped out and priming time was drawing near. The tobacco sleds were repaired. The barns were daubed and made more airtight for good curing.

On Saturday, July 30, Dad's crew tackled the spring field and then Uncle Nelson's home field. The two fields would be housed in Dad's barn.

The priming crew was Dad, Uncle Nelson, Joe, and John while the barn crew was Rose tying with Mom and Danny handing up. The second crew was Aunt Jo tying with Jane and Gray handing up. It would take a while for Danny and Gray to replace Elmer and Wayne, but for now, there was not a choice.

We made good progress today even though the barn crew ran behind all day. The barn was finished at 5:00 p.m.

After a good day of rest on Sunday, complete with naps on the pallets in the shade, Dad's crew hit the hill field for a big trial for the younger work crew. Dad had a 5:30 a.m. start as he thought it would be a long day to pull the six acres to go in the road barn.

"It looks wet! Let's hit it, boys!" Dad said as his primers hit it. Mr. Shore, as always, helped pull the first sled and drove the sleds. Then he handed up with Mom and Danny to Rose. The other tie team was Jane and Gray handing up to Aunt Jo.

It was, as Dad figured, a very long day with the barn being filled at 8:00 p.m. The hot, dog days of August were here. There would be many more of these days, starting tomorrow.

The hill field was completed along with the middle field on Tuesday, another long day with the finish at about 8:30 p.m. It was getting dark just as the last sticks were hung. With Elmer and Wayne being gone, it was Joe's job now to be the high hanger in the big barn. Dad or Uncle Nelson would be the bottom hanger.

"Boy, it's hot up here today!" Joe said as he mopped the sweat pouring down his face.

"It sure is," Dad said from the bottom half of the barn. The tight quarters of packing the barn full made it seem even hotter. Joe was ready for a dip in the creek. It would have to wait, though, as it would be too dark to go today.

On Wednesday, Uncle Nelson's woods field was primed to complete the round of first primings. These four acres were finished at 4:00 p.m. so Joe and John were going to the creek to cool off. Dad and Uncle Nelson and the whole crew decided to go along for the cool off. It was a fun time. Uncle Nelson was just like a kid.

Flat Top Haircut

The rest of the week was suckering time. Joe did not like to sucker tobacco. It was hot, hard, sticky work. Dad did manage to take Joe and John to Elkin on Saturday evening late to get a haircut. They wanted the new hairstyle, the flat top. The flat top haircut was popular all over the country. Joe loved it, even though his hair would not stand up very straight after he left Templeton's Barber Shop. Joe would wear a flat top haircut for the next five years until he went into the Army. Of course, the Army had their own hairstyle.

The Templeton Barber Shop had a familiar ring to it. Wonder if Mr. Templeton was related to the

Templeton's who owned the haunted house Mom and Dad used to live in before Joe was born.

Mom told us about the house. It seems that Mom used to lock and padlock the front door downstairs each night before going to bed. The next morning, the door would be standing open. Mom told Dad about it, but he said that she had forgotten to shut the door.

Aunt De Ette was spending the night with Mom and verified that the front door was locked and padlocked. In the morning, the door was standing open. They again told Dad about the door.

"We'll see about that door tonight," Dad said. "I'll shut it myself."

That night Dad locked and padlocked the door with Mom and Aunt De Ette looking on. The next morning, Dad was up first to check the door.

"It's wide open just like you said. Wow!" Dad said. "Sounds like this house is haunted."

That very day, Dad started looking and found an empty house at the Cooper place in Union Grove, the house where Joe was born. The story of the haunted house would close with Dad's family moving out immediately.

The priming cycle continued on Monday with the first of the second primings at the spring field and Nelson's home field. It would be a weekly routine now until all the tobacco was harvested. It was a long, grinding schedule with hard work and long hours. Many days would be from 3:00 a.m. to 9:00 p.m. This was farm life at the Little Farm on Brown Road.

Joe's in High School

School opened up on Monday, September 12, with half days the first week. Dad let all the youngins go to school the first day as the two acres at the spring field and Uncle Nelson's two acres could be finished by working late.

Danny was going to school today. He was excited as he waited for the bus. The first day of school is always a day of remembrance for any new first grader.

Joe was in high school, the ninth grade. It would be different this year having several different teachers and changing classes. Joe was excited. Mr. Joe Cash was his homeroom teacher. Mr. Cash also taught ninth and tenth grade English. Joe also had signed up for Geometry under Mr. Hoyt Reece. As it worked out, Joe did not like geometry and dropped out of the class in short order.

Joe also took Civics under Mr. O'Donnell who coached football. Mr. O'Donnell tried to get Joe to play football. He would have loved to, but Dad would not let him play. The farm work came first. Coach O'Donnell wanted to make a fullback out of Joe.

Joe's other classes were Business Math and World History. Joe loved history.

Old bus #63 got Joe and the other youngins home at 1:00 p.m. It was a fast dinner and on to the tobacco field and barn to complete Dad's barn by dark.

Dad kept Rose and Joe out of school on Tuesday, Wednesday, and Thursday, but let Jane and Danny go back to school. It was tough getting the tobacco finished each day, but somehow they did it with work past dark each day. The same school schedule would be for next week also as the tipping process would start on Monday at the spring field and would continue until Dad's crop would be tipped out on Wednesday at the middle field. Uncle Nelson's tips would be pulled on Thursday, September 22. Finally, the long harvest of 1955 was completed.

As was custom, yells of joy rang out from the field and then as an echo from the barn workers. It was good to be finished priming. A lot had been accomplished by a less experienced work crew with Elmer and Wayne being gone.

The wienie roast was planned over the last sled of tobacco. It would be on Saturday night, September 24, at 5:00 p.m.

Uncle Nelson didn't have much competition on hotdog eating at the annual end of tobacco priming wienie roast. His main foe in the past was Elmer who was far away in Texas in the Air Force. Elmer would be home next week for about fifteen days before the Air Force was sending him to Cornell University in Ithaca, New York, to study Romanian language before going to Germany.

Mr. Shore again paid for all the hotdogs, pop, and the trimmings. It was a fun time with Mrs. Shore, Mom, Dad, Rose, Joe, John, Jane, Danny, Uncle Nelson, Aunt Jo, Gray, Fay, and little "Debbie Dean" who was now almost 1 ½ years old. After a long, hard summer, it was nice to get together for a time of good food and fellowship.

The mad rush to get the tobacco ready for the market had already started. It would stretch out the next month. There was a lot of work to be done in grading of the tobacco and then tying it up before hauling it to Winston to Cook's Warehouse. As usual, Dad's youngins would spend the evenings after school as well as nights until 9:00 p.m. and all day Saturday in the packhouse. It was a steady job.

School was more demanding this year as should be expected of high school. Mr. O'Donnell was forever bugging Joe to play fullback for him on the football team.

"I'd like to play, Mr. O'Donnell, but my dad cannot spare me from the farm work," Joe said.

Joe's best friend, Archie, played on the team. He didn't have as much on him at home as Joe did. Archie realized that Joe could not play even though he wanted to play.

Gurn Johnson was again busy hauling Dad's tobacco. He would haul at least one load a week. Joe and the other youngins were excited when Dad came back with that good coconut candy. Joe's favorite was chocolate coconut, but Dad also brought home some strawberry coconut and vanilla coconut. Boy, was this good candy!

Cousin Jimmy was excited as his Brooklyn Dodgers finally won a World Series by beating Joe's Yankees four games to three. The Dodgers had never won before. Jimmy was all mouth about this feat. Joe had to take it in stride and say that we'd get you back next year. What else could you say?

Elmer left for assignment at Cornell University after being home for fifteen days. It was great to see Elmer again. We miss him.

The night air was getting nippy. It was getting closer to Dad's deadline to finish getting the tobacco ready for market. The last week of October saw Gurn haul two loads. One load went at 3:00 a.m. Tuesday to sell that day and then the last load was ready to go at 3:00 a.m. Thursday. Dad went with Gurn on the last load as he usually did. It was a banner year for Dad's money crop.

Chapter 20
Joe Makes Team

On Monday, October 31, Joe tried out for the basketball team at West Yadkin. In the past, he had only dreamed about it. Now was his chance. Joe was small at about 5'9" and 120 pounds, but he was wiry and tough. He had a good set shot, the shot of the day, and also shot about 85-90% on free throws.

Joe had a good shot at the team but was the last person cut. His friend Archie King made the team. Joe was heartbroken, even though he knew, at best, he was a long shot to make the team. Joe kept practicing hard at home every chance he got. He would be ready the next time.

The next time came sooner than Joe thought. He thought it would be next year, but one week later on Monday, November 14, Coach George Holmes saw Joe in the hall and asked him to come to his office during study hall. Joe went immediately the next class period to see Coach Holmes.

"Come in, Joe. Do you still want to play on the team?" Coach Holmes asked.

"I sure do, Coach!" Joe said.

"Here's your uniform. You're on the team. Clyde King did not make his grades and I had to drop him off the team," Coach Holmes said. "Can you practice this evening? We have our first game at Courtney tomorrow night."

"Yes, I can practice today. I left my shoes in my locker," Joe said. "I'll be ready for tomorrow night."

"See you at practice, Joe," Coach Holmes said.

Joe was so happy. He was on the team. He had to tell someone right away. Archie was in study hall with Joe.

"I'm on the team, Archie! Ain't that great?" Joe said in a whisper. "Can I thumb with you this evening after practice?"

"Sure you can. Congratulations, Joe!" Archie said.

Joe couldn't wait until practice this evening. It was good to be on the team. He had sent word home by Rose that he would be late. The team had a good practice. Coach Holmes told the team about Joe being on the team.

"Let's be ready to play tomorrow night at Courtney. The bus will leave here at 5:30 p.m. Don't be late!" Coach Holmes said.

Joe hurried to get dressed after practice. He and Archie headed to Highway 421 to try to catch a ride home. They would usually catch a ride with a Hanes worker or a Reynolds worker. Many people up Highway 421 worked at Winston and would give them a ride. Soon a car stopped and gave them a ride. Archie got out of the car at Marler Road.

"Thanks for the ride. See you tomorrow, Joe," Archie said.

"See you, Archie," Joe said. "I appreciate the ride, sir. I'll get out at Oak Grove. Thank you."

Joe quickly walked the one mile out Brown Road to the house. It was about 6:00 p.m. and time to milk the cows.

"Guess what, Mom?" Joe said excitedly. "I made the team. One player did not make his grades and Coach Holmes put me on the team. We play tomorrow at Courtney."

"That's good, Joe! Hurry up and get your milking done. Supper is about ready," Mom said. "I'm proud of you, Joe, for staying with it and not quitting."

Tuesday was a slow day. Joe was ready for the ballgame tonight, but the day would drag on and on. Finally, it was 2:00 p.m. and time for the team meeting in Coach Holmes' room. Coach Holmes would go over the game plan with the team.

All of the players had the last period of the day from 2:00 to 3:00 free to practice ball all year long or if they didn't play all sports, they would have a study hall period.

"We need to remember to work the ball around for a good shot. We don't have to rush and take a bad shot. Teamwork is the key. We'll take a fast break if it is available but, otherwise, we need to be patient. Now let's go over to the gym and practice our free throws for awhile," Coach Holmes said.

Joe loved shooting free throws. He could hit about eighteen out of twenty in practice. Today, however, he would just concentrate on passing the ball back to the starters to give them plenty of shots.

Some of these players were very good. Joe learned a lot from Jerry Dickerson, who was also a great pitcher in baseball, Marcus Allred, Joe Wright, Wayne Wagoner, Bobby Allen, and Jackie Reinhardt. Other members on the team, besides Joe, were Richard Money and, of course, Archie King.

Joe and Archie stayed around in the gym for about an hour after school practicing their shots. Joe was trying to learn the new shot in the game, the jump shot. It would take Joe awhile to learn this tough shot, but he knew he had to learn it to play on this team. Of course, Joe and Archie were realistic. They did not expect to play much, if any, tonight at Courtney.

After shooting hoops for awhile, Joe and Archie wandered down to the store down past the school,

West Yadkin Grocery. This was a hangout of school youngins. Many of them would eat dinner here everyday instead of eating in the school lunchroom. Joe could not afford to eat at either place. He still brought his dinner from home.

Dad had given Joe a quarter to get a snack to eat before the game tonight. Joe bought a bottle of pop and an oatmeal cookie for a dime, leaving him fifteen cents to spend after the game. He figured he would be hungrier later on tonight.

Finally, it was 5:30 p.m. and time to meet the activity bus up on the semi circle in front of the school. Both the girls' team and boys' team would ride to the games together. Joe didn't know any of the girls except ninth graders, Donna Johnson, Sonja Royal, and Nancy Reinhardt.

Joe sat with Archie on the long, slow ride to Courtney, which was a small school down in the southeast corner of Yadkin County. Courtney did not play football in our league as they still played the old six man game. They did not have enough players to compete in the eleven man game.

Courtney would play us in baseball and basketball and be competitive with us. West Yadkin also was a small school located in the southwest part of the county. One thing Joe would always remember about Courtney was a basketball player named Wilbur Baity who dyed his hair green to match their school colors. Green hair really looked weird in the 1950s.

The bus ride was down Highway 421 East to Yadkinville where we took Highway 601 South. We would turn off Highway 601 and go east on Courtney Road to get to the school.

We arrived at Courtney at 6:30 p.m. The girls' game would start at 7:00 with the boys' game to follow at 8:00 p.m. Joe would have mixed memories of Courtney, some good and some not so good, but funny.

The girls' basketball game in these days was the old game with six players on the court for each team. There would be three forwards and three guards for each team. The three forwards were offensive players while the three guards could only play defense. Neither player could cross the center court line. This way you put your best three defensive players on their best three offensive players. Then you put your three top scorers against their best defenders.

The game was a match of best players with individual showdowns but with great team play, too. No player could dribble over two dribbles without passing or shooting the ball. It was a great game. Joe hated to see the game changed later to the format that the boys played. He thought the change ruined a good girls' game.

West Yadkin High School was known for having great girls' teams during the 1940s and early 1950s. Mrs. Geneva Steelman had coached these teams to great success before retiring from coaching.

Tonight, the girls' game would not be close as the Golden Eagle girls would win by twenty points. Joe did not remember much about the game as he was so excited about his first game in the blue and gold for West Yadkin. Right after halftime of the girls' game, Joe and his teammates went to the dressing room to get dressed for the game.

Joe's First Game

Coach Holmes came in and talked again to the team before we went out for our warm-ups.

"We just want to play our game. Play good, solid defense and don't give up easy basketballs.

Work the ball for good shots. We are a team. Play team ball!" Coach Holmes said.

The girls' game was over. The West Yadkin cheerleaders were lined up for the team to come through and onto the floor led by our star player, Jerry Dickerson, who was the team captain.

"Let's go get 'em, team," Jerry said as he led us out. The Courtney gym was a small, cracker box type building. It had seats for maybe three to four hundred people. The crowd was very small tonight, even though Joe felt like there had to be at least five thousand people here. He was pumped up.

The team went through the usual warm-ups with lay-ups from the right, left, and then, center. Soon the teammates were shedding their blue warm-up jackets showing their deep blue colors. Joe always thought the blue and gold was a beautiful mixture of colors.

The buzzer sounded to start the game. Coach Holmes sent out his starters, Jerry Dickerson, Marcus Allred, Jackie Reinhardt, Joe Wright, and Bobby Allen. The team quickly matched up at center court to know who they had on defense. Jackie jumped center and the game was on.

West Yadkin got a quick jump on the green team as Jerry hit three fast jumpers. He had a simply beautiful jump shot. Joe was watching it and would try to copy the shot. At the end of the first quarter, we led Courtney 15-6. It looked like the rout was on.

Coach Holmes substituted freely in the second quarter with Wayne, Richard, and Archie playing a few minutes. Archie was a big, strong, husky boy who did not know his own strength. He played a lot of football and basketball for West Yadkin over these four years.

By halftime, the score was 32-14 as Jerry and Marcus were deadly with their jump shots. The team had played a good first half.

"Keep up the good work! We need to stay with our game plan no matter what the score is," Coach Holmes urged.

The third quarter was more of the same as the score grew to 48-20, a total rout. Joe was really enjoying this game. He would never forget his first game at Courtney.

The game was winding down in the fourth quarter. Joe was sitting down at the end of the bench enjoying the team's effort. All of a sudden, Joe heard his name.

"Joe! Joe!" Coach Holmes was calling his name. Joe quickly ran to the other end of the bench where Coach Holmes was standing.

"Joe, go in for Joe Wright at guard," Coach said as Joe's heart was about to pump its way out of his chest.

Joe ran to the scorer's table and into the game. He set up on defense as Jackie was shooting a foul shot. Joe was so happy. He couldn't believe he was actually playing. He looked over to Archie who was lined up for the foul shot and Archie smiled at him.

The time was down to one minute and thirty seconds as Joe eyed the old clock on the wall behind the basket. The time would go fast as Joe played defense and then brought the ball down on offense with Wayne. The ball went in the middle to Archie who missed a tough shot and then back on defense again. Joe stole the ball and passed to Wayne who made an easy shot just before the final buzzer. The game was over. West Yadkin won by a landslide, 66-32. Joe will never forget the thrill of playing in his first game at Courtney. It was fun.

The bus ride back to West Yadkin was a happy one as both teams had won big games. It sure felt good to win. Joe did not like to lose. He and Archie would later suffer through a terrible senior season in which the out manned team would not win a game.

Back at West Yadkin, Archie's sister was waiting for him. She was nice and gave Joe a ride all the way home. He tried to tell her he could walk from Oak Grove but she would not hear of it.

"Thank you for the ride, ma'am," Joe said as he got out under the beautiful, moonlit sky. It was almost as bright as day.

"See you tomorrow, Archie," Joe said as he ran into the dark house. Everyone was in bed as it was now 10:30 p.m. Joe drank a glass of milk and ate a chunk of cornbread. He was starved as he had not eaten since the 4:00 p.m. cookie.

Mom had heard Joe and walked into the kitchen to give him a hug. "Hey, Joe! How are you? Did you win?" Mom asked.

"I'm fine, Mom. We won! The score was 66-32. I got to play the last part of the fourth quarter. It sure was fun. Thanks for letting me play," Joe said.

"Get on to bed, Joe. You'll have trouble getting up in the morning," Mom said. "Good night."

"I'm in bed now," Joe said as he headed that way. "Good night, Mom!"

Guess what Joe dreamed tonight? He was playing basketball.

Basketball Dream

Joe and Archie were the stars of the team along with Jerry Dickerson. All three were seniors and were playing on an undefeated team. They had already beaten Jonesville for the Yadkin County championship and tonight they were playing Elkin for the district championship.

Coach Holmes had a smile on his face. This team was his best team ever. Early in the game, good defense helped West Yadkin score four easy baskets. Joe, Archie, and Jerry then each hit two straight jump shots from all around the circle. The rout was on and it was just the first quarter. The score was 24-6 at the end of the first quarter.

"Good job, team!" Coach said as there wasn't anything else to say. The machine was running smooth.

The rest of the game was more of the same. A good Elkin team led by 6'8" Jerry Steele was being out hustled and outplayed by the smaller, quicker Golden Eagles. Joe, Archie, and Jerry continued with the hot shooting, supported by a team effort on defense.

The final score was 86-48. Joe, Archie, and Jerry each scored over twenty points. What a game this was!

And then, as dreams go, Joe woke up to reality. Dad was waking him up. It was 5:30 a.m. and time to milk the cows. Joe had agreed to milk in the mornings when Dad had to milk for him at night. That was part of the basketball playing agreement.

Joe had no problem whatsoever with the agreement. He hopped out of bed and got to work. He was wide awake and hungry as a horse. He would lay away six of Mom's good biscuits with the eggs and gravy for breakfast.

Joe was early at the bus stop and told Rose and John all about the ballgame last night. He didn't mention his dream as he kept it all to himself. That is, except he had to tell Archie about it at school today. Joe and Archie would continue their close friendship throughout high school. They would spend a lot of time together.

On Friday night, West Yadkin had its second game of the year at home against Boonville. Again, both teams won, though the games were close. Joe got to play for the last minute of the game. He had an opportunity to score his first points ever, but, nervously, missed a one and one free throw. It definitely was a case of nerves as Joe was about automatic on free throws.

On Saturday morning, Dad's crew hit the fields at first light to finish pulling corn. Last Saturday's corn pile was shucked and in the corn crib. The corn was halfway finished. Dad, Rose, Joe, John, Jane, and Danny hopped on the wagon and headed over on the hill to the former Indian hunting grounds field.

Joe's mind wandered back to the dream he had about his Indian friends.

"Wouldn't it have been neat to live back when Indians were here, John?" Joe asked.

"I think it would have been fun," John said.

Dad interrupted their thoughts with a question for Joe. "Did ya'll win last night, Joe?" Dad asked.

"Yes, we won 62-54. I played the last minute and should have scored, but I missed a foul shot," Joe said.

"That's good. I'm glad ya'll are winning," Dad said. He didn't usually show any interest in Joe's sports. Dad never came to any games. Joe would have so loved for Dad to show an interest, but he did not. Obviously, Dad saw sports as a waste of time or something that took his youngins away from the farm work. That's why Joe was shocked when Dad asked about the game.

The corn pulling took all day as the crop was another good one. It would take all next week to finish the shucking. Work was a little slower this year as Dad's two oldest workers were gone.

Elmer had finished basic training and advanced training in Texas and then the Air Force sent him to Cornell University in New York to study the Romanian language. Soon, he would be heading to Germany for almost three years. We sure do miss Elmer.

Joe wasn't much help on the corn shucking the next week as he had basketball practice or a game every day. It would be late Saturday afternoon before the corn pile was finished. Joe had shucked corn all day. He was trying to make up for the past week.

"I'm sorry I haven't been much help to ya'll this week," Joe said. "I didn't know basketball would take so much time."

The two games this week were against Jonesville and Elkin, both were tough opponents. The boys lost both games and the girls lost to Jonesville and beat Elkin. The boys' record was now 2-2 while the girls were at 3-1.

The games next week were against Yadkinville on the road and Sparta at home. The boys bounced back by winning both games to move to 4-2. The girls lost at Yadkinville and beat Sparta at home to make their record 4-2, also.

December had blown in cold and damp. It was not going to be long before the snow would come. There was just a feel in the air.

With a short month, only two games were scheduled for the rest of December. We played East Bend at home and won both games. We played Dobson on the road and also won both games. The girls' and boys' teams had identical 7-2 records going into the Christmas break. Joe was pleased with the progress of the team and also with being able to play in four games so far.

Chapter 21
Christmas 1955

School was out on December 21 and would not reopen until Monday, January 2, 1956. Joe was ready for the break as the farm work, school, basketball practice, and basketball games were a big load. Joe was ready for some snow and some rabbit and squirrel hunting.

On Thursday morning, Leck Groce brought over his rabbit dogs to run a few rabbits. Leck, Dad, Joe, and John enjoyed a good spirited rabbit chase. They jumped six rabbits and shot four of them. It was fun to hear the dogs run. They were as good as Leck told us they were.

Joe made quick work with the skinning of the rabbits as Jane helped him. Soon the meat was in Mom's kitchen salted down and ready to cook for breakfast tomorrow morning.

Dad wanted to get the hogs killed, but the weather had moderated somewhat. Joe had been wrong about the snow for December. So far, the weather had stayed clear and warmer than normal.

A cold front moved through Friday night and on Saturday morning, snow flurries were blowing in from the north. Was there a white Christmas in the works? No! Not for now. The weather stayed cold but cleared up.

Elmer had given the family an early Christmas gift. He had entered a contest at Tom's Studio in Elkin and won a brand new seventeen inch screen television set. He proudly gave the TV set to his family. Now the youngins could watch the Lone Ranger, Hop Along Cassidy, and Roy Rogers at home without sneaking off to Uncle Lamar's to watch them.

Mom and Dad had said it was a sin to watch television so we did not ever get one. Slowly, Mom and Dad changed their view and would even go with us over to Uncle Lamar's to watch Alfred Hitchcock's scary mysteries. After this suspenseful show, the walk home down through the woods and down the hill to the spring and up the hill past the packhouse was a quick walk with over the shoulder looks behind us. It was spooky.

Now with our own TV, Dad would watch the good western shows and enjoy them. Gunsmoke would later be an all-time favorite.

Elmer was home for Christmas. Wouldn't you know it? He came in during the night of December 20 and got in bed without letting anyone know. Seems like he had pulled that trick before. Elmer was always full of tricks.

At 5:00 a.m. Sunday, Christmas morning, little feet hit the floor as Jane and Danny led the way into the front room to see what was in their shoe box. Jane was growing up. She got a pretty pocketbook along with the fruit, nuts, and candy.

Danny was happy with the cowboy outfit complete with a pair of six shooters and holsters. He didn't pay any attention to the goodies that were in the shoe box. He was ready for a quick draw.

Gifts were given out. It was a happy day at Mom and Dad's house, as the whole family was home. Joe got a neat new shirt and windbreaker jacket. He had been wanting a windbreaker. All of his friends at school seemed to have a windbreaker.

Just about the time Mom had breakfast ready, Grandpa Brown was knocking on the door.

"Merry Christmas, youngins!" Grandpa said.

"Merry Christmas, Grandpa!" all the youngins said as they headed to the breakfast table.

Mom prayed, "Heavenly Father, thank you for this day. Thank you for what it means to us. Thank you for keeping Elmer safe to come home. Thank you for this food and for providing for us each day. Be with the sick, shut-in, and the bereaved. Be with all of our family. Keep us in your will. Bless this food in Jesus' name. Amen. Amen."

"Grandpa, have some breakfast with us?" Mom said as she passed food around the table.

"No thanks, Gladys. Just a cup of American Ace coffee will be just fine," Grandpa said. He slowly drank his coffee and got up to go.

Mom got up and gave Grandpa his present and watched as he lit up one of those cigars.

"Thank ya'll for the coffee and the cigars," Grandpa said. He left in a puff of smoke on the way back up the driveway.

The morning went quickly and soon it was time to go to Grandpa Proctor's. Wayne and Elvie didn't go as they needed to go to her parents for Christmas.

"Still hasn't cut the weeds, has he?" Dad asked as he turned into Grandpa's driveway. As normal, the house was packed full of kinfolks who were loud and lively. They loved to get together and have a good time.

The evening of laughter, chatter, and songs went by quickly. The gifts were given out with wrapping paper scattered everywhere. It was departure time for the kin who would be going in all different directions. Everybody said their goodbyes and went their separate ways.

"We need to go, Gladys," Dad said. "We've got the chores to do and you know it's church night."

"Oh, me. I forgot today was Sunday, Clyde," Mom said as they quickly left for home.

Chores were done. Cows were milked and fed. Chickens were fed and watered and Dad's family was on their way to church for preaching. Training union did not meet today. Attendance was down as many people were out of town with their families for the holidays.

After a short preaching service, Dad drove home and it was to bed for everyone. Another big day had worn them out.

Trip to Greensboro

Wayne was out of work for a few days and would stay with us until Wednesday evening. They wanted Joe and John to go home with them for a few days. They would bring them back home on Saturday. Joe and John really wanted to go. Dad finally decided to let them go as they rarely ever got to go anywhere.

"I can handle the milking and chickens for a few days, I guess," Dad said. "Ya'll can go. Just have them back on Saturday," he added to Wayne.

"We'll be back Saturday evening," Wayne said as they headed out. Joe and John enjoyed the next three days. It was fun being in the city with an indoor bathroom, complete with a big bathtub. Joe would take his first ever bath in a bathtub while on this trip. It was nice to have an indoor bathroom.

"I like the bathroom and bathtub," Joe told Wayne. "It is nice."

Wayne and Elvie took Joe and John all over Greensboro showing them the town.

"It sure is bigger than Elkin, ain't it, Joe?" John said.

"Sure is!" Joe said.

The three days of being spoiled passed quickly. Joe and John ate hotdogs and hamburgers for three days. They really lived it up. But all good things must end. On Saturday morning, they got up and packed their belongings up and were ready to head back to the Little Farm on Brown Road. It had been a load of fun, but now it was over.

Joe and John were back home by 3:00 p.m. Mom met them at the door with a hug.

"I believe we were missed, John," Joe said as he gave Jane and Rose a hug.

"You sure were missed. You can't go next time unless we can go with you," Jane said.

Wayne and Elvie left to spend Saturday night with her folks. They would head back to Greensboro on Sunday evening.

"Where's Elmer?" Joe asked. "He hasn't gone back yet, has he?"

"No! He's up at Geraldine's. He'll have to head back on Monday, though," Mom said. Elmer had been dating Geraldine Huff from Elkin for over a year now. Everyone figured that they would have been married by now. Instead, he joined the Air Force.

Soon, it was chore time. Joe and John got their milking job back right away. Dad had been to Elkin and was just getting back when they finished milking.

"Good to see you boys are home," Dad said. "Your cows really missed you while you were gone."

At supper tonight, Joe ate a healthy portion of cornbread and milk. It was good to eat hotdogs and hamburgers, but you could not beat good old, country cooking. Cornbread and milk was tops.

"Well, tomorrow is 1956," Mom said at supper. "It sure was a fast year and a tough one, too. We lost two sons to the city this year."

"We'll be losing a couple more in the next three years, too, I imagine. Our family is really growing up," Dad said. "There's not too much on the farm to offer a youngin with a high school education. They have better opportunities in the big city."

"Dad, can we stay up for the new year tonight?" Joe asked.

"No, not this year! You have to get up to go to church tomorrow morning," Dad said.

It was Sunday, January 1, 1956. Another election year was here. Leap year was here again.

Pastor Hankins again preached on making a real commitment, not just a resolution.

"You need to fully commit your life to the Lord. Don't just make a January 1 promise that you won't keep. Not only commit to the Lord, but also to your family, your job, or your school work. Whatever you do, do it to the best of your ability and be faithful to it," Pastor Hankins said.

That's a good message, Joe thought to himself. Wonder how many people are really listening? Will it really make a difference to anyone? Joe was a thinker and he figured that most people were snoozing or thinking about their Sunday dinner.

School was back in session on Monday, January 2, 1956. Before we left for school, we told Elmer bye. He was leaving this morning for New York. We didn't know if we would see him again before he would be shipped out to Germany for his long tour of duty there.

"Write me sometime, Joe," Elmer said as we left. "It gets mighty lonesome away from home."

"I will! Bye," Joe said.

It was good to see Archie and other friends at school today, even though Joe could do without some of the schoolwork. It wasn't that bad, as Joe always managed to make A's and B's without fully applying himself.

Basketball practice was back on the agenda today and all week with a Friday night home game with Courtney on the schedule. Coach Holmes ran us a lot for the first two practices. We needed it as it had been a long two weeks since we had done any running.

"Boy, the running sure hurts after a couple of weeks off, doesn't it, Archie?" Joe said after practice on Tuesday.

"It sure does! It's hard to get your wind back," Archie said as they finally caught a ride home from practice.

It was another two victories on Friday night against Courtney. Neither game was close as both teams' records were now at 8-2. With only a little over a month left in the regular season, both teams were looking good.

The January birthdays were here. Danny was seven years old on January 18. He was enjoying his first year of school. On January 21, Joe was fifteen years old. Just think, he could get his driver's license next year. Dad celebrated his forty-second birthday on January 24. The week full of birthdays ended with a day out of school. Snow of four inches was on the ground.

The day out of school was enjoyed by all the youngins. Joe and John spent a big part of the day down on the spring hill with Jimmy and Avalon sledding on the fluffy snow. It sure was nice to be old enough to play in the snow. Joe remembers when Elmer and Wayne used to sled, but he was too little as Mom was afraid he'd get sick.

It stayed cold and the snow was laying around waiting for more to come down. It came down Tuesday evening after school, canceling the second straight basketball game. The snow accumulated another six inches to knock out school for the rest of the week.

February was here. Finally, the weather warmed slightly to allow school to reopen on Monday, February 6. The basketball schedule had been wiped out for the past two weeks. The Yadkin County tournament would start on Thursday night at Yadkinville.

Basketball Tournaments

The boys' team at 9-5 and the girls' team at 10-4 would play on Thursday night trying to move on to Friday night. The boys would play Courtney again while the girls would play East Bend.

Both teams easily advanced to the Friday night semifinals where they would have tougher games. The boys would play Boonville for the right to play top seed Jonesville. The girls would play Jonesville for the right to play top seed Yadkinville.

"We can beat this team tonight. We've already beaten them one time. Just play our game and we'll be okay," Coach Holmes said before the team hit the floor.

The game was close for the first half, but good, defensive play and timely shooting by Jerry and Marcus put West Yadkin ahead 45-38 at the end of the third quarter. The fourth quarter was more of the same and the final score was 60-48. Now it was on to the championship game with the dreaded Blue Jays. Sounds like a dream I've had, doesn't it? Now all we need is the same results!

The girls' team did not fare so well. They lost a close game to Jonesville, 49-48. It was a tough way to end a season as only the first and second place teams would advance to the district playoffs.

West Yadkin had already lost two games to Jonesville this year. They were a tough, veteran team who won the regular season championship. It would be an uphill battle, at best, for West Yadkin. We were big underdogs.

Jonesville jumped to a quick lead and held the upper hand at the end of the first quarter, 18-12.

"We've got to get back on defense. They're getting too many easy baskets. We cannot win without playing total team defense," Coach told us.

We played better defense in the second quarter and tightened up the game. At halftime, the score was 28-26, Jonesville. We were in the game.

A quick run by the Blue Jays to open the third quarter would be West Yadkin's downfall. They scored eight points before we knew what hit us. We made runs at the end of the quarter and again in the fourth quarter, but we would not get any closer than ten points. The final score was 61-50. The Blue Jays definitely were the best team. Next week, both teams would be in the district playoffs.

West Yadkin's game against Mountain Park was over just after center jump. Mountain Park was a tall team lead by 6'8" center Jerry Swift. He swatted the ball from center jump to a fast breaking guard and an easy lay-up with the game not yet five seconds old. Their height and quickness totally destroyed us. We lost 75-42, a dismal end to an, otherwise, good season. It had been a fun learning experience for Joe. The team finished with a record of 11-7 for the year.

Chapter 22
Chicken House Work

Friday was chicken pickup day again. The house of five thousand chickens were sixteen weeks old and ready to become fried chicken for someone. They were picked up while the youngins were at school today.

Cleanup would start immediately as the turn around time was one week. Dad had already started when Joe got home from school. Joe and John were put to work right away as Dad had also been working on getting the plant beds ready to sow on Saturday. Yes! It was that time again. Dad was planning on another large crop this year of fourteen acres.

By the end of the day on Saturday, the plant beds were sown and the chicken house was cleaned out and ready for the shavings for the floor. Chicken manure was scattered all over the pasture, the cornfield, and the garden area.

Rose and John had their seventeenth and thirteenth birthdays on Thursday, February 23. Rose was the oldest youngin at home now that Elmer and Wayne were gone. She didn't think that she was a youngin anymore, though. She thought that she was a grownup.

"Nee Nee is seventeen!" Joe said at suppertime. "Seems like only yesterday that she set that haystack on fire and then blamed me," Joe laughed. "I couldn't even reach the matches I was so small."

"Now, the both of you are our two oldest youngins," Mom said. "It's kinda sad as we see our family growing up and going off in every direction.

All we can do, though, is to teach you right from wrong and let the Lord watch over you."

"Train up a child in the way he should go: and when he is old, he will not depart from it," Mom quoted Proverbs 22:6. Mom not only quoted this verse, she believed it.

On Friday, February 24, the new batch of baby chicks, five thousand of them, arrived to spend the next sixteen weeks with us at the Little Farm on Brown Road. They would help provide additional training for Dad's work crew. Dad did not like for his youngins to have idle time. We did not. We had to look in the dictionary to even know how to spell idle.

February 29, leap year extra day, arrived the first time in four years. It was always a conversation day.

March came in windy like normal. Joe wanted to play baseball at school, but Dad could not spare him. Joe's dream of playing major league baseball looked like it was going down the drain. As in football, Joe did not get to play baseball until his junior and senior year. By then, Joe was hopeless in trying to hit the curve ball. He had never seen a curve ball before. In hindsight, Joe wished he had tried switch hitting as he could hit from both sides, but he did not. Joe needed someone to encourage him, but no one did.

April came with warmer weather. The plant bed covers were off and the tobacco plants were starting to grow. Dad had to water the plants two to three times a week.

May 1, barefoot day, came with bare feet in the tobacco field. Dad, Joe, and John were hustling to finish laying off the tobacco land for setting by late next week.

Grandpa Brown's strawberries looked the best this year than in the past few years. Grandpa kept saying that he was going to plow them up, but kept working them each year. After school on Thursday and Friday, Joe, Rose, Jane, and John helped pick for Grandpa to take to Wilkesboro on Friday and Saturday morning.

"The strawberries sure are sweet this year, Grandpa," Joe said. "They're mighty tasty."

"They are sweet!" Grandpa said. "They'll sell good, too. People like the sweeter berry rather than the tart ones."

Good rain showers helped the strawberries as they would bear for about three weeks this year. The rain also perked up the almost ready tobacco plants. Dad set a probable setting day for the spring field of Friday, May 11.

Setting Time Already

Tobacco setting day had arrived at the spring field. Dad had moved the two acres back to the lower spring field this year. He let Rose, Jane, and Danny go to school while he kept Joe and John home to help.

Dad, Joe, and John pulled plants while Mom straightened up the kitchen table after breakfast and got dinner started. The pinto beans would be done before she headed to the field to help with the setting. Taters would have to be cooked a little longer and biscuits would need to be made. It was a sight to sit at the table and watch Mom mix the flour, shortening, and milk together to make a batch of perfect biscuits. They would all turn out the same even though none of them were measured or cut with a biscuit cutter. Mom would shape each one by hand with love for her family.

Mom would then cook them a golden brown while always having her hands full of other things to do. Joe never remembers Mom burning the biscuits. They were always a work of art. On very few occasions, Mom would be so hurried in the tobacco field that she would not take the time to individually make those biscuits one by one. She would throw the whole cake in the pan and cook it. It still would be brown and good but not like the biscuits.

When all the youngins were at home and in their eating peak, Mom would bake about fifty biscuits for breakfast and fifty biscuits for dinner every day. We always had enough to eat. She knew exactly how many to cook. That was my mom taking care of her family. She would sing as she cooked. She was happy.

"In the sweet, by and by,
We shall meet on that beautiful shore.
In the sweet, by and by,
We shall meet on that beautiful shore."

Dad stuck his head in the door to let Mom know they were ready to start setting.

"Gladys, we are ready," Dad said as Joe and John ran through the kitchen and grabbed a leftover biscuit from breakfast. They were growing boys. They could eat all the time.

"I'm coming!" Mom yelled back to Dad as she grabbed her straw hat and hung her apron on the back of a chair. It was about 9:30 a.m. she noticed as she cut off the radio. She had been listening to Bro. Maze Jackson on the radio as she did everyday. She loved Bro. Maze. Later when Mom was sick, Bro. Maze would come with Joe to visit her. Joe would become good friends with Bro. Maze. He preached on about one hundred radio stations a day. He was a great man of God.

Dad had the wagon loaded with tobacco plants and water at the end of the lower spring field. He was rearing to go. He simply loved to work in tobacco and was like a kid who had lost his favorite toy for six months. He was ready to play with that toy now.

Mom dropped for Dad and John dropped for Joe. The sandy soil of the lower spring field was easy setting, more so than the red clay soil of the upper field of last year. Dad's crew, though only making a two row swipe across the field, still made good time. The click clack of the setters was playing Dad's music again.

It was a warm day with a cloudless sky. It was a perfect day to play baseball. Joe and John talked about playing next Sunday in their cow pasture league.

"We need to play together this summer," Joe said. "Avalon has grown a little and can play with Jimmy." Joe and John tossed the ball so much in the barnyard at the end of each day's work that they knew each other's moves and really played good together.

"I think we do, too. We can tear them up if we do," John said. "Let's tell Jimmy that's how we want to play."

After a break for dinner, the two setting crews were back at work at 1:00 p.m. The pace quickened considerably when the school youngins got home.

John switched to setting with Rose dropping and Jane dropped for Joe. Danny kept all setters in water and plants. With the click clack of a third setter echoing down the field towards the spring, the two acres were finished at 5:00 p.m. It was a good warm-up for the big field, which would be started on tomorrow.

Chores were done. Chickens were fed and watered. Joe and John milked the cows. Mom had supper ready right on time as the whole crew seemed to make their way in at the right time.

Mom and Dad still sat out front while Joe and Rose had been promoted to the seats at the end of the table where Elmer and Wayne used to sit. John, Jane, and Danny sat in back on the old homemade bench. My, if that old bench could talk, it could really tell some stories! It would have to include a bunch of giggles and a few tears, for sure.

Mom prayed, "Heavenly Father, thank you for this good day you've given us. Thank you for health and strength. We pray that you'd be with the sick, the shut-in, and the bereaved. Help them to look to you. We pray that you'd be with Elmer, Wayne, and Elvie. We pray that you'd bless this food to the nourishment of our body. We thank you in Jesus' name. Amen. Amen."

Dad's hungry crew quickly attacked the cornbread and milk. Joe and Rose could finally get a chunk of cornbread instead of all crumbs. Elmer and Wayne used to consume all the "corners" as we called the outside of the cake of cornbread. As if the cornbread was not reward enough for a good, hard day of work, Mom had stirred up a strawberry saunker. This treat was a surprise. Mom rarely fixed a dessert for supper.

"Boy, this saunker is good, Mom!" Joe said.

"It sure is!" Rose added as she poured a touch of milk in it to cool it.

"It's kind of musty," Dad said. "I must have more!" He laughed.

"I like strawberry saunker best of all," Jane said.

"I like peach best," John said.

"I like strawberry, too," Danny said.

"Thank you, all!" Mom said with a smile of happiness. She loved to please her family.

When supper was over, everyone helped Mom clean the kitchen up. They knew Mom was tired and to show their appreciation for the strawberry saunker, they told Mom to just sit down and tell them what to do.

Soon, everyone was in bed. A good night's sleep would be needed for the long day tomorrow.

Dad woke up Joe and John at 5:00 a.m. for chores. He wanted to be in the plant beds at 6:00 to try and get half of the hill field finished.

After Mom's usual blue ribbon breakfast, Dad's crew was in the plant beds pulling tobacco plants at 6:00 a.m. The wagon was loaded down with bushel baskets to be filled with plants. Water was hauled from the waterhole over near Mr. Shore's woods barn.

By 9:30 a.m., the setting began at the upper side of the hill field near Grandpa Brown's house. Again, three teams of tobacco setters started to work. Mom dropped for Dad while Jane dropped for Joe and Rose dropped for John. Danny manned the water and plant detail while also checking behind the busy setters for any loose soil around the newly set plants. If the soil was not firmed up enough, the plant would probably die.

Dad used all of his help. He was one person short of another setting team, but used Danny productively anyway. When Mom had to leave to get dinner finished, Danny would drop for Dad. Joe remembers all the good experience he got when he used to drop for Dad. It was all good learning for the future. Now, Joe had done it all. He had been setting for several years.

Chapter 23
Indoor Bathroom

Dad's setting day went according to plans. The hill field was set out just past the half mark when we ran out of plants at about 6:15 p.m.

It was on to chores and supper before the Saturday night baths.

"I hope to have the new bathroom, bathtub, and shower in before next week's baths," Dad announced. "That's my plan anyway." It had been a long time in the talking stages. Progress was being made.

Recently, Dad had added on a small bedroom with bunk beds for Joe and John. It was nice to have your own bed instead of having to sleep in the community bed as Joe's used to seem to be when the four boys shared a bed.

Dad planned the bathroom in the small area between the kitchen and the new bedroom. It was a small room but was just perfect for the indoor bathroom.

Rose was very happy. "I've been dreaming about the bathroom for a long time. I can't believe it's about to happen," she said.

Sunday was a welcome day of rest. Also, it was Mother's Day. We love our mom. After church and dinner, Mom and Dad headed down to Grandpa and Grandma Proctor's for their Sunday visit. Mom wanted to visit her mom.

"These weeds have an early start on him this year. They'll be whoppers by the end of the summer," Dad said as the weeds played music under the car that really annoyed him.

"Come in, youngins!" Grandma greeted everyone as she made her way to the kitchen to hand out her biscuits. As usual, the "cookie like" biscuits were better than cookies. Each youngin ate their fill of two or three before heading to the well in the enclosed screen porch to get a cold drink of water. The only way to drink cold well water is to drink from the old dipper hanging on the wall next to the well. Cold water was so refreshing.

"How's your tobacco setting coming along, Clyde?" Grandpa Proctor asked.

"Pretty good, so far! We've set out about half of our fourteen acres," Dad said. "How about yours?"

"I'm about through. I'll finish up tomorrow," Grandpa said.

Soon, other people were coming to see their mom. Uncle Porter, Aunt Nancy, Judy, and Benny came up the road from their nearby house which was actually a packhouse. They lived in the packhouse while they built their house. Aunt De Ette and Uncle Raymond were up from Winston. Aunt Hazel and Uncle Brice came in from Union Grove. Aunt Jane, and Uncle Phillip, and Cousin Pam came up from Winston and Aunt Dorothy and Uncle Parks also were home from Union Grove. Uncle Claude and Uncle Troy were not able to get home to see their mom on her special day.

Not long after the crowd rolled in, Dad was ready to go. It would be church time by the time chores were done.

"Bye, ya'll. We've got to go. It'll be church time soon," Mom said as she got up to leave.

Grandma hugged all the youngins and told them bye. "Ya'll come back soon. You hear?" Grandma said as they left.

"Bye, Grandma! We'll see you next time," all the youngins said.

"Mom, we sure do love you not only on Mother's Day, but every day," Joe said as they rode home.

"We sure do, Mom," Rose said.

"You are so good to us, Mom," Jane said.

"You're the best mom ever," John said.

"I love you, too, Mom," Danny said as all of the youngins had their say. But, of course, Mom already knew she was loved.

On Monday morning, it was back to the hill field to finish setting the eight acre field. Dad kept all of the youngins home to help as it would be another long day as Saturday had been.

By 9:30 a.m., the three setters were click clacking along moving across the hill field. The field was finished at 6:30 p.m., leaving one more long day of setting this year's crop out. Tuesday was another day with all youngins out of school. Mom and Dad would rather not keep them out of school, but they had no choice. The tobacco crop would not be set out in time without the help of the youngins.

The Tuesday setting of the middle field was a welcome day of completing the setting for the year. Joe liked to see progress. That's why he liked the tipping in the fall. It was the final stage of all the many steps of the tobacco in the field.

It was back to school on Wednesday. The school year was winding down. It had seemingly gone fast. Next Friday would be the last day of the ninth grade for Joe.

It was Wednesday, May 16, 1956. All the tobacco was set out. Now, Dad was going to make his family happy and fix an indoor bathroom complete with a bathtub and shower. Dad, being a jack of all trades, was doing the work himself. Uncle Nelson would help some while Joe was at school. Joe would help all he could when he was home. Dad stayed with it Wednesday, Thursday, and Friday. When the youngins got home from school on Friday, the bathroom was officially working.

"Ain't that a dream come true, Rose?" Mom asked as Rose and Jane checked out the bathtub. All the youngins would be able to try out the shower and bathtub tomorrow tonight. But as for now, the long walk to the outhouse was over. We could say bye-bye to all them spiders. Going in cold weather would not be so unpleasant now. Progress continued to come to the Little Farm on Brown Road.

On Saturday, Dad hit the tobacco field plowing the spring field, while Mom, Rose, Joe, John, Jane, and Danny chopped crabgrass and hoed tobacco all day long. The spring field was finished at 2:00 p.m., so the crew moved on to the hill field to work for the rest of the day. Dad had gone on earlier to plow. Mom stayed back at the house to cook Sunday dinner.

The hoeing went five rows at a clip starting at the upper side. Grandpa Brown came over to the edge of the field to talk with us as we hoed our way by him.

"Hey, youngins! Are you getting tired? Your grandma thinks that your Dad is killing you. I know you really work hard. One of these days you'll look back and thank him for getting you so prepared for the rest of your life," Grandpa said.

"We know, Grandpa. We'd like to be playing baseball but the work in the tobacco must be done," Joe said.

They hoed their way away from Grandpa and towards the other end, which was near the middle barn. They would wave to Grandpa and Grandma each time they got to the other end. Soon, they were out of sight on down in the field. They could only see the tin roof of Grandpa's house.

"Chore time, youngins!" Dad hollered as he rode his easy chair plow to the road end of the field where they were. They shouldered their hoes and made their way home.

Joe and John milked the cows while Rose and Jane fed and watered the chickens and Danny gathered the eggs. The chores were done and Dad was still not home. Supper was waiting.

Joe and John quickly took advantage of the little daylight left and tossed the baseball around until Dad got home. Joe always wanted to play ball. He and John recently got Dad to obligate to buy them a new ball glove this fall when the tobacco was sold.

Joe wanted a new first base mitt. John had a new glove in mind, too. Both of them were excited about Dad's deal. The new gloves should be bought about World Series time. Joe wanted to see the Yankees clobber the Dodgers in the series this year.

Sunday Evening Baseball

Sunday was a welcome day of rest. After church and dinner Joe, John, and Ralph Winters got their ball gloves and headed down to the cow pasture to play baseball with Jimmy and Avalon. So much for a day of rest!

To Joe and John, any time away from the tobacco field was rest. Playing ball was not work. It was fun. The boys played baseball all evening until about 5:00 p.m. when Dad whistled meaning it was time to get ready for church.

Joe, John, and Ralph washed up and changed clothes and were on the way church. It had been a fun day of rest.

It was the last week of school. The week went by quickly as the youngins were busy hoeing tobacco every day after school. The hill field was finished on Wednesday evening before prayer meeting. The middle field was started on Thursday morning by Mom and Dad. The youngins helped after school and then on Friday evening after they got out of school for the year at 12:00 noon.

Danny was promoted to the second grade and Jane to the fifth grade. John would be in the eighth grade while Joe would be in the tenth grade. Rose would be a senior in the fall. It would be her last year at West Yadkin. She was now starting her last summer at home. It was hard to believe that Nee Nee was now a big girl.

Hoeing was finished in the middle field late Saturday evening. So the first round was completed. There would be two or three more rounds before the tobacco would be laid by the end June.

The corn was planted. The garden was finished with plenty of popcorn planted. Then the hoeing cycle began all over again.

June came in hot and with long days in the scorching sun. Tobacco and corn always need attention. Dad was determined to keep his youngins busy.

Elmer's Home On Leave

There was special excitement in the house. Elmer's last letters said that he would be home for about a month from about June 10 to July 8. He was driving home in his 1953 Chevrolet, which he had with him in New York.

"He'll be in bed one morning when we get up," Joe said one night at supper.

"I expect he will, too," Mom said. "He likes to sneak in and surprise us."

Sure enough, on Sunday morning, June 10, when Mom and Dad got up, they found Elmer in the front bedroom fast asleep. He had come in at about 2:00 a.m.

"There's my boy," Mom said as she went over to the bed and gave him a big hug. Mom always called each one of us her boy or her girl. She loved us all so much. Soon the house was alive with happiness. We had a wonderful breakfast after Mom said the blessing.

"Heavenly Father, thank you for being so good to our family. Thank you for helping Elmer get home safely. Thank you for health and strength and for this food. Be with the sick, the shut-in, and the bereaved. Bless this food to the nourishment of our body. Thank you in Jesus' name. Amen. Amen."

A country breakfast of scrambled eggs, sausage, milk gravy, and biscuits was enjoyed by the whole family as Wayne and Elvie were also home.

"It sure is good to be home," Elmer said as he was eating like it was his last meal.

"It's good for all of us to be home together again," Mom said as she made sure no one ran out of biscuits.

"I miss your biscuits a lot, Mom," Elmer said.

"I have been eating yours and mine, too, big brother," Joe said with a laugh.

"You just about do that," Dad said. "I've been noticing."

"Well, I'm going to eat my share over the next three weeks," Elmer said as he pushed away from the table. He was in a hurry. He was going to pick up Geraldine for church and then spend the day with her.

Picnic With Huffs

"Elmer, see if Geraldine and her family want to go to the mountains with us next Sunday after church for a picnic," Mom said. "We won't get another chance to go for a while."

"That sounds like fun. I'll ask them," Elmer said.

The Huffs okayed the picnic and after church on Sunday, June 17, the Browns and the Huffs headed up Highway 268 towards Wilkesboro where they would turn west on Highway 421. By now, Joe was starving. He was ready to eat the picnic lunch at the church.

"It's going to be 2:00 p.m. before we eat," Joe said as the Browns and the Huffs continued their trek up the mountains. Joe liked the mountains but he did not like the winding S shaped roads.

Finally at 2:00 p.m., Dad pulled the car into a roadside park with picnic tables overlooking the Blue Ridge Parkway. We had found a place for the picnic to happen.

Mom and Mrs. Huff quickly unpacked fried chicken, banana sandwiches, potato salad, bologna sandwiches, ham biscuits, potato chips, Pepsis, cookies, and chocolate pound cake. Joe was sure there was more food there but he could not eat anymore.

Geraldine had two younger sisters, Katie Lee who was Joe's age and Hilda Gay who was John's age. Joe and John took a lot of kidding about the two sisters. Joe was too shy to do anything except speak to the girls. The girls were always nice and friendly to Joe and John.

Meanwhile back at the picnic, everyone had been starving and they were making food disappear fast. Mom's fried chicken was always good, but today, it seemed lifesaving good. It sure was quiet as everyone was eating food from both of these excellent cooks' favorite dishes. In about thirty minutes of serious eating, the food on the picnic table was just about gone.

No problem, though, as everyone was slowing down. They were filled up.

"This is the best fried chicken I've ever eat, Mrs. Brown," Mr. Huff said.

"I like that chocolate pound cake, Mrs. Huff," Dad said.

"I like it all," Elmer said with a laugh. "I haven't been eating good cooking for the past year. The Air Force doesn't cook like this. I've got a feeling that I won't eat like this in Germany either."

"I'll try to eat for me and you, too, Elmer," Joe said with a chuckling as he finished his second Pepsi. He, like everyone else, was full. The picnic table was shambles as it was almost bare.

"This has been fun, but we've got to get back down the mountain," Mr. Huff said.

"We need to go, too," Dad said. "It'll be church time soon."

Elmer and Geraldine rode with the Huffs and headed on down Highway 421 ahead of Dad's carload of youngins. Rose, Joe, John, and Danny were in the backseat while Jane rode up front with Mom and Dad. It was a quiet ride home as everyone except Mom and Dad took a nap.

Dad's family got home in time for a very short rest, and then it was back to church for the night service. After church, Dad's tired family was to bed as soon as they got home. Tomorrow was another work day.

On Monday morning, Dad wanted to finish the cleaning of the chicken house. The old chicken crop was picked up on Friday. Dad had a load of shavings coming late today and then the chicken house would be about ready for the new chicks on Friday.

On Tuesday, Dad had his crew dusting the tobacco with arsenic laced cornmeal to knock out any sign of the early worms in the bud of the tobacco plant. Joe was always leery of this dusting as he didn't want to get any of the arsenic in his face. He was glad that Dad always mixed the cornmeal with the arsenic. Joe would have to dip the homemade dispensers in the washtub to fill them up and that was close enough for him to get to the arsenic. He would always wash his hands carefully when he got close to the poison.

It was finally lay by week for the tobacco. The last plowing was here. The tobacco was growing rapidly and could not be plowed again. Dad put the large blades on the cultivator to pull more soil up around the base of the tobacco stalk.

Joe and John followed Dad's plow to uncover any lower leaves that had soil over them. Otherwise, those leaves would turn yellow and die. It was a slow, boring job, not hardly as bad as suckering, but not any fun.

Suckering? Oh, no. Joe could not believe it was about that time again. Suckering was the #1 job that all Dad's youngins despised.

Chapter 24
Elmer Leaves For Germany

July was here again. It was hot as July is supposed to be. This week was Elmer's last week at home. He was scheduled to go to New York for shipment to Germany on Sunday. It had been nice to have Elmer home for the past month. Even though he had been busy spending a lot of time with Geraldine, he still helped in the tobacco field, just like old times.

Blackberries were plentiful. Rose, Joe, John, Jane, and Danny fought chiggers, mosquitoes, pesky flies, and snakes to pick all Mom wanted and then a bunch to sell at the store. Joe and John had some money to spend on their favorite hobby, baseball cards.

"I got Yogi Berra," Joe said as he had a mouthful of the good bubblegum. This gum was better than regular bubblegum.

"I got Herb Score," John said with a mouthful of gum. "I have a Hank Bauer I'll trade with you. What Indian play do you have?"

"I'll trade Bobby Avila for Bauer," Joe said and the trade was made. Both Joe and John built the collection around their favorite team.

On Sunday evening after church, we said goodbye to Elmer for a long, almost three year tour of duty in Germany. He left as Wayne was taking him to the airport in Greensboro to fly to New York City. Elmer was going to see a lot of the world the next three years.

It was a sad day for all of our family. Mom shed tears as did Rose and Jane. The men folk were sad, but did not cry.

"Write me, Joe!" Elmer said as he left.

"I will, big brother. I'll be looking forward to seeing pictures of all the places you visit," Joe said.

Elmer was gone. The family watched the car pull out of the driveway. They waved until Wayne drove the car onto Brown Road and headed out towards Highway 421.

For the next three years, there was always an emptiness in the house. We missed Elmer. We thought of him a lot and Mom never prayed over a meal without mentioning her oldest son who was away serving his country.

We never knew exactly what job Elmer did. He had studied the Romanian language at Cornell University for almost a year to prepare him for some top secret job.

Elmer was faithful to write home. Mom wrote to him at least once a week. Joe wrote to him, but not as often as he should. It was very important when you're away from home serving your country to get mail. Joe would understand that feeling about four years later.

July was going quickly. We wished Mom happy birthday on Monday, July 16. The tobacco was ready to be topped out and here comes them dreaded suckers. The most hated job of the summer would occupy all of the daylight hours that priming didn't take.

Priming Time Again

The tobacco barns were checked out, chinked, and daubed for the upcoming curing. The Amoco oil man came by to fill up all the tanks with kerosene. The Amoco man would be a regular visitor to each barn as he had weekly checks. It would not do to run out of oil in the middle of curing a barn of tobacco.

The tobacco sleds were checked out and repaired getting ready for the upcoming first priming.

"Oh! My back hurts already," Joe kidded just thinking about first primings.

There is something new this year in the progress world. Mr. Shore had bought a tractor. It wasn't new but it sure was new to him and us. It was a M & M tractor. Mr. Shore loved his tractor and was forever seen riding down Shore Road and Brown Road.

Mr. Shore pulled the sleds from the field to the barn with the tractor. We still used Old Maude and Old Kate in the field to pull sleds.

Mr. Shore also used the tractor a bunch for plowing, sowing grain, cutting hay, raking hay, and baling hay. The tractor was here to stay. Dad was planning on buying a smaller tractor next summer to use at home. He would use Mr. Shore's tractor on the Shore's tobacco fields.

On Saturday, August 4, Dad's crew and Uncle Nelson's pulled the two acre spring field and Uncle Nelson's two acre home field. This year would be the third year of the swap with Uncle Nelson. It was a good working relationship. Our families were very close. Dad enjoyed working with Uncle Nelson as he, too, was a hard worker. They worked together in a lot of other things, too.

"Let's get in there and get wet, boys," Dad said as he looked at the tobacco with the heavy dew dripping off it.

"It's wet this morning, ain't it?" Uncle Nelson said.

"It'll wet you about like the pour-over would," Joe said as they got started. By the time they had pulled two rows with Old Bill pulling the sled, all of the primers were soaked to the bone.

"It's not very wet, is it?" Rose asked when Dad drove the first sled in to the barn.

"What are you talking about, youngin? It's wetter than the creek," Dad said. "It'll dry out fast, though. We're going to have a dog day, hot day today. It's getting hot already."

Humid weather was usually the order of the day when first primings were pulled. You had to go all the way to the ground where there didn't seem to be any air to breathe. It was stifling, especially when the hot sun was directly overhead.

"Ya'll keep up now. We're going to cover you up," Joe said as he headed back to the field wet as a hound dog in a thunderstorm.

The barn crew would keep up today as priming ground leaves was slower. Rose would tie with Mom and Danny handing up to her. Jane would also tie for the first time and was doing a good job with Aunt Jo, Gray, and Fay handing up. Fay was five years old and liked to hand up to both teams. She would move back and forth as needed.

Baby Debbie, "Debbie Dean" as we called her, was now a two year old toddler and "cute as a button." She was into everything. Joe and all of Dad's youngins loved Debbie like she was their own sister. She was so sweet.

By 10:00 a.m., the spring field was primed. The priming crew moved on to Uncle Nelson's field. The tobacco had to be kept separate at the barn. When it was hung in the barn, usually each batch took up two rooms in the old log barn. Dad and Uncle Nelson would share all the oil costs for curing.

Before dinner at about 11:30 a.m., all the spring field tobacco was hung in the barn. Joe hung the tobacco as Dad handed it up to him. Even though it was the lightest weight leaves on the stalk, the sticks were heavy to handle, especially when you reached down for them and then hung them up above your head.

It was get wet time again after finally drying out from the early morning bath of dew. The hanger would get soaked from sweat in the oven-like tin roofed barn and then get soaked by the dripping water from the tobacco hanging above. It was fun!

The best part of the day was the meals. Mom had a table full of pinto beans, taters, green beans, fried squash, biscuits, and a mom special surprise. She was full of good surprises. She had a simply mouth watering sarvis pie.

"Wow! What a meal you have, Mom! Did you stay up all night last night cooking?" Joe said.

"No! It's just a few things I threw together," Mom said as if this feast was nothing at all for her to fix.

Joe knew differently. He knew how hard Mom worked to feed her hardworking family. We could not work hard without these great meals.

"You can't beat pinto beans, Mom," Joe said as he had mashed up a big plateful of them. He was busy sopping up the bean juice with those perfect biscuits.

"That's right!" Dad said. "Pintos will give you the energy."

"That's not all they give you," John laughed.

"I like to mix them with the taters," Rose said.

"I like taters, too," Jane said. "But not mixed together."

"Me neither!" Danny said. "I'll let them mix in my belly."

The sarvis pie was the main event for Joe anyway. He loved this pie almost as much as he did Mom's sweet potato saunker, which was his all-time favorite. Soon, the meal was finished. Everyone was full and ready for a nap.

Guess what? No nap was in the plans for today. The barn of tobacco was waiting to be finished.

"Let's go, youngins!" Dad said as he heard Uncle Nelson's crew at the barn.

It was back to the field to pull only one remaining acre. That was fine with Joe. He was glad there weren't four acres to pull as hot as it was, at least 95 degrees. The tobacco was drooped down wilted from the scorching heat.

By 3:00 p.m., the priming crew was finished in the field. They made their way to the barn to help tie up the last sled. Joe gave Jane a break and tied the last sled for her. Joe and Rose had a tying race as the sled was crowded with plenty extra help handing up. It was fun to work in the shade and to work fast. The sled was empty and the tobacco was ready to hang.

Mom and Aunt Jo left to get their Sunday cooking done as we had plenty of help to tote the sticks into the barn. Uncle Nelson was feeling frisky and wanted to hang his tobacco.

"Is that okay with you, Joe?" Uncle Nelson asked.

"That's fine with me," Joe said. "Sweat some for me."

At half past four, the tobacco was housed and the barn was closed up for the curing. The first barn of the dreaded first primings was pulled. It was good to get started on this backbreaking task. Next week would finish all the ground leaves.

Finally, Sunday was here and a day of rest. The cow pasture league was in full swing after church and dinner.

Joe and John were playing together this summer against Jimmy and Avalon. It was a slugfest league as Joe and Jimmy were popping out homeruns in at least every other time at bat.

Joe kept stats on these games. These stats included the scores and team records with individual batting averages, hits, runs, RBI's, homeruns, errors, and pitcher's won and loss records. Joe kept all the records in his head during the game before making notes after the games. As many as six games would be played on any Sunday evening.

Joe always had a good memory and loved math and the calculations he needed to make for the different averages. No! We did not have calculators to do the math. It was done by longhand. The 1956 summer cow pasture league was not fun for the other side as Joe and John dominated. It was not very competitive. Joe and John's team had a record of 38-2. That's the reason that Joe and John had to split up to have a more competitive league.

"We can't keep playing them," Joe said. "They'll quit on us. It's not any fun to them."

"Yeah, I know," John said. "We'll have to go back to the other way. I'd rather not but we really don't have a choice."

On Monday, it was back to the first primings in the hill field. Monday and Tuesday were the two toughest days as six acres would be pulled each day. The road barn was filled on Monday and the middle barn was filled on Tuesday to finish Dad's first primings. Each day was a long 5:30 a.m. to 8:00 p.m. day. Days just don't get any harder, especially with the first primings.

On Wednesday, the first primings were finished for Uncle Nelson with the four acre woods field. It was a relatively easy day compared to Monday and Tuesday with an early finish time of 4:00 p.m. Just in time, too, as a thunderstorm moved in and rained cats and dogs for a solid hour. Water was standing all over the tobacco fields. The small branch near the tobacco barn was flooded over its banks.

Seining

"Hey, Dad, can we go seining? We have plenty of daylight left. What do you think?" Joe asked.

"Yeah, that sounds good, Joe," Dad said. "Run and see if Uncle Lamar wants to go."

"Do you want to go, Uncle Nelson?" Joe asked as he was hopping on his bike.

"Sounds like fun to me. I bet the creek is red muddy already," Uncle Nelson said.

Joe and John rode their bikes on the wet, slushy farm road back to Brown Road at the road barn. They went up the Shore hill past Grandpa Brown's and on down the road up the hill to Uncle Lamar's house.

"Do ya'll want to go seining?" Jimmy asked as Joe and John rode into the wet yard.

"How about that?" Joe said. "That's why we rode over here to see if ya'll can go."

"We're ready to go!" Uncle Lamar said. "We'll be right over to your house. The creek should be red muddy from all the rain we got."

Joe and John hurried back over to Grandpa Brown's house to see if he felt like going. It was so much more fun when Grandpa was with them.

"Do you want to go seining, Grandpa?" Joe asked as he stopped in the saturated yard near the back porch.

"I'd like to, Joe, but I just don't feel up to it today," Grandpa said. "Ya'll go ahead and have a good time. Watch out for them "hoop" snakes and mud turtles," he laughed.

Soon, Dad, Uncle Nelson, Joe, John, Uncle Lamar, Jimmy, and Avalon were on the way to

Hunting Creek. It was red muddy as they put in at the forks of the creeks.

"It looks like a good time to seine," Uncle Nelson said. He would help man the seine when Dad or Uncle Lamar grew tired. It was hard work holding on to the pole against the raging waters and moving around to the bank of the creek while the other man held the pole still.

Each time a half circle was made with the net, there would be catfish and suckers in the net. Sometimes the catch would be only three or four, but as the seining crew got close to the rock, business would pick up. The muddy, raging waters had roused the fish out of their hiding places.

Joe and Jimmy each carried a hemp sack to tote the fish. Uncle Nelson would help get the fish out of the net. Joe didn't have any trouble getting the suckers out, but the stinging catfish were for someone else to get.

The seining continued past the rock down to the pour-over. By now, both hemp sacks were heavy. There would be a good mess of fish for each of the three families for breakfast tomorrow morning.

The seining crew got out of the muddy creek and walked up to Uncle Lamar's house to divide the fish. Uncle Lamar and Uncle Nelson only wanted suckers while Dad liked the catfish better than the bone filled suckers. The two uncles each had twenty-two suckers while Dad had twenty-four catfish. It was quite a haul.

It was still drizzling with rain as Joe helped Dad skin the catfish. Mom salted them down while Joe and John milked the cows. Dad, Rose, and Danny fed and watered the chickens. Jane helped Mom with supper.

"It sure was fun going seining, Dad," Joe said as he ate his big bowl of cornbread with his big spoon. "Thank you for letting us go."

"You're welcome, son. It was fun. I'm glad we could go," Dad said.

"I had fun, too," John said.

"Can I go next time, Dad?" Danny asked.

"We'll have to wait awhile, Danny," Dad said. "The water is too deep for you. Someone would have to tote you."

Breakfast of catfish was good for a change, but Joe still would rather have the regular breakfast. He was always afraid of getting a fishbone in his throat.

The rainstorm put off second primings for a few days. It did not put off suckering, though. The suckers were growing even faster since the rain. It was an every day job. Joe was ready to get back to the priming schedule.

Second primings started back on Wednesday, August 15. From now on until the tobacco was tipped, each tobacco field would be pulled every week. Most of the time, the barns would have to be emptied first. That makes for a lot of long 3:00 a.m. to 8:00 p.m. days.

A little over half of the tobacco had been primed before school started up on Monday, September 10. It was Elmer's twenty-second birthday. We wish he was home with us. Joe wrote him a birthday letter.

Chapter 25
Joe – Tenth Grade

Joe was now in the tenth grade. Mr. Reece was his homeroom teacher. Joe was elected class president with Gail Swaim, vice president, Sue Wallace, treasurer, and Annette Hall, secretary.

Joe was taking English, US History, Biology, Business Math II, and Health. He wanted to take Shop or Agriculture, but this class was the last period of the day and Joe would practice basketball later in the winter in this period.

Coach O'Donnell was still trying to get Joe to come out and play on his football team. Joe again explained that he'd like to play, but Dad could not spare him out of the tobacco field.

Joe would miss school three days a week for the next three weeks to prime tobacco. Most of these days, Rose, John, and Jane would also miss. The tobacco had to harvested.

On Sunday, September 23, after church, Mom's family had the Proctor Reunion down at Grandpa and Grandma Proctor's house. It was dinner on the grounds. The normal sawbuck tables were set up out in the front yard near the driveway. The crowd was bigger than ever this year.

In attendance were Grandpa, Grandma, Mom's family, Uncle Claude's family including Larry and Bonnie, Aunt Dorothy's family, Aunt Hazel's family, Uncle Porter's family, Aunt De Ette's family, Uncle Paul, Aunt Lena, Lola Jean, Aunt Jane's family, and a lot of Mom's cousins from High Point.

Joe and John brought their ball and glove to toss the ball after the meal. Larry also was pitching the ball to Uncle Raymond. Larry had been a pitcher in his high school years and could still "bring it."

The table was spread with a variety of food. There was fried chicken of many flavors, country ham biscuits, green beans, corn on the cob, cooked corn, black-eyed peas, Crowder peas, pinto beans, fried squash, potato salad, tomato sandwiches, banana sandwiches, pimento cheese sandwiches, bologna sandwiches, deviled eggs, tomato pie, sauerkraut, pickles, beets, biscuits, cornbread, rolls, chocolate pie, chocolate cake, pound cake, bread pudding, coconut cake, lemon pie, egg custard, sweet potato pie, cherry pie, apple pie, peach pie, sweet potato saunker, apple cake, German chocolate cake, and many other desserts.

Certainly in this gathering of food, you could find plenty of whatever you wanted.

Joe did. He started on Grandma's country ham biscuits. He got four of them and ate two quickly so no one would think he was a little pig. Next was Mom's fried chicken, fried squash, corn on the cob, pinto beans, and deviled eggs.

Joe ate the first round quickly and refilled with more of the same. Grandma's biscuits were long gone. Someone probably took too large a portion for them to be gone so soon.

For sweets, Joe had chocolate pie, sweet potato saunker, and coconut cake. Boy, it sure was good! There was only one thing wrong. Joe was full. All the good food and two big Pepsis had done him in. It was time to stop and play ball.

Joe and John tossed the baseball for a long time until it was time to head home.

"Tell your mom we need to go," Dad told Joe. "It'll be church time soon." Byes were said and Dad was on the way out the driveway. Dad hadn't noticed that Grandpa had mowed the weeds down. Joe was getting ready to tell him.

"Wonder who mowed the weeds down?" Dad said right before he reached the end of the driveway.

It was Friday, September 28, and tip day for Dad's last field, the middle field. It was a good day, even though the official end of tobacco pulling would be tomorrow at Uncle Nelson's woods field.

At 4:00 p.m. on Saturday, September 29, yells of gladness rang out from the last tobacco field tipped. The yells were echoed over through the woods to the barn and back to the field. By 5:00 p.m., all tobacco was tied and hung in the barn. The 1956 crop was finished. It would be Rose's last tobacco priming as she was going to graduate from high school next May.

The tobacco cycle went to the packhouse for the next month. Dad's crew would again work after school each day and to 9:00 p.m. each night and all day on Saturday to get finished by the end of October.

The Yankees and the Dodgers went in the World Series again this year. With games tied at 2-2, Joe watched Don Larsen on TV at Cook's Warehouse as he pitched a perfect game, the only perfect game ever pitched in the World Series. It was a classic as Mickey Mantle homered and made a great running catch to preserve the gem for Larsen.

Even though the Yankees lost game six, they came back in game seven and won 9-0 to win the World Championship.

Joe wrote a poem about his team.

"The New York Yankees"

The Yankees are the best team in-the-east,
They win the most games and lose the least,
They win the pennant most every year,

And in the World Series you'll surely hear
The sound of the bats as they hit,
And drive their bewildered opponents nitwit.

As the Yankees take the field every day,
There is a big crowd to see them play,
The umpire says "play ball"
And the crowd rises, All---
For the first pitch of the game,
Those Cleveland Indians they're gonna tame.

When they come to bat the first time,
Their bats are – going to ring and chime,
The Yankees hit, and the Yankees win,
They have the pennant wrapped up again,
The Yankees play like they are told,
By Manager Stengel, hard, brave, and bold.

Jane was eleven years old on Sunday, Brown Reunion day. A good turnout and good food made for a good get together of the Brown clan. Thankfully, there was not another tornado like it was the last time Jane's birthday was on Brown Reunion day.

Another houseful of chickens was sixteen weeks old and sold on Friday, October 12. The chicken house business was like clockwork now. Dad's crew had the procedure down to an art.

"New chicks will be here Friday," Dad reminded Joe as the house was being cleaned out.

"We'll be ready, Dad," Joe said. "How're we doing on our tobacco selling target?"

"We're looking good," Dad said. "We should be through by the end of the month."

We were finished on Monday, October 29. Dad and Gurn loaded up a full load to go to the market on Tuesday morning at 3:00 a.m. The last of the tobacco would be sold today. Joe and John were also getting to go as today was ball glove day. The promise of the summer would come true today.

After the sale of the tobacco, Gurn drove Dad over by Sears where Joe and John picked out their gloves. Joe's Stan Musial first base mitt was a nice one. John got a Rocky Colavito outfield glove. We were tickled to death and could not wait to get home to try them out.

Team Without a Home

On Monday, November 5, basketball practice was starting. The team would be younger since the star of last year's team, Jerry Dickerson, had graduated. After a week of practice, Joe learned that he had made the team along with his best friend, Archie King, and Roger Swaim.

On November 6, President Eisenhower was re-elected for a second term in a landslide. He would be President for four more years.

It would be a long, rough year in many ways. The team suffered a blow when, after the first home game, the gym caught on fire and burned down.

"What happened?" Joe asked Archie at school the next morning as they stood and looked at the still smoldering rubble of what was a gym last night.

"I think some boys were hiding under the gym smoking and accidentally burned our gym," Archie said.

"What are we going to do now?" Joe asked.

Joe found out that evening as Coach Holmes had the team practicing on the outdoor court next to the sewage treatment plant. It was kind of smelly, but it was the best we could do.

"We'll practice here as long as the weather is good," Coach Holmes said. "Then we'll go to Elkin to practice when it gets cold. They've offered us the use of their court at the YMCA. It will be a lot of traveling this year. We won't play any home games."

It was a season to forget. We were a team without a home. It's ironic that this season was the last of Joe's favorite coach in high school. Coach Holmes would leave teaching to go into the insurance business where he was successful. He would later go into politics and serve in the General Assembly in Raleigh for many years.

The corn crop was up and in the corncrib. It was a good year. Popcorn was drying out for the wintertime snacks.

Happy birthday to Wayne. Wish you were here. You're now twenty years old.

Chapter 26
Winter

December came in with the feel of winter. According to the farmer, December is winter and all of the month, too.

The month rolled by quickly. It was December 19 and time for the Christmas break from school. The break would last until January 2. It was a welcome break for Joe.

The weather got hog killing cold as soon as school was out. Dad killed our three hogs and Uncle Nelson's two on Friday, December 21. Joe and John helped with the killing, which was finished by noontime.

Joe and John rode with Uncle Nelson and took the meat to Martin's Grocery to grind into sausage. Mr. Martin made quick work of the meat as he was an expert making sausage.

Joe got a chance to talk to Jerry while he was waiting.

"Sorry about your gym burning down, Joe," Jerry said. "That makes it tough on ya'll to practice and not playing any home games, doesn't it?"

"It sure does," Joe said. "We don't have a very good team this year." He hated to stare, but she was so beautiful.

He hoped she didn't think he was staring.

"You have another good team, don't you?" Joe asked.

"Yes, it's a good team. I hope we can beat Elkin this year," she said.

"Maybe you will, Jerry," Joe said as Mr. Martin had the sausage ready to go. "See you later."

"Bye, Joe," Jerry said.

"You sure are sweet on her, ain't you, Joe?" John said as soon as they had left the store.

"She's a nice girl," Joe said quickly.

A country breakfast after hog killing is a good time. On Saturday morning, Mom had sausage, eggs, gravy, and biscuits. What could be better?

Well, now, how about Sunday breakfast of tenderloin, eggs, gravy, biscuits, jam, jelly, and molasses? It was better than the good breakfast, as Joe's all-time favorite breakfast was tenderloin.

"This tenderloin is so good, Mom," Joe said. "You know that I love it, don't you?"

"Yes, I know, Joe. I can tell by the way you eat that you enjoy it," Mom said.

"It is good!" rang out from the other youngins around the table.

"Best breakfast ever, I'd say," Dad said as he was sopping another biscuit in the gravy. "If you don't like this food, you probably don't like to eat."

After church, it was a nap filled evening. The skies were overcast and it was still cold.

"Feels like Christmas weather," Dad said as he drove home from church. "Might be snowing soon, who knows?

Christmas

It was Christmas Eve. Wayne and Elvie were home for the big day tomorrow. Danny was excited about Santa. All the other youngins were looking for gifts, but only Danny was looking for Santa. He was wanting a ball glove so he could play ball with Joe and John.

On Christmas morning at precisely 5:00 a.m., Danny's feet hit the floor. He was followed by Rose, Joe, John, and Jane into the front room where he had left his shoe box for Santa to fill. Mom, Dad, Wayne, and Elvie were up and joined the early morning happenings.

"I got it! I got it!" Danny hollered as he picked up his ball glove and put it on. "Now I can play with you, Joe."

"You sure can, Danny. We'll need another player next summer when Jimmy is gone," Joe said.

Other gifts were exchanged. Joe got some new jeans and a dress shirt. He was ready to dress up now. It was a happy Christmas at our home even though we miss Elmer.

Grandpa came by and had a cup of American Ace coffee with us. He was feeling good and happy with his box of cigar. He always liked a good cigar and lit one up immediately as he headed back up to his house.

Wayne and Elvie left for her family's Christmas before dinner. We headed down to Mom's Christmas at Grandpa and Grandma Proctor's house.

"Weeds are growing again," Dad said as he drove down the driveway to the house. The crowd was large again as kinfolks from all over were home for Christmas.

"Hey, youngins!" Grandma said as she handed out her good biscuits. They were always a treat to Joe and the other youngins. They never grew tired of eating them no matter what time it was.

It was an evening of fun, family, and gifts. Mom's brothers and sisters were a close knit group who loved to come home to visit their parents and the more crowded the house was, the better they liked it. Mom truly enjoyed any visit back home. She didn't get to spend much time with her family.

Back at home, it was chore time in cold, threatening weather. It looked a lot like snow. The milking was finished. The chickens were fed. Supper was finished and now snow was falling. It would snow all night and into midday Wednesday.

The snowfall was about six inches deep. The cold wind continued to swirl the rest of the day.

It was a sit by the fire day. Except for chores, Joe would stay in all day.

The cold snap lasted through the weekend. The roads were still a mess. Snow doesn't melt with the temperature staying below freezing. 'Snow laying around waiting for more to come down.' We did not get out to go to church on Sunday.

Monday, New Year's Eve, warmed up slightly as the sun was shining brightly. It was a good night to eat popcorn and crackerjacks by the fire. Dad popped a bowl for each youngin and everyone ate their fill.

"Can we stay up until the new year comes in, Dad?" Joe asked as Dad was getting up to go to bed.

"I guess you can since it's not a school night," Dad said.

Rose, Joe, John, and Jane stayed up. Danny bombed out at 9:00 p.m. It was fun, sleepy, but fun. As soon as the Times Square ball fell, everyone was in bed and fast asleep.

New Year 1957

It was January 1, 1957. Another new year was here. This year would mark the halfway point of Elmer's four years in the Air Force. Everyone missed Elmer so much.

On Wednesday, January 2, it was back to school. Cold, dreary weather with thoughts of more snow stayed around all month.

Here comes the January birthdays with Danny who was eight years old on January 18. Joe turned the magical year of sixteen years old on January

21. He was now old enough to get his driver's license.

For some reason, Dad didn't seem to be in any hurry for Joe to get his license. Dad took him to get a permit about the middle of February, but Joe would not get his license until September 13.

Dad also celebrated his forty-third birthday on January 24. The big birthday month would end with snow on the ground for most of the month.

February continued the cold weather. The old groundhog, for sure, saw his shadow on February 2, which would mean six more weeks of wintertime. Joe sure hoped the "hog" was wrong this time. He was ready for warm weather and baseball season.

The latest house of chickens graduated on February 8. They were sixteen weeks old. The chicken house cycle continued with a new house of five thousand chicks on February 15.

Signs of spring were starting to appear. The weather warmed up enough and dried up to allow the plant beds to be sown on Saturday, February 16. Dad was happy about the coming tobacco season. He couldn't wait to get us youngins back out in that hot sun working in his favorite spot, the tobacco field.

So much for warmer weather as snow fell all day Sunday. As it often happens, the plant beds got a good, slow snowfall to soak the newly sowed money crop. By midweek, it was fifty degrees and all the snow was gone.

Rose was eighteen years old on February 23. She was now a beautiful, young woman who would not be home much longer. John was now fourteen years old and growing up.

"We don't have any little youngins anymore, Clyde. They're all growing up too fast," Mom said. "Time just moves too fast for our family."

"Time goes on, Gladys," Dad said. "We can't keep them here forever."

Springtime

March blew in warm air. It was blustery the whole month. The plant beds had to be weeded continually. They were looking good as April showers came around.

Dad was getting the fields ready for the tobacco and corn crops. Progress just keeps a coming. Dad bought his first tractor, a Ford, which was not new. He immediately broke the tractor in by plowing our tobacco field and cornfield. He would use Mr. Shore's M & M tractor to plow the twelve acres there.

The tractor sure did speed up things. It was so much faster than the old turn plow being pulled by a horse. What would be the next innovation at the Little Farm on Brown Road?

May 1, barefoot day, came cooler than normal, but it was barefoot day and we went barefooted. That is, we did after we made the rounds and did our glass pickup. Mom required a glass pickup before we could barefoot.

Even with a glass pickup day, we still got our cuts and gashes from glass.

Joe remembers one time he was six years old when he was running wide open through the orchard to the north of our house and ran right through a broken pop bottle. He got a nasty gash in the bottom of his left foot. Mom quickly went to the kitchen and came back with a big slice of a beet that she was getting ready to cook.

After carefully cleaning Joe's cut foot, Mom tied the slice of beet to his foot with a strip of white cloth which she wrapped round and round to make sure the beet was tightly secure to the cut. The beet would take the poison out of the wound to eliminate a chance of infection.

"What a neat idea, Mom! I didn't know beets were medicine," Joe said.

"Learning from the old folks was critical to know how to handle situations as we came up," Mom said. "In the old days, we did not have doctors and hospitals on every corner. We had to make do with what we had or what we grew."

From that day on, Joe did not eat beets as he considered it medicine. Who wanted to eat medicine?

Tobacco setting time was drawing near. Joe and John were helping Dad get the land ready to set. The tractor again was used to lay off the rows. It moved considerably faster than the horse moved.

Joe still did not have his driver's license. Dad did take him back to renew his learner's permit. Joe's friend, Archie King, had his driver's license. His dad had taken him on his birthday back on February 4. Archie would come by to get Joe and John on Saturday nights and they'd go to Elkin to ride around. It was good to have a set of wheels. With a dollar's worth of gas, you could drive around all weekend.

Tobacco setting time had arrived. Dad was happy. He was his happiest when he and all of his youngins were out on that hot tobacco field.

Dad kept all of his help home from school today. It was a must. The money crop had to be set.

After a big, healthy breakfast of milk, scrambled eggs, canned sausage, milk gravy, biscuits, jam, jelly, and molasses, who couldn't get out and work hard? Joe again ate his usual seven biscuits to get himself going. At least this meal would keep him charged up until dinnertime.

Dad's plan for today was to set the two acre field at home, which this year was down near the big maple tree and then some of the hill field. Dad had moved the tobacco this year as some of last year's crop diseased and had died. He sowed the spring field in pasture this year.

So the big maple field was started at about 9:30 after three and a half hours pulling plants. Mom dropped for Dad while Rose, who was in her final year on the tobacco farm, dropped for John. Jane dropped for Joe and Danny kept up water and plants.

The echoes of the tobacco setters were click clacking down past the big maple and the little branch that ran during wet weather and dried up during dry weather. Dad's music was going again. The cloudy skies were threatening, but Dad was hoping to get at least this field set before rain came.

By 2:00 p.m., the three teams of setters had finished the big maple field. With the rain holding off, Dad moved on to the hill field to get a start there. A steady three rows at a clip moved on down the hill. Plants held out and the rains held off giving us a good start on this eight acre field. It looked like about two acres were set out by the end of plants at 7:00 p.m. We had a good shower during the night.

Saturday morning was more of the same. Setting began about 9:00 a.m. after an early start in the plants beds at 5:30 a.m. Dad had a full day planned for his work crew today.

The steady click clack was moving the setting crews quickly down the hill field.

"We're going to miss you, Nee Nee," Joe said to Rose. "Will you miss us a little bit?"

"I sure will," Rose said. "But one thing I won't miss is this hot sun and the tobacco field."

"I know what you mean, Rose. I'll be out of here in two more years," Joe said. "I'm like you. I'll be looking to get me an inside job and get out of this hot sun."

"I hate to see ya'll leave, but the farm cannot compete with the city for high school graduates," Dad said sadly. He so wanted someone to stay on the farm with him. By day's end at 7:00 p.m., the hill field was within two acres of being finished. It had been two long days of setting and Sunday, a day of rest, was a welcome sight.

It was Mother's Day, May 12. All of Mom's youngins, except Elmer, were at church with her this morning at the preaching service.

"All of you children go to your mom now and give her a big hug and tell her how much you love her!" Pastor Hankins said at the end of the invitation. Quickly, the aisles were full as youngins made their way to their mom.

"I love you, Mom!" each one of us told Mom as she got all teary eyed with us.

"I love you, too," Mom said in reply.

We had quite a mom and we were forever letting her know that she was so special.

Dad would later take Mom to see her mom. What a good tradition this was to let our mom know how we feel! Mother's Day to Joe was as special as Christmas was. No one could take the place of Mom.

On Monday, Dad's crew would have to miss school again. Four more acres would be set out, two acres to complete the hill field and two acres in the middle field. It was another long day with an almost dark finish.

On Tuesday, Dad let Rose, Jane, and Danny go to school. We only had two acres to set and Dad felt like two setting crews could finish this field up. They did and the setting was over for this year.

It was back to school for all the youngins on Wednesday. Dad was busy planting corn. Grandpa Brown was picking strawberries to take to Wilkesboro on Thursday morning. Joe, John, Jane, and Danny helped Grandpa pick from school bus time to almost dark. It was good to get some change to jingle in your pocket.

Dad's schedule had us hoeing tobacco for the next three to four weeks. We continued to walk Rose through her farewell trip through the tobacco field. She would be missed, that's for sure.

"You'll come back to see us often, won't you, Rose?" Jane asked of her only sister.

"I sure will! I'll probably be home about every weekend," Rose said.

Chapter 27
Rose Graduates - Marries

It was the last day of school, a short day until noon. Rose's graduation was at 11:00 a.m. She was so happy. She was now off the farm. Her tobacco working days were over.

Rose would leave for Greensboro on Saturday, June 1. She would stay the next week at Wayne and Elvie's while she looked for a job.

Rose returned home on Saturday, June 8, and was married to her boyfriend of the past several months, Billy "Tip" Gregory. Tip worked at the Pepsi Cola plant in Greensboro. Her departure left only four youngins at home. Joe was now the oldest. The heavy load of fourteen acres of tobacco, with three less workers than three years ago, would be on Joe's shoulders. He would have to be Dad's lead worker and show the way for the rest of the youngins.

Joe was determined to do the job that Dad expected of him. He had more responsibility and he handled it well. With that work load, Joe also wanted to do some things at school that he had not been able to do in prior years. With only two more years of high school left, Joe was determined to play football his last two years. He and John were lobbying Dad for a chance to play. Archie helped as he had been playing already for two years and wanted Joe to play.

Dad liked Archie and was influenced by him. Also, Uncle Nelson and Mr. Shore influenced Dad's final decision to let Joe and John play.

"The boys don't have much time left with you, Clyde. They work hard and would really appreciate you letting them play," Uncle Nelson said. Joe could have hugged him for what he said.

Mr. Shore said, "The boys are top workers, Clyde. They are not your average workers. They are special and they won't get this chance to play ever again."

Mr. Shore had offered to pay for Joe to go to the college of his choice if Joe would work for him these last two years and then each summer. Joe did not take him up on his offer as he only wanted to get out of school and to get out of the hot sun. Mr. Shore had made an invaluable offer to Joe. Joe often wondered what might have happened if he had gone on to school.

It was Monday morning and the hoeing in the tobacco field was not so bad for Joe and John. Dad had told them over the weekend that they could play football this fall. Joe would play for his last two years and John would get to play all of his four years in high school. It made for a happier work crew as Jane and Danny knew that Dad's decision would affect them when they got to high school.

Another house of chickens was sold last week. The hoeing was interrupted a couple of days to get the house in shape for new chicks on June 14.

Any break in the tobacco schedule was always a welcome sight. Joe and John simply loved these rare summer days when it would set in raining. Dad would always find more work to do, but not in the hot sun.

July came hot as usual. It was hay time. Joe and John also helped Mr. Shore get up hay. Mr. Shore would bale all of his hay and straw. It was easier to get up than the loose hay as we had to do at home.

When Mr. Shore had his wheat and oats combined, Joe and John would be waiting around to get up the straw. As the combine was nearing finishing each field, Joe and John would get to chase and sometimes catch rabbits in the last grain. Rabbits are very fast but they could be caught if they were pinned in or scared. It was fun. We would always let the rabbits go as they were not eatable because of "wolves" (worms) that they had in hot weather. Old timers would warn not to eat rabbits with "wolves."

"Happy birthday, Mom," everyone said at breakfast on July 16, to the sweetest person in the whole world. "We love you!"

"May Pops"

In addition to picking blackberries to sell, Joe and John used to sell "may pops." May pops were a running plant that grew in or around gardens, cornfields, and tobacco fields. When the may pop was ready to eat, the fruit which was about the size of a lemon was very sweet. We would pull up the vines and let the vines and roots lay out in the sun to dry. The roots were the selling interest of the plant.

May pops were plentiful on our farm. You would need a bunch of them to get any weight as they were light as feathers when they dried out. We were told that the roots were used in some kind of medicine. Many roots were used on the farm over the years. Country people used them to make their homemade remedies for whatever would ail them. We would take our may pops down Highway 21 to Houstonville to sell.

It was nearing that time of the year again. The tobacco was topped out and suckers were starting to grow. If the tobacco stalk would grow as fast as those hateful old suckers, the tobacco season would be cut in half.

Suckering was in full blast. It was late July. All tobacco barns were checked out, chinked, and daubed for airtight heat control. The old sleds were repaired and some were replaced by new sleds. Everything would be checked out before the priming started. Now was the time to get all equipment in tip top shape. We didn't need to wait and have problems on priming day.

It was Thursday, August 1, and first priming day again at the big maple field and Uncle Nelson's home field. The backbreaking job was dreaded by all primers, no matter what their age was. Imagine standing bent over with your head near the ground all day long.

"My back never gets used to this job," Joe said as the first sled was finished.

"It never will either!" Uncle Nelson said as he rubbed his back. He was already soaked from head to toe by the heavy dew on the tobacco.

"The best thing about first primings is the end of the day," Dad laughed as he took the first sled to the barn with his tractor. The priming crew could then go ahead with their job without waiting for Dad to return.

Dad's Crew Minus Three

Dad, Uncle Nelson, Joe, and John primed while the barn crew was Jane tying with Mom and Danny handing up. Aunt Jo tied with a young crew of Gray and Fay handing up. The barn crew would have a rough year. The days of the barn crew keeping up were only a memory. Everyone was doing their best but the workers were younger. We missed Rose! The day would be a long one with Dad's barn being full to the top at about 7:00 p.m. Tomorrow would be a better day. We would have Mr. Shore at the barn.

It was to the hill field and a 5:30 a.m. start on Friday morning. Dad had to get this crew started early if we were to fill the road barn before dark today.

Jane tied with Mom and Danny handing up. Aunt Jo tied with Mr. Shore, Gray, and Fay handing up. It went much smoother with Mr. Shore helping but the priming crew still stayed ahead all day. They had to push hard to get the six acres in to-day. They did and they did. It was another rough day with a carbon copy to come again tomorrow.

Dog day #3 was Saturday with another 5:30 a.m. start. The hill field two acres were finished and then it was on to the middle field for four more acres to fill the middle barn. These were three of the toughest days Joe can remember. The barn would not be completed until it was pitch dark. The final sticks were hung by car lights and flash-lights. It was good to finally get this barn behind us.

Chores were done by lights. The cows had about given up on us. They were already laying down when we went to milk them. Dad and Danny took care of the chickens before supper, which to-night was at 9:00 p.m.

Dad's crew was tired and starved. They ate supper quietly as they wiped out all the cornbread and leftover biscuits and then went straight to bed.

Sunday was here and finally a day of rest after a draining three days of first primings. After church, naps were in order for everyone. Joe and John skipped their usual Sunday evening baseball game to rest up. First primings would do that to you.

Monday was the last day of first primings at Uncle Nelson's woods field. It was an easier day with only four acres to prime. Joe was hoping for a little rain after today to give us a break before second primings started. He got his wish but a little early. The rain moved in at noontime and the rest of the day was wet. It felt good as the humid weather had taken its toll on the field workers.

The rain would last the rest of Monday and all day Tuesday. At least we got a one day break from suckering tobacco and a one week break on priming.

From now on, the rest of priming season would be a weekly cycle in each field. The 3:00 a.m. to 9:00 p.m. days would be here until we completed the tobacco harvesting. The barn would have to be emptied each day before it was refilled the same day. We had a busy schedule.

Archie came by on Saturday night, August 31, to let us know about football practice starting on Monday night at 6:00 p.m. Joe and John were excited. They had looked forward to playing on the same football team all summer.

"We have a new coach. You know Coach Donnell left. Our new coach is Mr. Shull," Archie said as they headed to Elkin to go the Reeves Theatre to see a Lone Ranger movie. It was nice to go to town and relax after another tough week.

The tobacco crop was halfway home now. Four more weeks, four more primings and it would be finished.

Chapter 28
Sandy Dies

Sunday, September 1, was a very sad day for Dad's family. Sandy, our dog, had been feeling poorly for a while and just kind of wore out. He died this evening after church. We buried him down near the big maple tree where we used to play with him so much.

Sandy would go with us to the creek when we went swimming. He would go with us when we went on a muscadine eating trip. It was usually on Sunday evening at the creek or high in the big maple. Sandy would wait patiently looking up at us as if to say, "Be careful and don't fall."

Sandy was a master of bringing up the cows and Old Bill when we needed them. They always knew that Sandy meant business. He was so good at his job that it was effortless. Sandy was so gentle with all of the youngins, yet he could get mean real quick if one of them was threatened by man or beast. Sandy would grab a snake by the neck and break it instantly.

Strangers should not wander into our yard uninvited. Sandy would put them back in their cars. Neighbors and family could come in anytime as Sandy knew them. What in the world would we do without our best dog ever, Sandy? He was just like a member of the family. You could not ask for a smarter dog than Sandy. It would be tough for a long time, knowing that we no longer had the guard dog at our front door and at our back door. He was everywhere. Remember when he would leap skyward to get the old towel on the tree limb? What a jumper Sandy was! What a great dog Sandy was! Sandy was the best.

Joe wrote this poem about Sandy:

"Sandy is the best dog we have had, ever.
Bite, fight one of us, he has never.
He has a sandy coat of hair
And we always wish we had a pair
Of dogs that to us is such a friend
Who we all will love to the end.
He helps us work and do all the chores
And makes people ask, Is he yours?
Yes! He is ours. Sandy, we do own
And had I rather suffer, than hear him groan.
He has always been a kind and gentle dog
Who doesn't eat as most dogs (like a hog).
Every evening after school
Sandy has but one rule
To wait patiently for us
And bark with joy when he sees the bus.
He greets us the same way everyday
And barks joyously as if to say,
Hello! I wait again for you.
Isn't that what a good dog should do?
Sandy, such a dog I've never seen,
With his eyes a brownish green,
His golden hair and wagging tail.
Here he comes running just when we yell.
If we need him, say to chase a cat,
Here he'll come and do just that.
When we go to do the chores everyday
Sandy is always there, not in the way,
But to help us, he is trying.
And this I'm not denying
That for us it is swell
Just to see him wag his tail.
He stands very straight and firm
And not like some dogs, does he squirm.
He always seems happy and glad
And never is he angry and mad.

It makes us want to shout with glee
To know we own a dog like he.
Sandy acts as good as some humans I know
And bad actions he has yet to show.
Most dogs are incomparable to him by me
They appear as a weed, to a very tall tree."

Football

It was Labor Day, Monday, September 2. Everyday was labor day at the Little Farm on Brown Road. Today was the big day when football practice would start.

Football practice would have to wait a few hours, though, as the fifth primings were being pulled at the big maple field and Uncle Nelson's field. It was a good day with the barn being filled by 5:00 p.m.

Soon, Archie came by to give Joe and John a ride to their first football practice. It was hot, but they were anxious to get to work with the pigskin.

Coach Shull was on hand to greet all prospective players. He was a short, slender, starting to bald man who was probably about thirty-five years old. He had a dry sense of humor. There were about twenty-five people trying out for the team.

West Yadkin was a small school and always had trouble getting ballplayers when there was farm work to do. We never got some of the better athletes to play. There was too much work at home that had to be done.

Joe got his practice uniform and pads on and was looking for a helmet. His first helmet was a leather one which was called a "pumpkin" helmet.

"We'll get you a real helmet in a few days, son," Coach Shull said as he checked out Joe's old outdated helmet. Before the end of the week, Joe had a real helmet to protect his head.

The first few days were mostly running and exercise. Then the contact gradually came. Joe was always a running back. He didn't particularly like to tackle or to be tackled. He liked to use his speed to elude tacklers. However, in tackling drills, everyone had to hit and be hit. It was the nature of the drill.

Joe would be a backup running back and defensive back this year. He also would play about any other position as needed. John would play backup positions, also.

Archie was a three year player and started at tackle on both offense and defense. In the old days, most all players played both offense and defense. Another good friend, Roger Swaim, would start on both sides of the ball, too.

Driver's License at Last

With two hard weeks of practice, the first game was Friday night, September 13. This day would be memorable for Joe as Dad finally took him to get his driver's license. That night was Joe's first high school football game at home against a tough Sparta team. They were a tough mountain team and beat us by two touchdowns.

West Yadkin's best players were quarterback Joe Wright, end Marcus Allred, running back/linebacker Wayne Wagoner, and Archie King on the line. Joe did not get to play any in this game. He would not see much playing time all year except in spot situations or when someone was hurt.

School started on Monday, September 9, with half days the first week. Joe was now a junior. He had English with Mrs. Helen Wishon, a great teacher whom Joe liked and respected very much. Mrs. Wishon had already taught Elmer, Wayne, and

Rose and knew about our family. Joe also had Mr. Shull in History, Mr. Peele in Chemistry, and Mr. Moretz in Business Math.

Joe was again elected a class officer, treasurer, with Brenda Swaim, secretary, Gene Williams, president, and Willodean Shore, vice president. It was an honor to be elected by your fellow classmates.

Ernest Pretzel

Joe loved history and chemistry. In History, Mr. Shull was always picking on the "Elvis Presley" crazed girls. Mr. Shull called Elvis "Ernest Pretzel" which really burned up the girls. They were all in love with Elvis.

Mr. Shull said, "I don't see what all of you girls see in that "Ernest Pretzel." He probably doesn't know anything about history and couldn't even pass my test. He doesn't know music. All he does is stand up there and shake himself, bang on a guitar, and make a racket. I don't call that music. It's just a noise."

Mr. Shull would repeat this Elvis bashing at least once or twice a week. Joe and the other guys in the class loved it, but the girls did not care for Mr. Shull's opinions.

In Chemistry, Mr. Peele was always doing experiments creating funny smells in the lab. Most people had trouble with the formulas and code names for the different chemicals, but Joe loved this type work.

Some of the senior girls in the class would like to sit near Joe so he could help them with their projects. Most of them just did not want to study and do their homework.

Frog Gigging

Joe, Archie, and several of the other boys got along good with Mr. Peele. They liked the projects of cutting up the frogs to see what made them tick. Somehow the subject came up that Mr. Peele liked frog legs so the boys would go frog gigging with him.

Mr. Peele lived near Flat Rock Baptist Church so the boys would go gigging at a couple of ponds nearby. Mr. Peele would have a high powered flashlight to shine into the pond to blind the frogs and then, instead of gigging them, he would shoot them between their eyes with his 22 caliber pistol. It was so neat. Joe would usually shine the light for Mr. Peele. We always had so much fun and would get a sack of frogs each time we went.

Joe did not try to eat the frog legs at that time, but would try them years later. They were okay, but Joe did not use them to replace his fried chicken. Mr. Peele would only stay at West Yadkin for one year.

Now that Joe had his driver's license, he would get to drive Elmer's 1953 Chevrolet some. He liked to drive Elmer's car better than Dad's old Plymouth.

Tobacco was finally tipped out the week of September 23 with the final day being September 26 at Uncle Nelson's woods field.

"Yes! Yes!" hollered Joe and John as the last leaves were pulled.

The echo from the barn came back across the woods and branch, which ran, between the field and the barn.

"Yes! Yes! Yes!" the barn crew hollered back as they, too, were happy that the priming was done for this year.

The annual end of tobacco priming wienie roast was planned for Saturday, September 28, at 6:00 p.m. As usual, the wienie roast was held at the road barn. Mr. and Mrs. Shore, Mom, Dad, Joe, John, Jane, Danny, Uncle Nelson, Aunt Jo, Gray, Fay, and Debbie, now about 3 ½ years old, were in attendance.

Uncle Nelson won the big eater award "hands down" as Joe could not come close to eating the eight hotdogs. Joe ate four hotdogs and that was enough for him. It was a good time of fun and food for a well deserved work crew. Everyone appreciated Mr. Shore for giving us the time of fun.

Farmer Brown

After the wienie roast, Archie came by and went with Joe and John to visit Farmer Brown. Farmer was Grandpa Brown's first cousin who lived by himself in a little shack out across Highway 421 from Paul Dobbins' store. Farmer was a hermit who, from his early childhood, was different. He was not all there mentally but was smarter than many people gave him credit.

Farmer was an attraction of people from all over the state and adjoining states. People would visit Farmer and listen to him talk and play his self playing piano. When he talked, he repeated his lines.

"Hey, Farmer! How're you doing?" Joe said as he knocked on the door.

"Hey, Joe! Are you doing alright, now are you?" Farmer said. "Will you come in, now will you?"

Farmer knew us as Dad always let Farmer ride with us to the Brown Reunion in Statesville each summer.

"Farmer, this is my friend, Archie King. He wanted to come by to see you with us," Joe said.

"Would you be Miles King's boy, now would you?" Farmer asked.

"That's me!" Archie said as he shook Farmer's hand.

"I've knowed your Dad for years, I sure have," Farmer said.

"Can you play some songs for us, Farmer?" John asked. "We like to see you play."

Farmer started playing the self playing piano, but in his mind, he was playing it himself.

"When the saints go marching in.
When the saints go marching in.
Oh, Lord, I want to be in that number
When the saints go marching in."

"That's good, Farmer!" Archie said. "I play the piano, too."

"You do, now do you?" Farmer said as he played another song.

"Rock of Ages, cleft for me,
Let me hide myself in Thee;
Let the waters and the blood,
From thy wounded side which flowed,
Be of sin, the double cure,
Save from wrath and make me pure."

"That's Cousin Henry's favorite song, it is," Farmer said. He was talking about Grandpa Brown.

"Well, we've got to go, Farmer. You've got more company coming to the door," Joe said. "Bye, Farmer."

"Bye, Farmer," John said.

"Bye, ya'll. Tell Miles I said hey, now will you?" Farmer said to Archie.

"Joe, you and John, tell Clyde and Gladys I said hey, now will you?" Farmer said. "Ya'll come back to see me soon."

Archie spoke up as he started the car, "Farmer is smarter that most people think. He remembered Dad. I bet he knows a lot of people."

"I know he does," Joe said. "He goes everywhere. You can see him walking all over the country."

"He gets around alright. He walks to church every Sunday all the way over to Asbury. That's a long walk from here," John said as they headed home. It was getting late.

"See ya'll Monday at school," Archie said as he dropped us off.

"See ya!" Joe and John said.

Monday football practice was brutal. After a loss, Coach Shull would drill us with extra head on tackling. We had now lost three games in a row and the tackling had been sloppy.

"Hit and drive him back!" Coach was yelling. Each player would get to tackle and then would switch lines and get tackled.

It seemed like Joe was always getting matched up with the bigger boys on the team. Joe was 5' 10" tall, but only weighed 130 pounds soaking wet. He was wiry, but he was light. He preferred to outrun them, not run over them.

"Boy, that was a tough practice!" Joe said as he, Archie, John, and Roger Swaim lined up on Highway 421 to thumb a ride home after practice.

"It sure was!" Roger said. "I think Coach is trying to get our attention after Boonville and Yadkinville made our record 0-3."

Joe and John walked the mile out Brown Road from Highway 421. It was 6:00 p.m. and chore time. Then after supper, it would be work in the packhouse until 9:00 p.m. Joe and John did not mind working late as this was the only way they would be able to play football. The next month would be more of the same to meet Dad's deadline on selling the tobacco.

Jonesville made West Yadkin 0-4 as they beat us, 26-6, on Friday night. Jonesville had a much better team, but we did play better.

On Sunday, October 6, it was Brown Reunion time again at Grandpa Brown's after church at 1:00 p.m. We had another good turnout with plenty of good food. It was always a good time of food and family fun.

The packhouse was moving along at a good pace. Dad was letting Mr. Shore haul our tobacco to the market along with Uncle Nelson's. Gurn Johnson, who had been hauling our tobacco as long as Joe could remember, had quit hauling. Mr. Shore had bought a big truck and could haul lots more than Gurn's old truck.

Another house of chickens was sold last week and five thousand new chicks arrived. The chicken cycle brought needed extra money in.

It was school, football practice, and packhouse work every day. It was a better football game on Friday night as West Yadkin beat Dodson, 27-13. It was good to finally win a game.

Chapter 29
Joe's First Start

It was two wins in a row as West Yadkin beat Pilot Mountain up there, 13-6. A tough win, but any win is good. The record was now 2-4 with a trip to the mountains to play Lansing and then Elkin at our place.

We won at Lansing, 19-12, to move to 3-4. Three wins in a row made us feel good about playing Elkin at home. Joe had a good week in practice playing the Elkin aggressive defense against our first team. Joe would shoot the gap between the center and guards from his linebacker position creating havoc in practice.

"That's the way to play defense, Joe!" Coach said. "Can't anyone block that guy?" he scowled at his offensive line.

Joe was happy with his week of practice and would be ready to play some Friday night, if needed.

On Friday night, November 1, the West Yadkin bleachers were filling up early. It was a good crowd, hoping to see the underdog Eagles beat the 7-1 Bucking Elks. The Elkin radio station, WIFM was getting set up to broadcast the game.

Coach Shull was having his talk with the team before they headed out on the field.

"We need to play aggressive defense. This team is good. They don't need for us to make mistakes and give them points. They can score a bunch on their own. We simply cannot win if we make mistakes," Coach said.

"We have another problem! Clyde hurt his leg and cannot play middle linebacker. I guess we'll let Gary stay in and play defense." Gary was our one player who played offense only at center. Gary was about 6′ 7″ tall, but was slender and slow.

"No! We won't either," Coach said. "Joe, you'll go in and play defense like you played all week."

Joe couldn't believe what he'd heard. He was finally going to get a start on defense. He was excited. He quickly snapped on his helmet and had fire in his eyes.

"I'm ready, Coach!" Joe said as the team headed down the sidewalk out past the Ag building and ran onto the field to the rousing approval of the crowd. Joe was pumped up. He hoped Elkin got the ball first so he could get going.

Elkin won the toss and received the kickoff. Now they had it first down at their twenty-five yard line. Two running plays into the line got Elkin only a couple of yards. Joe had been working on the center in both of these plays, first to the left and then to the right.

The Sack

"Okay, it's third and eight. Let's stop them here," Captain Wayne Wagoner, a vicious hitter, said.

Elkin quarterback Wally Holcomb took the snap and went back to pass. Joe saw a gap to the right of center and hit it quickly. No one picked him up. In a flash, Joe was all over the quarterback who was scrambling to get away. Joe grabbed his jersey by one hand and his passing arm by the other hand and rudely flung him to the ground.

The quarterback slowly got to his feet, looked at Joe, and said, "Good play. You were all over me before I knew what hit me."

"Thanks!" Joe said as he headed back to his position and got ready for the punt.

"Good play, Joe," came from all of his teammates. Archie gave Joe a pat on the back.

"You got him good, Joe," Archie said.

West Yadkin played the good Elkin team close before losing by a score of 18-12. Joe was active the whole night as he moved around the line to keep hitting them from different angles.

Coach Shull talked about our play after the game. "We played a good game tonight, team! I'm proud of you. I wish we could keep on playing. We're playing good now."

The season was over and already Joe was looking forward to next year when he would be a senior and one of the team leaders.

One of Joe's classmates, Gene Williams, was not at the game and heard it on the radio. He was telling Joe about the announcer talking about the time Joe sacked the quarterback. His play by play was, "And there's Wally Holcomb back to pass. He's being rushed. He scrambles and there little Joe Brown hitting him and throwing him to the ground. What a play the youngster has made, sacking Wally Holcomb!"

Joe laughed and said, "I wish I could have heard that."

All the tobacco was gone. The final sale was last Wednesday on October 30. It was good to have the 1957 crop behind us. Dad had thought about tending less tobacco next year, but would not say, for sure, for two to three months. It had been a hard, tough year, but every year seemed to be that way. It was never easy and most farmers did not expect or seek the easy life. Farmers knew that they had to battle the elements year in and year out to survive.

A Sad Day

One of Dad's cousins in Statesville, J.T. Brown, worked as a North Carolina state patrolman. Tonight, November 5, Trooper Brown was making a routine stop of a suspicious vehicle. The driver of this vehicle was an escaped patient from a mental institution named Frank Wetzel. Wetzel shot Trooper Brown before he was later captured. Trooper Brown died while undergoing surgery at the hospital.

The mental patient, Wetzel, had earlier killed another state patrolman, W.L. Reece in Richmond County. Trooper Reece had stopped Wetzel for speeding.

It was a sad time for the Brown family. Dad took all of his family to the funeral in Statesville on Saturday, November 9. Joe remembers the funeral as one of the saddest he had ever attended. At the end of the funeral, the Highway Patrol Honor Guard fired their weapons in the air in honor of the fallen trooper. Then a lonely bugler blew taps that seemed to go through the cool November air and pierce right to the heart. It was such a sad, lonely sound.

We kept the family in our prayers for a long time. The murderer, Wetzel, would go on trial and be convicted of first degree murder on both counts. Wetzel would only get life on both counts because he was a mental patient. Dad always said he should have been "hanged by the neck" until dead immediately after the trial. Joe felt the same way about the "cold blooded" killer.

It was a waste of precious lives by someone whom the taxpayers would end up supporting for the rest of his life, which has been almost fifty years now. Again, this is a waste. The money spent to keep such trash alive should be spent to help the families of the two troopers killed. We cannot bring them back, but we could help their families instead of helping the "cold blooded" killer. It seems like some of our judicial ways are somewhat messed up.

Certainly, Joe would remember this tragedy for a long, long time. He wanted to be a state patrolman for awhile after his cousin's death, but would later change his mind. Joe realized that the judicial system was against law officers and were responsible indirectly for the deaths of many officers in line of duty. It was a field of work that would continually get tougher.

Pastor Hankins made mention of the death of Dad's first cousin and had a special prayer for the families of both of the state troopers during church on Sunday morning.

After church, Joe, John, Jane, and Danny went up to Grandpa Brown's house for a visit. It was a nice evening, not warm, but not cold. Grandpa was out on the front porch with his light jacket on.

Story About Justice

Grandpa was stirred up about the death of his nephew and Trooper Reece. He knew that Wetzel, a mental patient, had gunned both of them down in cold blood.

Grandpa started, "We need to give this "thug" a fast trial next week. We don't need to wait around about it and have some "fancy pants" lawyer get him off with anything less than hanging by the neck until death. It's very obvious that the man is guilty. We need to get it over with and let the families have the satisfaction of knowing that justice has prevailed."

Grandpa continued, "That's what would have happened in the old days. The accused got a speedy, but fair trial, and was then punished accordingly. If we did things that way today, we wouldn't have all of this crime. Justice corrects crime!"

"I remember when I was a youngin about eight years old. Some man down about Yadkinville got mad and stabbed his next door neighbor who died on the spot. The victim's wife was a witness to the killing. She was right there in the same room at the time. The sheriff arrested the killer and put him in the county jail in Yadkinville."

"The killing happened on Friday night. By the middle of the next week, a trial was set and a jury was selected. It was an airtight case with only one witness available. No one else had seen the killing."

"The verdict was guilty of premeditated murder. The sentence was to be hanged by the neck until dead on Friday morning at dawn. So the sentence was to be carried out in less than a week after the crime had been committed. Such justice sends a fast message that if you commit a crime in our county, you will pay for that crime quickly and with your life if you take a life in a premeditated manner."

"People from all over the county converged in Yadkinville on Friday morning. School was out for the day. It was a day of justice. It was the first time I had seen anyone hanged. I saw two more later but the sight of the hanging had a lingering effect on everyone in attendance."

"It truly was an awful sight, but the death penalty works. It has an effect on crime when it is allowed to work. That's what needs to happen to this Wetzel guy. Then criminals everywhere will sit up and take note. But if we just put him in jail for the rest of his life, what has he lost? He's better off in jail than where he was. He has not lost anything and has not paid and never will pay for his terrible crimes," Grandpa said.

"You have it pegged just right, Grandpa," Joe said. "I'm afraid that they won't burn him for these murders. He should visit the electric chair in Raleigh, but I don't think he will."

With football season over, Joe and Dad decided that Joe would not play basketball, at least, at the beginning of the season. Joe would concentrate on helping get all the work around the farm caught up. Dad had carried much of the load during football season and Joe appreciated it.

The corn crop had to be pulled and shucked before bad weather hit. Corn that hung in the field in rainy, bad weather for a long time would rot and not be any good. We had put too much work and money into the crop to see it waste. Some people would let it hang in the field all winter. Seeing this happen would really bother Dad. He could not stand to see waste.

November was gone. December, the farmer's beginning of winter, was here. There was a nip in the air.

Joe went with Archie to most of the basketball games. He missed playing.

"Dad, do you think it'll be okay if I start back playing basketball after Christmas? We seem to have the work caught up pretty good," Joe asked at supper before leaving for a game.

"I don't see why not," Dad said. "You've worked hard to get things done since football season ended. Can you get on the team? I thought the team was already chosen."

"Coach Shull said he had an opening. Someone failed their grades." Joe said. "I'll tell him I'll be at practice after the Christmas break. Thanks, Dad!"

Joe talked to Coach Shull at the game tonight. It was all set. Joe would start practice on Thursday, January 2. Coach knew why Joe had not been playing and understood that farm work had to come first.

"That's good, Joe," Archie said on the way home. "We need some help."

School was out on Friday, December 20, for the Christmas break until Thursday, January 2. Joe looked forward to the time away from the books.

Joe's First Date

On Saturday night, December 21, Joe had his first date. Ralph Winters and his date Eunice Peoples lined Joe up with a blind date. Joe was a nervous wreck. He was so shy. Joe cleaned up Elmer's 1953 Chevrolet and was on the way to pick up Ralph at 6:00 p.m. We then picked up Ralph's date, Eunice, who lived down Highway 67 about halfway to Boonville. From there, we drove back to Jonesville to pick up Joe's date, Jean Jarvis, who lived on Highway 67 near the Minute Grill.

Joe went to the door with Ralph and Eunice who introduced Joe. They spent the next three hours riding around through Elkin and eating a hamburger at the Grill. Jean seemed to be a nice girl, but Joe sure was glad Ralph and Eunice were there to carry the conversation.

Dad had reluctantly let Joe have the car.

"You need to be home by 9:30 p.m.," Dad said before Joe left.

"That's too early," Joe pleaded with Dad.

"No! It's 9:30 p.m.," Dad said.

It was now past 10:00. Joe didn't have the nerve to tell Ralph about the 9:30 p.m. curfew. Ralph would laugh.

Finally, about 10:15, Joe took Jean home and then Eunice, and, finally, Ralph at about 10:30 p.m. Joe was in trouble as he motored down Swan

Creek Road arriving home at 11:00 p.m. He was 1 ½ hours late.

Dad was waiting for Joe as he hurried into the house.

"Where have you been? You're 1 ½ hours late! You'll never get the car again!" Dad ranted.

"I'm sorry, Dad. It was so much driving and time got away from me," Joe said. "I just couldn't get back at 9:30. That's so early."

Dad went to bed still raising cane about Joe being so late. Joe figured he'd never get the car again.

"I'm probably grounded for a while, Ralph," Joe told him at church on Sunday. "I didn't get home until 11:00 last night."

"Oh, boy! That's bad! I think Jean likes you," Ralph said.

Ralph and Eunice would continue dating and later get married. Joe would date Jean a couple more times, but he was too shy to date very much.

Christmas 1957

It was Christmas Eve. Wayne, Elvie, Rose, and Tip were home for Christmas. It was like old times around the fire with popcorn, crackerjacks, and Mom's "better than bought" chocolate candy. Everyone ate their fill.

At 5:00 a.m. on Christmas morning, feet hit the floor, as always, at the Little Farm on Brown Road. For the first time in many years, there weren't any shoe boxes out. Danny thought that he was too big to play Santa anymore. It was kind of sad. All of Mom and Dad's youngins were now Santa broke. Where did time go?

Christmas morning was still an exciting time. Gifts were exchanged. It was a lot of fun. We miss Elmer again this year. We sent his gifts about three weeks ago and had received his gifts last week. Of course, they could not be opened until today.

Joe was happy with his new jeans and dress shoes. It was good to see everyone happy on this special day. This day would not have been complete without the knock on the door by Grandpa Brown.

"Merry Christmas, youngins!" Grandpa said. "How are ya'll doing today?"

"We're doing good, Grandpa," Joe said. "Hope you're feeling good."

"I'm okay," Grandpa said as he poured a cup of American Ace coffee and sat down at the breakfast table. "This is good coffee, Gladys, and a good tenderloin biscuit, too."

Mom had fixed up a breakfast for kings today, with tenderloin, sausage, liver mush, scrambled eggs, gravy, biscuits, jelly, jam, and molasses. Everyone ate quietly as the food was too good to spend time talking.

You could certainly tell that we had just killed hogs. The artic air last week was perfect hog killing weather. The smokehouse was filled with plenty, even if we were to have a long, rough winter.

Soon, Grandpa was ready to go. Joe gave him the usual box of long cigars and Grandpa was happily on the way in a puff of smoke.

After dinner, Mom and Dad headed down to Grandpa Proctor's with Joe, John, Jane, and Danny.

"He needs to cut these weeds. The frost sure hasn't knocked them down," Dad said as he drove down the Proctor's driveway.

It was a regular houseful of company. Grandma stayed busy making her rounds giving everyone of her grandchildren a hug and a couple of her biscuits. A trip to Grandma Proctor's would not be complete without a biscuit or two or three or more.

It was a fun evening, but soon it was time to head home. Days were short and it was chore time.

The time out of school passed quickly. It was New Year's Eve with Joe, John, and Archie. It was 12:01, 1958. Another new year was here.

"See ya'll at school Thursday," Archie said as he sleepily left for home.

"See ya!" Joe said and was immediately asleep.

Basketball Team

School was back in session on Thursday, January 2, 1958. Joe was glad to be back at basketball practice. Two players had failed their grades and Joe was on the team. It was good to be playing again with Roger Swaim, Archie, and the other guys. The team still did not have a home gym. A new one was being built and would be ready next year. The practices would again be at the YMCA in Elkin. That would make for a lot of time on the old bus back and forth to Elkin.

The starting lineup for the team was Marcus Allred, Archie King, Jackie Reinhardt, Joe Wright, and Wayne Wagoner. Joe was happy to play in a backup role. He looked forward to next year when he was sure to be a starter.

This team, like last year's team, hustled and scraped for their points, but we were not a good team. The best team was Joe's freshman season. His sophomore and his junior years were down. And, sadly to say, his senior year would be the worst team of all. But Joe enjoyed playing. The fun will be remembered forever even if the losses were hard to take.

It's January birthday time again. Danny is nine on January 18, while Joe celebrates his seventeenth on January 21. It's hard to imagine that Joe is getting ready for his last full year at home. Dad is forty-four on January 24.

Another house of chickens graduated to become fryers on January 24. The chicken house was quickly cleared out for the next five thousand chicks, which would arrive on January 31. The chicken cycle continues as January ends on a snowy note.

February is cold and snowy to begin. The sun would pop through long enough for the groundhog to see his shadow on his day. Six more weeks of winter was the prediction made by the old "hog."

Chapter 30
Tobacco Time

On Saturday, February 15, it was plant bed sowing day. Dad had decided to continue to raise fourteen acres of tobacco again this year. By the end of the day, the plant beds were sown, covered, and ready for the usual bad weather.

The weather was right to script as it started snowing on Sunday evening and snowed all night. School was out Monday and Tuesday with the six inches of snow.

"The moisture is good for the plant beds," Dad said at supper on Tuesday night. "School will run tomorrow, though. The roads are in pretty good shape."

On February 23, John turned fifteen years old. Rose was now nineteen.

March came in windy, as usual. The weather was starting to warm up. Springtime was coming.

April was warmer. The showers were good for the tobacco plant beds. Plant beds required a lot of water. When it did not rain often enough, we kept them watered by hand.

April was a weed pulling month at the plant beds. Dad believed in keeping the fertilizer at work on the tobacco plants instead of weeds. If Dad saw a weed, we got busy with our weeding.

Dad was busy getting the land turned, harrowed, and then laid off for tobacco. The corn land and garden was turned, also. The fun time of wrestling with the two hundred pound bags of fertilizer was here again. Joe and John could give a two hundred pound bag a tussle now that they had grown up.

Joe remembers the times that he and John were at Paul Dobbins' store when the eighteen wheeler fertilizer truck arrived. Paul also had a feed, seed, and fertilizer business in addition to the store. Paul would pay Joe and John $2.00 each to unload the truck. They would use a hand truck to unload what seemed to be thousands of bags of fertilizer. By the time the truck was unloaded, Joe and John both would be soaking wet with sweat as if they had been hanging tobacco in the top of a barn on a one hundred degree day.

"Thank you, boys!" Paul would say as he paid them $2.00 each.

"You're welcome!" Joe and John would say as they hurried home with their fortune in their pocket.

It was May 1, 1958. Barefoot day was here again. The school year was winding down. Soon, Joe would only have one year left at good old West Yadkin High School. Where in the world has time gone?

The junior class would lose a few students within the next year. Some of Joe's classmates this year would not graduate with him. Some would quit and not graduate at all.

This year's class was Margaret Allen, Collen Ashley, Annette Hall Brooks, Joe, Roger Caudle, Jo Ella Chandler, Brenda Cheek, Sue Dwiggins, Elaine Everidge, Doretha Gardner, Max Gough, Tony Hobson, Hazel Hudson, Wayne Huffman, Donna Johnson, Archie King, Bonnie Livingood, Polly Martin, Mary Bryant, Nancy Reinhardt, Sonja Royal, Tommy Seagraves, Margaret Shore, Willodean Shore, JoAnn Simpson, Brenda Swaim, Gail Swaim, Harold Swaim, Sylvia Trivette, Billy Turner, Jerleen Turner, Dina Underwood, Patty Vestal, Mary Leigh Walker, Gene Williams, Margaret Wilkins, and Terry Windsor.

Our class sponsors were Miss Beamer and Mr. Reece. It had been a good year for our class.

After a week of strawberry picking with Grandpa Brown, Joe, John, Jane, and Danny were all set for the start of tobacco setting for 1958. Dad wanted to set the big maple field on Friday to allow more time for the hill field on Saturday, a non school day.

Joe drove Elmer's car to school so he could leave at noon and bring the other youngins home early to start setting. Dad's crew ate dinner and were in the field before 1:00 p.m. Mom dropped for Dad and Jane dropped for Joe while Danny dropped for John. Three setting teams were click clacking across the big maple field.

By 4:00 p.m., the big maple field was finished. Dad had plants left over and moved his crews to the hill field to get a start there. About one acre was set out by 7:00 p.m. when we ran out of plants.

Dad had his crew in the plant beds at 5:30 a.m. pulling plants for the long day of setting. At 9:30, the crews started setting in the hill field again. It was an overcast day with a pleasant breeze.

"This is a good day for setting," Joe said as they began the click clack of the setters. "I like it when it's not so hot."

"Maybe we can get all of our plants set out to-day and get a good shower tonight," Dad said as he gazed at the threatening clouds.

The weather stayed about the same all day, threatening, but no rain came. By days end, about six acres of the eight acre field was set out. The tobacco plants were setting up good as it had been a cool day. Normally when new plants are set out, the sun will cause them to droop down by the end of the day. Today's setting leaves six more acres to set out on Monday and Tuesday. It was good to be over halfway through.

Mother's Day Note

Sunday, May 11, was Mother's Day.

"I love you, Mom!" Joe said at breakfast. "Happy Mother's Day."

"Love you, Mom," John said.

"I love you, too, Mom," Jane said.

"I love you, Mom," Danny said as he was the last to give Mom her hug.

"Thank you, youngins! I love you all, too!" Mom said. "Look what I found, Joe. Here's a Mother's Day note you gave me when you were in the second grade in 1949. It reads, 'For My Mother.'"

"My mother does so many things
That it would be a sin
For her to work and me to play
When I could help her every day.
Signed Joe."'

"Isn't that sweet?" Mom said.

"I still feel that way, Mom!" Joe said.

At church, our new pastor of one month, Preacher Culler, recognized all mothers with a good sermon from Proverbs 31. "In closing, I want all children to go to their mom and tell her that you love her. Give her a hug," Pastor Culler said.

Mom was a little teary eyed after Joe, John, Jane, and Danny came by to give her another hug. It was, as always, a sweet, loving time.

Monday was a no school day for Dad's crew. It was another 5:30 a.m. to 7:00 p.m. day. We had a real good day finishing the hill field by 2:00 p.m. Next was the four acre middle field which was a little over half finished by quitting time at 7:00. Dad and Mom would have plants pulled and setting started before the youngins got home from school on Tuesday. The field would be finished by 6:00 p.m. It was good to have another crop of tobacco set out.

The weather had been cooperating nicely as we had showers over the weekend and then again Monday night. This rain made the newly set out tobacco perk up and start to growing right away.

Bus Driver

On Wednesday morning at school, Joe and three other boys were told to report to Mr. Wright's office at 10:00 a.m. Joe wondered what he had done, but Mr. Wright assured them all nothing was wrong.

"We need some school bus drivers! We're short of substitutes and need to get some of you four licensed today. Mr. Hatcher from the state licensing office is here to take ya'll out on a road test," Mr. Wright said.

Mr. Hatcher stood up and led the four boys to bus #7, one of the newer buses.

"Hop in, boys and let's take a ride!" Mr. Hatcher said as he drove up Highway 421. After driving for about a mile, he stopped and let each of the four potential drivers drive a school bus for the first time.

"It's your time, Joe," Mr. Hatcher said. "Get a feel for the gears. They're kind of like a truck. Drive until I tell you to stop."

"Stop! Put out your stop sign," Joe stopped as a car behind him honked its horn at a school bus stopped on the highway at this time of the day. Joe looked to Mr. Hatcher.

"Just sit here! Let him wait! We're not in any hurry. We're carrying precious cargo," Mr. Hatcher said.

"Go ahead now, Joe, and we'll let Mr. Honker pass us on this straight stretch," Mr. Hatcher continued. The car passed giving us a hard look and two long blasts from his horn. Mr. Hatcher waved at him.

Joe liked Mr. Hatcher who was in charge of the situation. He did not get in a hurry. He let all four "soon to be licensed" school bus drivers drive several times to get familiar with the school bus. Joe was already hoping to get a school bus route for next year. The pay was $25.00 a month. That kind of money could buy Joe a lot of gas for the 1953 Chevrolet.

Gas was selling for about $.18 per gallon with prices as low as $.15 when there were gas wars.

After about one and a half hours of going up and down Highway 421, Mr. Hatcher took us back to West Yadkin.

"These boys are okay to drive, Mr. Wright," Mr. Hatcher said. "I believe they'll do a good job for you."

"Good! I need someone to drive #63 this evening," Mr. Wright said. "That's your bus, Joe. You go ahead and drive it."

Joe could not believe it. He had every bit of twenty minutes behind the wheel of a new school bus and he was going to drive old #63 today.

"Yes sir!" Joe said as he headed back to his classroom to continue school. He still could not believe that he was going to drive a bus today. Boy, would Mom and Dad be surprised!

Joe hurried to the bus after the 3:00 p.m. buzzer. To everyone's surprise, Joe was sitting behind the wheel of old #63 when they got on the bus.

"What are you doing behind the wheel?" Cousin Lorene asked when she got on the bus.

"I'm the driver today. I'm an official school bus driver as of today," Joe said.

"That's cool!" Lorene said as she sat in one of the front seats. "I didn't know you were getting your license."

"I didn't, either, until today," Joe said with a laugh.

"Are you driving our bus?" John asked as he got on the bus.

"Are you driving?" Danny asked.

"My big brother is driving our bus!" Jane told her friends. She was proud of her brother.

"Yes! I'm driving old #63!" Joe assured all of them. He found out real soon that old #63 did not drive like the new #7.

Joe had never driven anything that had to be double-clutched, but old #63 did. He scraped the gears about every time he changed them for awhile. Gradually, he would get used to the bus and do a better job. But on this first experience with old #63, Joe had his hands full. He enjoyed driving and would drive several times this year for the regular driver, Marcus Allred.

Mom and Dad were surprised to see old #63 coming down the driveway with Joe behind the wheel. Joe pulled back behind the house and turned around so he would be ready to go in the morning.

"Last stop for today!" Joe told John, Jane, and Danny as he opened the door.

"When in the world did you get your bus license, Joe?" Mom asked as she came out to see what all the noise was.

"Today at school, Mom, I became a bus driver. Mr. Hatcher came up and gave the road test to four of us. I was put to work today. Mr. Wright needed a driver," Joe said.

Joe would drive for someone about every evening the rest of the school year. He really hoped to get a bus route for next year.

At supper tonight, Joe had to explain how he rode to school on #63 this morning and then drove the bus home this evening.

"Mr. Wright needed some drivers fast and Mr. Hatcher came up and certified us," Joe told Dad. "I'm real careful, Dad. I know I'm carrying a bunch of youngins."

"I'm proud of you, son," Dad said as he ate his cornbread and milk.

It was Saturday, May 17, and time to start the process of cultivating and hoeing tobacco at the big maple field. Dad had the field plowed by the time the youngins got home from school. Yes, it had been a make-up day in school today. All the snow days had to be made up.

The big maple field was hoed out Monday evening after school. Dad had moved on to the hill field to his riding plow. He simply loved that riding plow. Joe admits that this plow was faster in that it plowed one full row each time, whereby the old horse plow only did half a row.

Dad was using the tractor to plow our tobacco at home, but he liked the riding plow pulled by Old Kate and Old Maude better. Maybe Dad was resisting progress.

On Friday, May 23, Holly Farms picked up our five thousand chickens and left us a house to get cleaned up by next Friday when new chicks would arrive. As usual, Dad was busy and the house was clean and ready by midweek.

On Thursday, May 29, school was out for the year. Joe was now officially a senior with only one year to go. John was a tenth grader, Jane was a seventh grader, while Danny would be in the fourth grade.

The tobacco was coming along nicely. We had just finished the second round of plowing and hoeing all of the fourteen acres. The cycle would continue for the next three weeks until the tobacco was laid by.

Chapter 31
The Battleground

It was Sunday, June 1, 1958. Dad drove all of us down to Greensboro to visit Wayne, Elvie, Rose, and Tip. We packed a picnic lunch and they did, too. We met them at Battleground Park, which is where some of the historic battles of the American Revolutionary War were fought.

Today would be different for Joe. After eating a great meal of fried chicken, deviled eggs, sandwiches, Pepsis, chips, hotdogs, hamburgers, cookies, ham biscuits, chocolate pie, and banana pudding, Joe was just standing around in the wooded area wishing he could go swimming. It was hot, about ninety degrees.

Suddenly, Joe saw a swarm of yellow jackets around his feet. He had stirred up a nest of yellow jackets and they were in a foul mood. Joe was immediately stung by about ten or twelve of them on his feet and ankles. He was fortunate to have been wearing long pants, shoes, and socks or the stings would have been worse.

Everyone else scattered except Dad. He came to Joe's rescue by swatting the varmints off Joe with his straw hat. Joe had been doing a dance since the stings began. He and Dad finally managed to chase off all the yellow jackets. Joe was afraid that they were going to go up his pants legs and that would have been even more trouble.

Joe's feet and ankles were really hurting now. We left the Battleground Park soon and went to the Greensboro Airport to watch airplanes for awhile. We made a stop on the way to get a bottle of rubbing alcohol to put on Joe's feet and ankles, which by now were swollen a lot. The alcohol was a temporary relief, but he was still in a lot of pain.

Joe was not in any frame of mind to watch the airplanes today. He stayed in the car and kept applying the alcohol to his wounds received at the battleground. The park was properly named as it had certainly been a battleground for Joe today. He would always remember that day at the park. It was forever a conversation piece in our family.

"I'm just glad the yellow jackets didn't go up your pants legs," Dad said. "I thought they probably had when I saw so many of them."

"I'm glad they didn't, either. It was bad enough as it was, but it could have been much worse," Joe said.

Within a couple of days, Joe was back to normal. He didn't miss any work. It took something major to miss work with Dad.

It was Saturday evening, June 7, about 2:00 p.m. Joe and John had talked Dad into stopping early today after another long week of hoeing tobacco and chopping crabgrass.

Archie was coming by to go swimming at Roger Swaim's Grandpa Redding's pond. It was a good day for it as it was about ninety-five degrees. Mr. Redding lived up off Highway 421 on Dennyville Road just over the county line into Wilkes County.

Roger would invite us up to swim anytime we wanted to go. It was always fun. Roger would spend a lot of the summer at his Grandpa's place. Who wouldn't with such a nice pond to fish or to swim?

Joe, John, Archie, and Roger would spend the next two hours in the cool waters of the pond. They would dive or jump off the diving board that Roger fixed up on the near side of the pond. Joe didn't know how to dive, so he usually did a "belly flop" or just jumped in with a big splash.

Soon, the boys were trying to see who could make the biggest splash. Archie usually won that game as he was the biggest of the boys with Roger running a close second.

At about 5:00 p.m., it was storm time as the "corn wagons" were starting to roll in the not too distant west. The thunder was getting closer. It was time to take shelter.

"We'd better go!" Joe said as everyone was headed towards the car. "We'll see you later, Roger."

"See you, Roger!" Archie said.

"Ya'll come back the first of the week if you can," Roger said.

The Natural Athlete

Roger was Joe and Archie's best friend. They had gone to school and played ball together since early grades. Roger was a natural athlete. He could hit a baseball farther than anyone Joe knew. He was the only person Joe had ever seen hit a ball over the right field fence and into the semi circle past where the buses parked.

Roger had such a smooth, graceful swing. It seemed so effortless. Joe, on the other hand, worked hard and tried his best, but without an opportunity to play baseball due to the work on the farm, he never did learn to hit the curve ball.

Roger also did not like to study at school. He would get behind in his work and, eventually, not be able to graduate with Joe and Archie. We tried to encourage Roger to work on his schoolwork, but he never did take it serious. What a shame it was as Roger had all the athletic ability in the world!

Joe and John hurried with the chores while Archie waited. They were going to Elkin to take in a "shoot 'em up" western movie at the Reeves Theatre.

Mom had supper ready and invited Archie to eat with us.

"Archie, come on in and eat with the "poor folks" if you will," Mom said.

"Okay!" Archie said as he sat down and ate a big bowl of cornbread and milk with us. "I love cornbread and milk, Mrs. Brown. Thanks for supper. It sure was good."

Soon, Joe, John, and Archie were headed to Elkin for a time of fun. Joe and Archie were such good friends and John was always with them.

It was late June. The tobacco had been laid by. The hay crop was cut and baled up. Yes, that's right! For the first time, Dad got our hay baled. Joe was so glad. It was so much easier than handling the loose hay.

It was July and time for the harvesting of the wheat and oats and getting up hundreds of bales of straw with Mr. Shore. It was now a fun job. Joe and John would love to ride on top of a load of straw or a load of bags of wheat from the field up at Pea Ridge. The ride by tractor down busy Highway 421 was a slow three mile trek.

"Happy birthday, Mom!" everyone said at the breakfast table on Wednesday morning, July 16.

"Thank you!" Mom said as she hurried to get Dad's work crew ready for the tobacco field. It was a tobacco topping day. Soon, the suckers would be growing again. Joe and John were experimenting again on their anti-sucker substances.

Joe and John could get the secret recipe to kill suckers, but it also would make the tobacco plants look sick. They never quite put in the correct potion to do the job.

The rest of the week was spent on tobacco topping which was a time consuming job and then all the barns were checked out and daubed up for the curing season. The sleds were checked out and repaired. Everything needed to be ready.

Laying Blocks

On Monday morning, July 21, Dad had a three day block laying job in Jonesville. An old house was being remodeled. It was kind of fun to get a break from the tobacco work. Dad was still very demanding, even in his block laying. Joe and John would carry blocks and make mud or mortar for the block laying. Dad had to have the blocks in just the right place and the mud where he could easily get a trowel full quickly.

Dad was an excellent block mason and very fast. He had to have all of his needed supplies in the right place.

Joe remembers this three day job, especially. He found an old 1881 Indian head penny. He has since been an avid collector of Indian head pennies.

Mom packed dinner for us on Monday and Tuesday, but on Wednesday, Dad said we would go to the store and get us a big Pepsi, a pack of nabs, and an oatmeal cookie. That sure was a treat for Joe and John.

But the three day job was over and it was back to the tobacco field as the suckers were growing and had to be pulled. The sucker cycle would go on for the next two months or until the priming season ended. It was a never ending battle.

Joe's Last Season

On Friday, August 1, it was first priming day all over again at the big maple field and Uncle Nelson's field. Slowly, but surely, Uncle Nelson's workers were growing up. Gray was now nine years old and Fay was now seven. Little Debbie was now four years old and about two years away from helping at the barn.

Dad, Uncle Nelson, Joe, and John again were the primers while the barn crew was Jane tying for Mom and Danny. Aunt Jo also tied for Gray and Fay. The barn crew would be faster, but still would not be able to stay up with the fast primers.

"Here we go to stand on our heads again," Joe said as they started the backbreaking task.

"Ain't it fun, though?" Uncle Nelson asked. "Where in the world could you have so much fun with a good group of people?"

"It is good people, but I could have more fun playing baseball," Joe said.

"Me, too!" John said.

"Let's all get wet now," Dad said as the heavy dew was dripping off the tall tobacco.

By the end of the first sled, none of the primers could find a dry spot of clothing. They were all soaked to the bone.

It was a good productive morning. The big maple field was pulled by 10:00 a.m. and hanged in the barn by 11:00. The primers went on to Uncle Nelson's field to pull his two acres.

Mom had a typical tobacco priming dinner today with pinto beans, taters, fried squash, biscuits, and a surprise cherry saunker. Joe ate his fill of pinto beans mashed up and with biscuits to sop the bean juice. After biscuit #7, or was it #8, Joe was ready for the delicious saunker.

"This is good, Mom!" Joe said. "I don't think you'll have any of it left over."

"It's good, Gladys," Dad said as he burped his approval.

"The cherries are tart enough to make it a little better, Mom," Jane said.

"I like it better sweeter ," John said as he drank his milk from a quart jar. John had this thing about wanting to drink his milk from a jar.

"It's just plain good, Mom," Danny said.

It was back to the field at 1:00 p.m. The sun was bearing down hot and humid. It was about ninety degrees in the shade and the primers definitely were not in the shade. Joe was glad that they didn't have to prime all evening. He was also hoping for cooler weather before tomorrow.

The priming was finished by 3:30 p.m. The primers then pitched in to help the barn crew finish tying. The hanging was completed by about 5:00 p.m. The first barn of the year was now in and ready to cure.

On Saturday, August 2, it was more of the same except even more. The hill field was being housed at the road barn. Today's job would be to get six acres of the eight acre field primed. It was a long day, but the job would be completed by about 7:00 p.m. It sure helped to have Mr. Shore driving sleds and helping at the barn.

Mr. Shore surprised everyone with a snack of a Pepsi and a pack of nabs at 10:00 a.m. That sure was a good treat that really hit the spot.

The Picture

Also, the Agrico fertilizer salesman came by to take a picture of Dad's crew in the hill field. Paul Dobbins sent him out to see us as we were one of his biggest customers. The picture was of Dad, Mom, Joe, John, Jane, and Danny and, of course, Debbie had to get in the picture as she was just like our baby sister. Jane held Debbie for the picture.

The Agrico salesman would later bring the picture to Dad. We kept it up on the mantle for a long time.

After a long, hard, hot day, the road barn was full. It was going to be good to have a day of rest after priming ten acres of first primings in these two days.

Monday morning, August 4, was another typical dog day. It was hot, humid, and dusty dry. We needed some rain. The primers started at 5:30 a.m. hoping to beat the heat, but it was already hot.

The hill field was pulled by 9:30 a.m. and it was on to the middle field for the rest of the day. It was a full day of work to finish this field and to fill the middle barn. A lot of sweat dropped today both in the field and then later in the stifling, hot barn. Joe got his share of the hot as he hanged tobacco in the top of the tinned roof oven like barn.

The first primings were finished on Tuesday in Uncle Nelson's woods field. The woods barn was filled by 3:00 p.m. It was nice to finish early and to take a dip in the cool waters at the pour-over. How refreshing the water felt!

On Wednesday, Joe and John hired out to help Lon Cheek prime his first primings. Dad thought it was okay for them to hire out to make a little cash. The boys would earn fifty cents per hour. They rode their bikes out to the Cheek's house and worked all day.

At dinnertime, Joe and John went to Paul Dobbins' store and had a dinner of a Pepsi, a nab, and an oatmeal cake. They would eat under the big oak trees at Oak Grove Church. It was nice to be able to work and to get paid for it.

On Thursday, Joe and John helped Miles King prime tobacco. Archie had earlier asked Dad if they could hire his two best primers. Dad said yes and Joe and John were busy priming for the sixth day in the past seven days.

Mrs. King had a delicious meal prepared for all the workers. It was pinto beans, green beans, corn on the cob, taters, biscuits, and apple cobbler. She called it a cobbler, but it looked like one of Mom's saunkers.

It was fun hiring out. Joe and John would hire out to the same two farms all summer long. Joe enjoyed, especially, helping Archie. The two good friends were inseparable.

It was an unusual crop of tobacco as it was ripening faster than ever. The normal few days of rest between the first and second primings did not happen this year. Second primings kept the pace going on the same schedule as the first had started. Maybe that would mean an early end to the tobacco pulling this year. Hopefully, it would mean less school missed.

Chapter 32
Football – Senior Year

The tobacco priming went like clockwork with five primings being pulled by September 1, the date of the first football practice. Archie came by to get Joe and John a little past 5:00 p.m. Practice was scheduled for 6:00.

The turnout was light for the first practice. There were eighteen players ready to play. It sure was tough trying to practice right in the middle of tobacco priming. Coach Shull and Assistant Coach Don Carter met with the new team and greeted them with high expectations for the upcoming season.

Coach Shull noted that Joe had gained a few pounds from last year. He mentioned that Joe looked stronger in the legs. He was planning on Joe to be a major ball carrier this year.

The first week of practice was tough as expected. Coach ran us a lot and had a bunch of head on tackling. By the week's end, five or six players were nicked up and could not practice. It was going to be a tough year.

Joe, Archie, and Roger Swaim were the only seniors on the team. They were elected tri-captains by the team. It was an honor that Joe tried to live up to as the example to younger players on the team.

School started on Monday, September 8, 1958. It would be a memorable year for Joe as your senior year should be. School was only a half day for the first week. Joe missed some school, but not as much as last year. With football practice under the lights, Joe did not miss practice. He was an early choice of Coach Shull to be the left halfback.

Roger Swaim was fullback and Chicken King was right halfback. Bruce Ashburn was the quarterback with Dalton Coram and Nolan Brown at ends. Archie King and Benny Ashley were tackles, with Rudy Pardue and Gray Pinnix at guards. Bud Everidge was the center. Joe Doss, Johnny Shore, and Luther Vanhoy played a lot, also.

The first game was set for Friday, September 12, at West Yadkin. We had a good crowd on hand and we played a decent game, but we could not score any points. We lost 13-0 to an always tough Sparta team. Joe ran the ball five times for fifteen yards as our injury plagued line could not block.

Monday's practice worked on both run blocking and pass blocking. We had to improve in that area to win some ballgames this year. Outside of Archie, our line had no size whatsoever. They were small and, for the most part, inexperienced, too.

We had a rough game coming up this week with our old rival, Jonesville. We worked hard in practice to get ready for their powerful team. Their main runner was Roy Lee Shore who used to go to church at Mineral Springs, but had not been coming of late. He was a speedy halfback who gave opposing teams problems.

Jonesville was too good for us on Friday night. They beat us badly, 41-6, as their team was big and fast, a combination that is hard to beat. Roy Lee Shore ran wild as he must have gained two hundred yards on the ground. He was as good as had been advertised. Joe hardly saw the ball all night on offense, only carrying three times for fifteen yards.

"They were too good for us! Forget this game and let's move on to the next one at Boonville next week," Coach Shull said. Our injuries were piling up. Roger Swaim had a bad leg and would not play a lot the rest of the year. Our line was nicked and beat up. Coach Shull didn't have many subs to use as we only had eighteen players dressed out. John was already getting playing time in the line and he was small at about one hundred twenty pounds.

Joe and Archie talked about our line and what we could do to get some blocking for our running game.

"What can we do, Archie? By the time I get the ball, someone is already on top of me," Joe said.

"I know! You could get some yardage if we would give you some holes to run through. I can't seem to get the younger players to understand it," Archie said.

It had been busy since the Jonesville game. The chickens were picked up and a new crop of five thousand chicks were due next Friday. The house would be ready, but it was a struggle with tips being pulled on Friday, Saturday, Monday, and Tuesday.

When the last leaves were pulled at about 3:00 p.m. on Tuesday, September 23, cheers of joy once again filled the air.

"Yea! Yea! Yea hoo!" came the wild cries from the field.

Not to be outdone, the barn crew echoed, "Yea! Yea! Yea!" It was the highlight of the year as the tips were hanged in the barn and Joe and John were on their way to football practice.

Practice this week was a lot of running sprints and also going through the routine of plays. Contact was held to a minimum due to the frail condition of our line. With Roger Swaim injured, Joe Doss would play fullback this week.

Boonville was a tough place to play. They had rowdy fans and a physically tough bunch of players. We played tough, but we were out manned. Boonville won 19-6. Joe carried the ball seven times for twenty-eight yards. Joe Doss, playing fullback in place of Roger Swaim who had a leg injury, was also injured early in the game. He sprained his ankle and would not play next week at Yadkinville. Our record was now 0-3. We needed some healthy players.

It was life in the packhouse for the next month. We had a bunch of tobacco to get ready for the market. Everyday after school working late at night and all day on Saturdays would be required to get the tobacco to market before the end of October.

On Saturday night, September 29, we had our annual end of tobacco priming wienie roast. It was always a fun time.

"Anybody going to give me any competition this year?" Uncle Nelson asked as he began to eat the first of his eight hotdogs. No one could challenge him. He again was the big eater. Joe and Dad ate four hotdogs each, but did not care to eat anymore.

"I guess you're the big pig again!" Joe told Uncle Nelson as they shared a good laugh. Joe, John, Jane, and Danny were very close to Uncle Nelson and kidded him a lot. He was a fun loving man who was always kidding around.

Football practice this week was more of the same with emphasis on play running and running sprints. Joe was the only healthy running back this week. Roger Swaim and Joe Doss were out. Right halfback Chicken King was nicked up but would play some. Quarterback Bruce Ashburn was nicked up also, but would play.

The game with Yadkinville was another tough, physical game. Their defense was as tough as Boonville and later, Elkin. They were fierce. To make matters worse, Joe had to play all four backfield positions as the nicked up players were decoys. In this game, Joe would run plays from quarterback, fullback, left halfback, and right halfback. Soon, the defense was keying on Joe as he was the only healthy running back. He took a beating in this game.

Yadkinville won 25-0 as they were dominating. Joe ran the ball fifteen times for forty-five yards. It was a tough forty-five yards. Oh, what Joe would give for about five Archie's in the line in front of him. Our record fell to 0-4. We needed a win badly, and we had to get some players healthy soon.

The tobacco was moving quickly from the packhouse to the market. A big load on Mr. Shore's truck would go to Cook's Warehouse each week. What a good sign this was! Joe was ready to finish the 1958 crop. It had been a long year.

After a good week of practice, our team was optimistic for this week's game with Walnut Cove.

"This is a team we can beat!" Coach Shull said all week. "We have been out manned for the past three weeks. We almost got Joe killed last week carrying the ball. Let's take the fight to this team tonight. We'll have Roger back at fullback with Bruce and Chicken feeling better. We can win this game. We're going to run our trick plays from short punt formation to try to open up the field."

The trick plays were double-reverse plays for the halfbacks from short punt formation. This play was Joe's favorite play. He got a chance to use his speed. The ball would be snapped direct to the quarterback who was in short punt formation. The quarterback would run the ball towards the fullback and then hand the ball off to the fullback who would run from the opposite side of the quarterback towards the halfback who would be split out slightly as a wingback.

The play would look like a reverse play, quarterback to fullback, until the last second when the fullback would hand the ball off to the halfback. By then, the defense would be sucked in to that side of the field. The fleet footed halfback would have an alley of blocking setup around the opposite end. Usually, all Joe would want is just one first block and he would be gone.

At least that's how this play was drawn up on the chalkboard. The play did not always work on the field. Linesman had to block a little bit.

About the middle of the first quarter, Coach Shull sent the play in by a sub, "double reverse L," which meant the ball would go to Joe at left halfback. Joe was excited. He had run this play before, but this time he would have a chance to run against a team of equal players.

The ball was snapped to Bruce who ran right and handed the ball to Roger Swaim, who headed left to sell his run to the defense and then handed the ball to Joe who was heading quickly to the right. There was only one big problem. Roger did not give the ball to Joe cleanly. He missed Joe's pocket and the ball bounced to the ground. Joe quickly dove on the loose ball as he was immediately hit in the back by knees, elbows, and helmets.

"Oh!" Joe hollered as the referees had missed some late hits.

"Sorry about that, Joe. I missed your pocket," Roger said as we went back to the huddle.

"Sorry, Joe" John said. "My man was one of those who hit you in the back. I'll get him next time."

"No problem!" Joe said as he winced in pain.

Coach Shull waited awhile as he stuck to straight ahead plays and short passes. Bruce passed the last ten yards to Dalton Coram for a touchdown. West Yadkin led 7-0 after Roger ran the extra point.

"Good drive, team!" Archie said. "Let's get the ball back now."

Archie and Benny Ashley hit the Walnut Cove running back on both sides and the ball popped loose at the West Yadkin thirty-four yard line. Roger Swaim recovered the fumble. We were in business again.

Double Reverse Works

Coach Shull again called Joe's play, "double reverse L." Joe was ready. He looked to John in the huddle and winked.

"No missed blocks this time, please," Joe said as John smiled.

The ball went to Bruce who ran right and handed off to Roger who ran left and again handed off to Joe who was moving to the right. Guess what? Again, the pocket was missed and the ball hit the ground. Should I dive on the ball? Joe thought. Go for it!

Quick as a cat, Joe picked up the ball and headed around right end in a sprint. The defense had been sucked in when they saw the fumble. Joe was on the way down the sidelines. No one was within thirty yards of him. He was going, going, gone. It was a sixty-six yard run for the first touchdown of Joe's career. He did not see many touchdowns so he was very happy as were his teammates who met him in the end zone.

After the extra point, which was run in by Bruce, the score was 14-0. The final was 20-6. We had won our first game. Our record was now 1-4. Joe ran for 124 yards that night.

"Great game, boys!" Coach Shull said in the locker room. "It feels good, doesn't it? Way to stick with it, Joe."

"It sure does!" Joe said. "Thanks, Coach!"

Chapter 33
Homecoming

Practice was more fun this week. A win sure can liven up a team. This week was going to be a big week. It was homecoming week. Joe and Archie were looking forward to crowning the queen. Roger Swaim was hurt again and did not want to participate in the queen kissing ceremony. Joe was excited. What a nice week to be captain of the football team!

It would be a big week for our band and for all the students of good old West Yadkin High School. Homecoming would draw the biggest crowd of the year. People who hadn't been to a game all year would be here this week.

The cheerleading squad of Judy Pardue, Rhoda Morrison, Peggy Ireland, Sue Money, Doretha Gardner, Mildred Pardue, Jean Brown, Shirley Burgess, Sue Doss, Sylvia Trivette, Vena Carpenter, Vonda Groce, Fairy Bray, and Cousin Lorene Brown did a great job all year and really enjoyed this week.

The homecoming court was made up of Cynthia Allen and Kay Brown of the freshman class and Jean Brown and Libby Golden of the sophomore class. The junior class was represented by Earline Reavis and Linda Brown while the senior attendants were Nancy Reinhardt and Sonja Royal. The homecoming queen was the friendliest girl in school, Donna Johnson, whom Joe had known since the first grade in Mrs. Gough's class. Joe and Archie took a lot of ribbing from the team during the week. Everyone was wondering about how long the kiss for the queen would last. It was all in fun.

"Ya'll are just jealous!" Joe said.

"You got that right!" Nolan Brown said. "We envy you." Nolan was a good friend and not related to Joe and John.

It was Friday night, October 17, 1958, and homecoming at West Yadkin High School. We had a lot of fun planned for this night, but we knew we had a tough football game ahead of us. Pilot Mountain was a big, strong, mountain team. They were good on offense and on defense.

Joe knew it was going to be a tough night after he was clobbered on the opening kickoff. He had to return all of the kickoffs as other players had their nicks and bruises again. Roger Swaim was gone for the year. West Yadkin could not get much going in the first half and were down 13-0 at halftime.

Coach Shull talked to us for a few minutes in the end zone while waiting for the halftime festivities to start. Joe and Archie left the squad to take their place with the senior class representatives.

One by one the attendants and escorts were introduced to the overflow crowd. The freshman class went first followed by the sophomore class. Then the junior class attendants were announced to the cheering crowd. Finally, the senior class representatives were escorted out to midfield.

Now it was time for Joe and Archie to escort Donna Johnson, our beautiful queen, onto the field. Joe had Donna's left arm while Archie had her right arm. They slowly made their way to midfield, enjoying every moment.

Kiss for the Queen

Mr. Wright handed Joe the crown to place on Donna's head. Joe slowly and carefully placed the crown on her head and then planted a kiss on her that drew "oohs" and "aahs" from the cheering crowd.

"Congratulations, Donna! You are a beautiful queen," Joe said.

"Thank you, Joe," Donna said.

Next it was Archie's turn to kiss the queen. He kissed her and the ceremony was over. Halftime that you would remember forever was now history. It was time to get back to the football game.

We showed a little more life in the second half scoring on a pass play to Dalton Coram to cut the score to 13-7. But it was short lived as Pilot Mountain marched back downfield and scored quickly to move ahead by 20-7. They would add another touchdown in the fourth quarter to win by 26-7. They had too much size on us. We could not handle them.

Joe had a decent game with thirty-five yards on five carries. The bruised offensive line was again a sore spot for the night. Our record fell to 1-5.

We had two weeks before our next game against the toughest opponent yet, Elkin. We could use two weeks to try and heal up before this game in Elkin. We had good practices and needed them to help build up our spirits for this game in which Elkin would be a heavy favorite.

We tied up a lot of tobacco these last two weeks. Finally on Thursday, October 30, Mr. Shore took our last load to the market. The tobacco had been selling good and it was a big relief to get all of it to the market before November 1. This year's sale would be the last time that Joe would go to the market. He would not be around for the summer season next year.

No Blocking

It was Friday night, October 31, 1958. West Yadkin traveled to Elkin to meet the "Bucking Elks." It was not much of a game as we were outclassed from the beginning. The final score was 41-6. Joe was beat up like he was during the Yadkinville game. Joe carried the ball ten times for forty yards, but we could not generate any consistent offense against Elkin's tough defense.

"Elkin and Yadkinville hit me harder than anyone else all year," Joe told Archie after the game.

"Sorry we didn't give you more blocking, Joe," Archie said. "We just need some more players!"

At school on Monday, Coach pointed out that this was another game to forget.

Let's concentrate on this week's game up in the mountains," Coach said. "It'll be cold up there, football weather, and we can win. Now get dressed for practice."

Horse Play - Injury

Joe was getting dressed. He had on his shoulder pads, pants, and was moving over to sit down to put on his football cleats when all of a sudden, a couple of players were horse playing around. They turned over a bench, which hit Joe's left foot on top immediately rupturing a blood vein. The blood vein instantly rose up the size of an egg.

Joe was in pain and horrified at the egg size knot on his foot. Nolan Brown ran quickly to get Coach Shull who got ice on the foot right away. Coach looked towards the two culprits without saying a word. He didn't have to as their heads were hanging down.

"A couple of you guys carry Joe out to one of the buses out front. I'll go to the office and get a driver to take him down to Dr. Bell," Coach said as Archie and Nolan assisted Joe to the bus.

Joe had played all year without injury and today was injured in the dressing room by the horse playing of a couple of pranksters.

"How in the world did you get this egg on your foot, Joe?" Dr. Bell asked. "Were you playing football barefooted?"

"No! I got it in the locker room. A couple of boys were horsing around and knocked a bench over on my foot," Joe said.

"I bet I could guess who the two boys are. They are always into something," Dr. Bell said.

Dr. Bell was West Yadkin's biggest fan. He always supported the school. He loved sports and always took good care of the players. Joe has many fond memories of Dr. Bell and his association with the school. The athletic field would soon bear Dr. Bell's name. It was an honor, which was well deserved.

"You'll need to stay off this foot for a week or so, Joe. I don't imagine you will be able to play this week. Come back to me about Thursday and I'll check it out. About all we can do is to use ice today and then stay off of it to let the swelling and soreness heal up."

Joe went back to school and got dressed as the team was finishing their practice for the day.

"Dr. Bell wants me to come back Thursday, Coach. He says I probably won't be playing this week. I don't want to miss but we have to wait till Thursday and see," Joe said.

"Okay, Joe. It's a tough break, but it could have broken your foot," Coach said.

Archie took Joe home and was really steamed up about the horse play. "Coach has been telling those two all year to stop that horse play. He should kick them off the team," Archie said in a riled tone.

"See you tomorrow, Archie. Thanks for the ride," Joe said.

"I'll come by and get you in the morning so you won't have to mess with the old bus," Archie said as he left.

"What happened to you?" Jane asked as she saw Joe's bandaged left foot as he hopped in the door.

"What's wrong with my boy?" Mom asked.

"Were you playing football without your shoes, Joe?' Danny asked.

"Where's Dad?" Joe asked as he wanted to tell his story only one time.

"He's milking the cows," Mom said. Soon, Dad was in the kitchen and supper was on the table. He hadn't noticed Joe's foot.

Mom prayed, "Heavenly Father, thank you for this good day and for health and strength. Thank you for this food. We pray that you'd bless it. Be with the sick, the shut-in, and the bereaved. We pray that you'd be with Elmer. Keep him safe. We pray you'd help Joe's foot to get better. Thanks for all your goodness. We thank you in Jesus' name. Amen. Amen."

"What's wrong with Joe's foot?" Dad asked in a curious voice. "Did I miss something?"

Joe told his story about what happened. They were all amazed that he did not get hurt on the football field but in the locker room because of horse play.

"I agree with Archie! The two players should be kicked off the team," Mom said.

"They sure should be!" Dad agreed.

On Thursday evening, Joe went back to see Dr. Bell to get word on the game tomorrow.

"You need to miss the game, Joe, and get rest so you can be ready for next week," Dr. Bell said after looking at the black and blue bruised foot. "You won't do the team any good this week no better than you're moving around."

Joe relayed the message to Coach Shull who was not surprised.

"You need to stay off your feet as much as you can, Joe. Maybe you'll be okay for next week's game. That'll be your last game," Coach Shull said.

Joe stayed off his feet all he could. He didn't even go to the game at Lansing. John gave him a report on the game about midnight when he got home.

"We won 19-13! Boy, was it cold up there in them mountains!" John said as he got in the top bunk bed and was asleep immediately.

"That makes our record 2-6!" Joe said as John was out of it already. "We need a good game next week to finish 3-6."

On Monday, Joe was still limping a little, but his foot felt better. He moved slowly and carefully in practice Monday and Tuesday before going near top speed on Wednesday. By Thursday evening's light practice, Joe was feeling good.

Chapter 34
Joe's Best Game

Coach Shull spoke to his team in skull practice. On Friday. "This is it, boys! We have an excellent chance to win this week. Let's close the season with a good, strong win. Think and run the plays like we do in practice. Win!"

It was a fun bus ride to Dobson, which is located between Elkin and Mount Airy in Surry County. It would be the last football game for Archie and Joe. They were pumped up and ready to play.

"Let's close out with a win, Joe!" Archie said as they sat together on the bus. "We can do it!"

"We will do the job tonight. I have a feeling," Joe said. "It's good to have Roger playing again." Roger Swaim was going to play his last game also after earlier being listed as out for the year. He would not be full speed but he would be a big help.

The first quarter was 0-0. We moved the ball but could not score. Joe was running the best he had run all year. The double-reverse was working every time it was tried. On the first play of the second quarter, Joe scored a touchdown on a one yard plunge. With the extra point, the score was 7-0. Joe had run the double-reverse play two times on this drive gaining thirty yards each time.

Dodson took the kickoff and went downfield quickly to our forty yard line. They tried to tie the score on the next play on a long pass down to their right end. The pass was overthrown and Joe intercepted it at the ten yard line. He headed back the other way first to his left, then across the middle and, finally, following blocks by Archie and Roger to the right and in the clear about the fifty yard line.

Joe had clear sailing the rest of the way and scored to make the score 13-0. The extra point made it 14-0. There was joy on the visiting sidelines as we were getting ready to open this game up. Roger Swaim made the score 21-0 with a two yard run and the extra point pass to Dalton Coram.

Double Reverse - Again

With about four minutes left in the first half, we got the ball back at our thirty yard line. The play call was double-reverse left again. Joe was ready. He got the ball and broke into the clear around right end. He was galloping like a pony when he was hit from the blind side after a forty yard gain.

Joe was winded and almost knocked out by the blow. He lay on the ground in pain. He couldn't breathe and felt like his ribs were cracked. In a couple of minutes, Joe got to his feet and was helped off the field by his two best friends, Archie and Roger.

"You okay, Joe?" they both asked. "Boy, you sure have been running the ball!"

"I'll be okay," Joe said. He couldn't breathe very good yet as he received a big hand from the West Yadkin sidelines. He sat down on the bench and would watch the rest of the game from the sidelines. His high school football career was now over.

Joe had his best game ever in less than two quarters because of the injury. He had run the double-reverse five times for a total of one hundred fifty yards and gained thirty yards in five other runs. He ran back one kickoff and two punts for forty-five yards and the ninety yards on the interception for a total combined yardage of three hundred fifteen yards.

Joe's ribs were hurting and he would be sore for a few days, but he was happy with his last game. We won 41-7 as Bruce, Chicken, and Johnny Shore would score a touchdown in the last half for the final total of forty-one points, our best game of the year by far.

Joe would remember sitting on the beach the last half and listening to the fans. It had been a long year and they were going to enjoy this game.

"Good run, Roger!" Joe heard someone say. Someone had arrived late and had missed the first half.

Peggy Ireland, one of the freshman cheerleaders, was telling them about the first half. "You should have seen Joe Brown when he intercepted a pass down close to the goal and ran it all the way back for a touchdown. He ran all over the field. But he got hurt right before halftime and has not played anymore."

The bus ride was fun on the way back. Even in pain, Joe enjoyed the fun with the team. What great memories he had from this year playing football! He was going to miss the good times.

Joe was sore the next morning as Dad headed his work crew to the cornfield. It was the second Saturday of corn pulling. Last week's work had been shucked along with the good popcorn crop.

"You're moving kind of funny, Joe. Are you okay?" Dad asked as they were starting to pull the first load of the day.

"I'm okay, Dad. My ribs are sore. I got popped real good last night," Joe said.

"I know! John told me about it. He also said you ran wild with the ball and scored two times. That's good," Dad said.

The soreness would not hurt so much after a day of pulling corn. By the time Archie came over to make the usual run to Elkin, Joe was feeling good. The hot shower sure did help.

"Are you okay, Joe?" Archie asked as he and Roger Swaim were ready to go to town.

"You seem to be moving okay now, Joe," Roger said.

"I'm doing better. The long day in the cornfield helped loosen me up," Joe said as he and John got in the car to head to Elkin.

"You got your name in the paper, Joe," Archie said. "Did you see it?"

"Yes! I saw it. They sure messed up your name, didn't they, Roger?" Joe laughed. "They think that your name is Ben."

"Is it Ben Roger or Roger Ben?" John joked with Roger.

On Monday, November 17, basketball practice was under way. No matter how good shape you think you're in, each sport is different and you hurt when getting ready. Joe always dreaded the first week of any practice. The wind sprints could be painful.

After two weeks of practice, Joe again felt like his Dad needed him at home to help. Joe knew that he would not be home much longer and wanted to help all he could. So he talked with Coach Shull and again decided to wait until after the Christmas break to play basketball. Coach Shull understood Joe's position and respected it.

Joe was scheduled to be a starter and was after returning to the team in January. In the meantime, Joe and John put in a lot of time getting the work done around the farm. The chicken house work was always time consuming. By the first of the year, Joe and Dad figured that the work that had got behind during football season would all be caught up.

Monday, December 1, came in cold as you would expect. School was going good and, as hard as it was to believe, Joe's days at West Yadkin were winding down.

"We won't be here much longer, Joe," Archie said at school. "Our time here is about gone. I'll be glad when you get back out here where you belong on our basketball team. We're not doing very good at all."

The boys' team was winless after the first four games. The girls' team was good with a 3-1 record. Donna Johnson and Sonja Royal were a scoring machine and fun to watch. They seemed to always score over twenty points a game each.

The girls' game was one of the most interesting sports events you could watch. The team was made up of three guards who only played defense and three forwards who played offense. Neither could cross over center court to the other end. A player could dribble only two times before either shooting or passing the ball. Under this format, each team would put their best scorers against the other team's best defensive players.

The good girls' team would have one or two tall players who would get the ball on the inside and hold the ball high above everyone else and score at will. Donna and Sonja both were taller than average, but they were good athletes and good shooters, too.

School closed down for Christmas on Friday, December 19, 1958, and would reopen on Thursday, January 1, 1959. It would be an enjoyable time off with Joe doing a little rabbit hunting and squirrel hunting. Joe, Archie, and John would spend a lot of time in Elkin "dragging" Main Street. That was the thing to do on Friday and Saturday nights.

Elmer would be spending his last Christmas in Germany this year. The whole family was looking forward to his return to North Carolina in April. It seemed like he had been gone for so long.

Christmas 1958

At 5:00 a.m. on December 25, the Brown household was alive, as always, on Christmas day. It was a time of happiness as Wayne, Elvie, Rose, and Tip were home to enjoy Christmas with us. Gift opening was a fun time as it always was. Joe got mostly clothes this year and was well pleased with everything.

"Merry Christmas!" Grandpa said as he made his usual Christmas morning visit. He had slowed down a lot in the past few years, but he loved his Christmas morning visit. He had his cup of Maxwell House coffee with us before he left with one of those long cigars in his mouth. He was happy, even though he did not feel good.

"We'll see you later, youngins!" Grandpa said.

"Bye, Grandpa! See you a little later," Joe said.

After dinner, it was time to go to Grandpa and Grandma Proctor's for the Christmas gathering.

"He still hasn't cut the long weeds down. I guess he's waiting for the snow to knock them down," Dad made his usual comments as he drove down the driveway to the house.

The house was packed with most of Mom's brothers and sisters with their families. Grandma ushered all of us into her kitchen to get a couple of her "better than good" biscuits. They were tastier than ever.

"You sure do make a tasty biscuit, Grandma," Joe said as he was on #3.

"Thank you, Joe! I'm glad you like them," Grandma said.

"I don't just like them. I love them, Grandma!" Joe said as they made their way into the front room where music and gifts filled the room. What a good time of fun this was! The family was growing all the time. Grandma so loved having her house full of kin.

"It sure was good to see my family," Mom said on the way home. "I wish I could see them more often. Some of them I don't see but once or twice a year. Everybody stays so busy."

"Families used to live closer together, didn't they, Mom?" Joe asked.

"Yes! They did back when everyone was farming. Those were the good, old days. Now, everybody seems to be scattered out all over the country," Mom said.

On Wednesday, December 31, 1958, Dad's family went to prayer meeting as was normal at Mineral Springs Baptist Church. It was a long night for Joe, John, and Archie who stayed up to bring in the new year, 1959.

"It sure was a short night's sleep!" Joe told Archie at school on January 1, 1959. The new year was here. Joe's senior year continued to disappear. Joe and Archie were counting the days. Soon, the senior trip to Washington would be here.

The Long Season

On Monday, January 5, Joe was back at basketball practice. It was good to be back. Joe loved all sports and competition. He would enjoy the last two months of basketball, even though the team was awful.

"It's good to see you back, Joe," Archie said as he gave Joe a ride home.

"Maybe we can win a couple of games now," Roger said as he also was catching a ride with Archie.

It was not to be with this team. They played good in spurts, but could not play consistently. The team was so small with Archie and Roger as the biggest players. They were not tall compared to other teams we played.

Soon, Joe was back in the starting lineup with Archie, Roger, Larry Allred, and Joe Doss. Joe had been working hard on his jump shot. He had to have the outside shot as short as he was. He was never much on driving with the ball.

"You're going to start tonight, Joe," Sue Money told him out in the hall. It seems like she, Brenda Swaim, and Willodean Shore had been bugging Coach Shull to start Joe. Sue and Joe used to date, but were not now.

"Can I ride to the game with you, Joe?" Sue asked.

"Sure. I'll be by to get you at 6:15 p.m. Will that get you here soon enough?" Joe asked. Sue was a cheerleader.

"Yes! That's good," Sue said.

Joe did start tonight and had a decent game of six points in another losing effort. The losses continued to mount for this team, which could not get a break.

"We're still having fun, I know, but I'd like to win a few games," Joe told Archie and Roger.

"That sure would be nice!" Archie said.

"All we can do is to keep hustling and play our best," Roger said. Still the team continued to lose. Coach Shull tried to keep us loose, but the losses did not help with our attitudes. We would scrape and sometimes have words in practice, all out of frustration over losing.

On Wednesday, January 21, Joe was eighteen years old. He couldn't believe he was finally eighteen.

The Funny Date

Joe also dated another cheerleader, Wanda Brown, two or three times. Wanda had been dating Bruce Ashburn for a long time but they were not dating now.

Joe remembers one particular date with Wanda that was funny. We were playing at Courtney. Joe picked up Wanda at her house up in Ramcat. He drove her to the game and after playing, Joe got dressed and came out of the dressing room to take his date home. He did not see Wanda anywhere.

"I have a message for you, Joe," Nolan Brown said as he saw Joe looking around.

"Wanda left with Bruce a little while ago. Sorry!"

"No problem. I figured they would get back together," Joe said. He wasn't going to worry about it.

"She shouldn't have done you this way," Nolan said. "That's not very nice."

"It's okay," Joe added. It was kind of funny.

The next day in the hall, Wanda came up to Joe.

"I'm sorry about last night, Joe," Wanda said. "I did you wrong and I'm sorry."

"It's okay. No hard feelings," Joe said. Wanda and Bruce would later get married.

So Close

Was Friday the thirteenth a good day for West Yadkin to snap their season long losing streak? It looked like it most of the game as we led all the way with Joe, Archie, Roger, and Larry Allred leading the way. Joe tapped in a miss by Larry with thirty seconds left in the game to give West Yadkin a 39-38 lead. Joe had scored eight points.

The gym was rocking and loud as Sparta brought the ball down for the last shot. Cheerleaders were biting their nails, holding their breath, while all the time, they were trying to cheer.

Sparta's big man got the ball in the middle and made an easy lay up with only two seconds left. A long frustration shot by Roger missed and the losing streak would continue.

The Yadkin County tournament next week would be the last chance for this team to win. Wouldn't it be nice to pull an upset in the tournament?

Meanwhile back on the farm, it was plant bed sowing day. The last crop of tobacco that Joe would help set out was to start today. It was a good, warm day, especially for February. The plant beds were sowed and covered. Dad's crop for this year was cut back to twelve acres. Mr. Shore's allotment was cut back some by the government flue cured program.

Dad thought twelve acres would be a plenty for this crew, as he knew Joe would be gone at the end of May.

"I sure wish you'd stay and help me, Joe," Dad said. "I'd let you have four acres and you'd do okay with it."

"I don't think there's much of a future anymore on the farm. The government keeps cutting the acreage for the "little man" and soon the big farms will completely run the little man out of business. It's a sad state of affairs, I think," Joe said.

"You're right! The farm is not what it used to be," Dad said. "You can do much better in the city with your education."

It was February 19, 1959, and the Yadkin County basketball tournament was under way in Yadkinville. Joe started at guard and played one of his best all around games in another losing effort. He scored six points as the team lost to Courtney and was eliminated from the tournament. The season ended at a woeful 0-19. What a nightmare this season was!

The girls' team had fared much better this year. They lost out on Friday night in the semifinals but had a great season with a winning record. Would it be great to have a winning record, Joe thought.

On Monday, February 23, John turned the magical sixteen years old. He was now old enough to get his driver's license. Where has time gone?

In school assembly today, February 27, the girls' basketball team challenged the boys' team to a game. The gym was filled as the boys had to wear a "sack" dress and play the girls' rules. Joe had a lot of laughs and got a lot of laughs as he literally wore a "sack." Mom had converted one of Dad's old fertilizer sacks for Joe to wear.

"Now that's what I call a sack dress, Joe!" Donna kidded Joe.

Joe, Archie, and Roger led the boys as they played a good game, which was nip and tuck all the way until Joe and Archie hit late baskets to lead the boys to a close win. It was so much fun and seemed to be enjoyed by all who attended the game.

Baseball season was under way. Joe could not play because of the farm work, but he enjoyed attending many of the games and helping out Coach Carter by being the official scorer. West Yadkin always had a good baseball team. This year's team was very young, but were good.

Tommy Wilmoth, a freshman, was the best pitcher on the team. Dalton Coram and his brother Benny were also good pitchers who could catch and play other positions as well. Joe's friend, Gene Williams, was the regular catcher who had always been a good player, but, like Joe, he had never learned to hit the curve ball.

Joe so regrets that he did not have the opportunity to play Little League ball and learn in organized ball how to play. He was never able to play because of the farm work. He understood how he was needed on the farm, but he still had wanted to, at least, have a chance to learn and play on the high school team and maybe have a long shot at his dream.

It was windy March again. The weather was warming up. The school year was winding down. Dad was getting the land turned for the tobacco and corn crops.

Elmer Is Home

Elmer is home from Germany and out of the Air Force. As normal, Elmer came in during the night and got in bed. Mom knew that time was close and had been expecting him soon.

"There's my boy!" Mom said as she gave him a big hug. "You're early. I didn't expect you until the end of the month."

"I got out early because of all the leave that I didn't take," Elmer said. "It's good to be home."

"It's good to see you, too, son," Mom said with a tear in her eyes.

Elmer could not believe how much Joe and John had grown.

"You have just shot up and you're taller than me now!" Elmer said in his Yankee accent he had picked up.

It was good to see Elmer. He stayed around the rest of the week and then headed to Greensboro where he started to work for Burlington Industries in the mailroom. He would be home every Friday night and stay until Sunday evening when he would have to return to Greensboro. Elmer, Wayne, and Rose were in Greensboro and soon, Joe would move there, too.

The New York Yankees

On Friday, March 27, 1959, Joe, Archie, Gene Williams, and James Nicholson went to Winston to Ernie Shore Field to see the New York Yankees play an exhibition game against the Philadelphia Phillies. It was a big thrill for Joe to see his role model, heroes, play. He got his picture taken with Yankee catcher, Yogi Berra. What a feeling it was!

"Thank you, Yogi," Joe said after the picture. He could not get anywhere close to his hero, Mickey Mantle, who was always followed by a horde of fans.

Joe got pictures of the great manager, Casey Stengel, and also a distant picture of Mantle and Hank Bauer. He also got several autographs, not Mantle, unfortunately. He could not get close to him. The autographs included Yogi Berra and the World Series perfect game pitcher, Don Larsen. The game was thoroughly enjoyed by Joe. What a big moment this was in his life!

Joe remembered that Ernie Shore, for whom the field was named, used to pitch for the Yankees also back in the mid-twenties. He was a great pitcher who, along with Babe Ruth, another great pitcher who could also hit, helped build the Yankee dynasty.

Chapter 35
Washington Trip

It was Monday, March 30, 1959, and the day the senior class had been waiting for all year. The trip to Washington, D.C., a senior tradition for years was finally here. Joe, Archie, Tommy Seagraves, and James Nicholson were the only boys in the class going on the trip. All other boys were busy working or not interested in going. The price of the trip was pretty steep at about $35.00, not including food.

Our class was honored by the fact that our principal, Mr. C.C. Wright and Mrs. Wright were going along as chaperones. Mr. Wright had always been close to our class as we were his first class as principal. It was going to be a good, fun trip.

The boys were greatly outnumbered by the girls. Joe liked the odds. He would get to know many of his classmates better on this trip away from schoolwork and teachers. Mr. and Mrs. Wright were excellent chaperones and loosened up and really enjoyed the trip.

898 Steps Up, 898 Steps Down

Joe and Donna Johnson had always been friends and they would pal around together on this trip. The whole week they would sit together and make all the tours with each other. Joe remembers especially the visit to the Washington Monument. Donna did not want to ride the elevator that took all the others to the top, so she and Joe made the hike to the top of the monument, all 898 steps.

After a short stop for the viewing from atop the monument, Joe and Donna made the 898 steps back down. They were both soaking wet from the hike. It was fun, though, as we were the only ones in the class who could say that they had walked all the way up and back down. Everyone else was packed into the elevator for the ride up and down. How dull that sounds!

"We did it, Joe! Do you believe we walked all those 898 steps up and down? Boy, am I tired!" Donna said.

"I'm tired, too! It was quite a hike, wasn't it?" Joe said. "We will always remember all those steps, won't we?" It would always be a conversation piece for them. They would never forget.

Our class stayed at the Burlington Hotel on New York Avenue for the week. All of the four boys roomed together and decided that they would not sleep all week. It was a trial of patience for each one of them. Every time one of them would doze off, they would get hit with shaving cream on their hands or their toes. What a mess this makes when they were tickled under the nose!

On other occasions, you might find a doughnut around your big toe when you dozed. We were just determined not to go to sleep. By the end of the week, there could be some very sleepy and somewhat ill boys. It was all in fun, though.

The four boys all bought rebel hats on the way to D.C. and wore them for the whole trip. They wanted to let D.C. know where we were from, as if the accent would not let them know.

Girl Scouts

Joe ran into a group of girls scouts in the hotel lobby. The girls seemed to fall for Joe.

"My, you're handsome!" one of the ten year old girls told Joe.

"Thank you!" Joe said as he fascinated the youngsters from New York City. They loved to hear Joe talk.

Joe's classmates kidded him the whole trip about his girl scout friends. The girl scouts left after a couple of days. Joe hated to see them go.

"I'm surprised they didn't take you with them," Brenda Swaim said to Joe. "They really did fall for you."

"They were sweet girls," Joe said with a smile.

The fun week continued with great trips to the Treasury Department where all of our money was made.

"If I could spend an hour in here, I think I'd be okay," Joe said. "Just think how much money I could pocket."

The trip to the F.B.I. was another interesting one. Joe had always liked J. Edgar Hoover, the long time director of the F.B.I.

"Watch them fingerprint all of us while we're here," Tommy said with a laugh.

The Lincoln Memorial was another great visit. All the history that was being taken in this week was amazing. This week could be more of an education than all the history they ever learned in the classroom.

"You will remember this trip and its history more than anything you ever learned from a book," Mr. Wright told us. "It's quite an opportunity for ya'll."

The Washington Zoo was a fun visit, too. Animals of all kinds were here from all over the world. The monkeys were funny looking and entertaining. Tommy allowed as how some of them look like a few of our classmates.

"Don't say a word, Tommy!" Doretha Gardner said. "I see one over there that looks exactly like you."

The visit to the White House, Capitol, and Congress in session was a highlight of the trip. Imagine being in here with all the history of the past one hundred seventy-five years.

"Just think about all the presidents who have lived here over the years," Joe said as he walked through the White House. "I would have liked to have been here back in the days of Washington, Adams, and Jefferson."

"I can just see you, Joe!" James said.

"Me, too, Joe!" Archie said. "You might have been president, too."

Seeing Congress in session and the Supreme Court in action was a completion of the three branches of government at work. The Supreme Court seemed pomp and British like in their tradition, Joe thought.

"They seem like they are royalty!" Joe said as he closely observed them.

The whole Washington trip was so much fun and a learning experience for everyone. The monument was a favorite part, but Joe enjoyed the whole week. The visit to the Smithsonian Institute was seeing a lot of different parts of our country in action. This institute had memories from the past of about every walk of life imaginable. You name it and it was there. From the first airplane flight to today's advanced flying machine, all were displayed.

Pictures or models of heroes from the past were here for visitors to see everyday. This attraction was always a favorite of visitors in our nation's capital.

And, of course, Washington, D.C. on the banks of the Potomac River was beautiful with its magnificent cherry trees blooming. Their fragrance lit up the air throughout the city. You wondered about the story of George Washington and his famous cherry tree that he chopped down.

Joe always imagined and dreamed about living in the old days. He thought it would have been so cool to have been with the minutemen or with George Washington's troops at Valley Forge. History was so exciting! This trip was also an exciting part of Joe's life. He learned so much in the short week in the nation's capital.

The week passed by so quickly. Joe, Archie, Tommy, and James were sleepy eyed each day and by the end of the week, they could barely keep their eyes open. Everyone stayed up late, but we just stayed up. The whole group was so close by week's end, we were just all buddies. We thought we knew each other after twelve years in school together but we really got to know one another this week.

The girls on the trip, Doretha Gardner, Donna Johnson, Margaret Allen, Gail Swaim, Sonja Royal, Mary Leigh Walker, Hazel Hudson, Margaret Wilkins, Sylvia Trivette, Brenda Swaim, Willodean Shore, Margaret Shore, and Mildred Pardue were kind of like our sisters. Unlike most classes, there were not any dating couples in this class. We all liked each other, some better than others, of course, but we all would have done anything for a classmate in need.

The last night in Washington, everyone gathered in one of the rooms to talk, sing, and just cut up. Mr. and Mrs. Wright were not with us, but, no matter, as we behaved as if they were there. We talked about how much fun this week had been and how much we all thought about each other.

Our class "house mother" Doretha Gardner was our storyteller and told a story. She was great to make up stories.

Soon, it was curfew time and all the girls were in their rooms getting packed up to return home tomorrow. The boys were in their room ready for another all night session of nothing but fun.

"Can you believe that we've stayed up all week?" Joe asked as he was trying to keep his eyes open.

"I believe it!" Archie said. "I'm about dead."

"I think we can make it, Joe," Tommy said.

"Let's go for it!" James said as he was breaking open another box of doughnuts. We ate doughnuts all week.

"Remember we have to be on the bus at 7:00 in the morning," Joe said. "Mr. Wright wants us to leave on time so we can get back home before late tomorrow."

"We'll still be up. No problem!" Tommy said.

Sleepyheads

Next morning at 7:00, there was a problem as Mr. Wright was taking head count on the bus.

"Where are the boys?" Mr. Wright said. "Has anyone seen them this morning?" No one had seen them this morning. Mr. Wright proceeded to go knock on their door. After several knocks, Archie opened the door.

"We're waiting on you, boys!" Mr. Wright said as the boys scrambled to get going. They did not make it on the last night. They had fallen asleep sometime in the wee hours of the morning.

"I bet we're in trouble," Joe said as they washed their faces and brushed their teeth hurriedly.

"Wonder when we went to sleep?" Tommy asked.

"Last time I noticed, it was 5:05!" Joe said. "I guess we bombed out about that time."

Joe, Archie, Tommy, and James ran to the bus and got aboard to a round of cheers from all over the bus.

"Sleepy head, sleepy head, couldn't get out of bed! Sleepy head, sleepy head!" the girls said as Mr. and Mrs. Wright and the bus driver laughed.

Donna had saved Joe a seat and greeted him with a smile.

"I knew you couldn't go without sleep forever, Joe!" she said. "When you weren't here, I knew that you had overslept."

Joe slept a good part of the way home after breakfast in Washington. After a stop at Thomas Jefferson's Monticello in Charlottesville, Va., and lunch nearby, the last leg of the trip was under way. Joe and Donna talked the rest of the way home as they reflected on the fun week.

"This trip has been so much fun, hasn't it?" Donna said.

"It sure has! I hate to see it end. Soon, our senior year will be over. We have a lot to do when we get back with our class play, class night, our banquets, and then graduation. Can you believe it?" Joe said.

"It's really hard to believe. It's about over!" Donna said.

At 4:00 p.m., the bus pulled into the semi circle of good, old West Yadkin High School. The dream week was over. It was time to get back to schoolwork to complete the year. Their lives would never be the same. This week would live on in their minds for the rest of their lives.

Roger Swaim was waiting to give Joe and Archie a ride home.

"Thank you, Mr. and Mrs. Wright for going with us on this trip. It was nice of you to go," Joe told them as everyone was leaving.

"We enjoyed the trip. You are a good group. We will always be close to this group of students," Mr. Wright said.

"Did you see Ike?" Roger asked as soon as we were on our way home.

"No, but we saw where he lives," Joe said. "It sure was a fun trip. Wish you could have gone with us."

"I like your hats!" Roger said as he drove along. "Where did you get them?"

"We got them in Richmond on the way up to Washington," Archie said. "We wanted everyone to know that we're rebels."

Roger dropped Joe off first and started to leave.

"Do ya'll want to go to Elkin tonight?" Archie asked.

"Sure!" Joe said and Roger nodded okay.

"I'll be back over about 6:30 to get you and John then!" Archie said.

"Thanks for the ride!" Joe told Roger.

It was good to be home. Joe went inside to give Mom and Jane a hug. Joe and John did the chores and were soon ready to go to town. John asked Joe and Archie questions all the way about their trip.

"You'll have a good time in two years when you go, John," Archie said. "You've got it to look forward to in 1961."

Chapter 36
The End Nears

The school year seemed to fly after "the trip." We had many things to get ready for over the next month and a half. There was the senior play to learn parts in a short period of time. Joe didn't have to worry about learning lines. He was a ghost in the play and all he had to do was to come through the house at just the right time and let out a blood curdling laugh. All that took was a little practice and Joe made a perfect ghost, or so he was told.

On Friday morning, May 8, West Yadkin held their annual athletic banquet. Joe always enjoyed this banquet which recognized the achievements of all the many athletes who had lettered in football, basketball, baseball, and cheerleading.

Coach Shull was the master of ceremonies for the banquet. He and Mr. Carter awarded letters and trophies for most valuable players.

Archie King was most valuable lineman while Roger Swaim was named most valuable back.

"I don't deserve this trophy, Joe. You do. You led the team all year. I missed so many games," Roger told Joe as he came back to the table. Roger put the trophy in the dash of his car and left it there for weeks before he took it in the house. It didn't matter all that much to him. Roger also won the most valuable award in baseball. He could hit the ball harder and faster than anyone Joe had seen play at West Yadkin.

It was a fun night, especially after a bad start. Joe had a date with a cheerleader, Fairy Bray. They had already dated a couple of times. She was a sweet girl.

The Fall

When Joe went to Fairy's house to pick her up, it was raining cats and dogs, complete with thunder and lightning. Joe pulled the car up in front of the house and made a dash for the front porch where Fairy and her mom and dad were waiting. Joe made quick football like moves through the muddy yard and then fell flat on his face right in front of the Bray family.

Joe was so embarrassed! He wanted to stay face down, but he quickly got up and onto the porch.

"I did a trick for you, didn't I?" Joe said as he did not know anything better to say.

"I'm sorry, Joe," Fairy said as she tried to wipe off the mud from Joe's neat banquet jacket.

"Don't bother with it!" Joe said. "I'm going to have to go back home and change clothes. This outfit has had it. If you're ready, we'll go. We'll have to hurry."

Joe drove back home and miracle working Mom helped him get another dashing outfit ready. Fairy sat in the front room and talked to Jane.

Later after the banquet, Joe and Fairy laughed about Joe's fall. Joe was so glad that she did not laugh at him when he fell.

Only three weeks of school remained for Joe. It was hard to imagine after twelve long years, that it was about to end.

Class Play

The class play was coming up Friday night. Play practice had been so much fun. Joe, Archie, Donna, Sonja, Brenda, Gail, Doretha, Carolyn Whitaker, Billy Turner, Tommy Seagraves, Gene Williams, James Nicholson, and others were drawn so much closer by the good times and bad times of play practice. Practice was nightly for the past two weeks.

Mrs. Wishon and Mr. John Moretz, our class sponsors, were patient with us and guided the cast to learn their lines and to do a great job. After practice, we enjoyed fun of snacks down at Brooks Crossroads and then made our way home up the new but unopened Highway 421.

What a bunch of laughs this class had with the play. Joe was glad to be a scary part of it.

"Joe, I want you to meet my niece," Carolyn Whitaker said at practice. "I told her about you and she's coming to the play Friday night." Carolyn was a new student at West Yadkin this year. She was married and had moved into our area at the beginning of the school year. She was witty, full of nervous energy, and a barrel of fun.

"Great! I'm looking forward to meeting her, Carolyn. What is her name?" Joe asked.

"Judy Evans, and she goes to school at Jonesville. She's a pretty little auburn, red headed girl," Carolyn said.

Joe was ready to meet Judy. He was waiting to meet a girl from another school. It seemed like there were problems dating girls from your own school. People talked too much.

On Friday, May 15, it was senior play night. The auditorium was filled to capacity. Joe and all his classmates had the usual jitters, but the play went well. Joe came on the scene one time in each of the three acts of the play sending chills up the spines of the people in attendance with his ghostly laugh.

"Ah hahahahahahahahahaha. Ah hahahahahahahaha!"

Mom loved the play and told Joe that he sure did make a spooky sounding ghost. She was proud of him.

The laugh even sent chills through the girls in the play even though they had heard it often in practice.

"That laugh scares me and I have heard it over and over!" Brenda said. "I'd hate to think how it'd scare me if I saw you in your black cape in the dark of the night."

After the play, Joe was introduced to Judy Evans, Carolyn's niece. Joe quickly made a date with the cute redhead for Saturday night. No use wasting time as he wasn't going to be around long.

The Last Setting

On Saturday, May 16, it was tobacco setting time again. This year would be the last round of setting for Joe. He was glad but it was also with a note of sadness. Dad was slowly losing all of his work crew.

Dad's crew was in the plant beds at 5:30 a.m. to pull plants for about four acres. The big maple field was set first with Mom dropping plants for Dad while Jane dropped for Joe and Danny dropped for John. The click clack of the setters echoed down the field towards the big maple tree. It seemed that the click clack was telling Joe, "This is it! Time to move on!"

The big maple field was finished at 2:00 p.m. and Dad's efficient setting crews moved on to the hill field to set two acres of the eight acre field before 6:00 p.m.

Joe quickly helped do the chores, showered, and headed to Jonesville for his first date with Judy Evans. It was a get acquainted date as they sat around at her house and talked. She was a nice girl. Joe liked her. He made another date with her for next Friday night to go to class night and then also on Saturday night.

"How'd it go Saturday night, Joe?" Carolyn asked Monday night at school for class night rehearsal. Joe had missed school to set tobacco.

"Good! I think she's a sweet girl," Joe said.

"That's great! She likes you and thinks you are cute," Carolyn said.

Joe, John, Jane, and Danny missed school again on Tuesday as the tobacco crop was finished. Twelve acres were set out. Joe was going to miss his family, but he would not miss the hot sun and the long, hard days. He appreciated all he learned growing up on the farm. Under different circumstances, he would enjoy having a farm of his own, but it seemed that the odds were stacked against the small farmer. They did not stand a chance anymore.

Grandpa Brown

Grandpa Brown was sick. He had been in the Elkin Hospital for the last few days. Tonight, Dad was sitting up with him as he had been very sick. He could not get out of bed and needed someone with him. Joe went with Dad and sat up with him. Some of the longest hours Joe ever spent had to be in the hospital when Grandpa was sick. It was so sad to see Grandpa hurting. He had always been so full of life. He would improve and come home at the end of the week, but he would never be well again.

Class Night

On Thursday night, the seniors practiced for the class night exercise again. They also practiced marching in and out of the auditorium as Sunday would be the Baccalaureate sermon. Only one more week and our school days at good, old West Yadkin High School would be over with forever. The best and most memorable days of our lives were about gone.

On Friday, May 22, it was time for class night, a program to reflect on our years in school and, especially this year. Every graduating senior participated in the fun. On the lighter side, Joe and Billy Turner did a comedy skit as the country music couple, Homer and Jethro. Billy played the accordion as he and Joe sang:

"On top of Old Smoky - all covered with trees.
I stood in the water - plumb up to my ankles."

"But, Homer, that don't rhyme!" Billy said.

"I know, but you see the water wasn't deep enough," Joe said.

"Her hair was silky and smooth as silk
She got that from shampooing in dragon milk."

"How do you get dragon milk?" Billy asked.

"You get that from a short legged cow," Joe said.

The skit went on for four verses, which seemed to be enjoyed by all. Joe and Billy had also dressed for the occasion in their bib overalls and straw hats. They were a sight.

Mrs. Wishon and Mr. Moretz introduced the superlatives of the graduating class. Joe was selected as most studious with Jerleen Turner, most dependable with Doretha Gardner, best all-around with Gail Swaim, and most likely to succeed with Margaret Shore. Our class thanked Mrs. Wishon and Mr. Moretz for being good sponsors and gave them a gift as a token of our appreciation. It was a fun night remembering all the good times and accomplishments of our class.

"That was a good program, Joe," Judy said as Joe drove her home. "Your skit was good and very funny. Maybe you need to go to Nashville and try to give Homer and Jethro some competition instead of going into the Marines."

Joe was considering going into the Marines when he got out of school. He didn't really want to, but he knew that he would have to fulfill his military obligation before he could get a good job.

It was Sunday, May 24, 1959. At church today, Pastor Culler recognized the graduating class of 1959. The church gave Joe a Bible with his name engraved on it.

Pastor Culler challenged the seniors to make a commitment to serve the Lord and stay true to His Word.

"The world will lead you astray. Stay in God's Word and He will guide you every day," Pastor said.

At 3:00 p.m. at West Yadkin, it was the Baccalaureate sermon for the twenty-eight graduates to be. The realization of graduating was starting to sink in as we marched into the auditorium in our caps and gowns.

The congregation sang "Fairest Lord Jesus" and Mr. Wright, our principal for all of our twelve years in school, prayed.

Mr. Joe Cash, English teacher, sang "I am Thy God" followed by the sermon on "Opportunity, Fidelity, and Reward" by Rev. R.E. Hildebrandt. The graduates listened intently for any advice that would help them in their soon to be life after school.

Soon, the remarks of advice were followed by the benediction and the seniors marched out of the auditorium led by the marshals of the junior class. The end of the school year draws closer. The next three days would only be a formality and rehearsing for graduation on Thursday. It was nice to be able to go to school and just have a good time.

"I think it's kind of nice to be able to socialize a little, don't you, Joe?" Brenda asked.

"I sure do! I think we should have earned that right by now," Joe said.

Chapter 37
Appreciation – Memories

Joe worked in the tobacco on Monday, Tuesday, and Wednesday after school. It was hoeing time.

"Your hoeing days are about over, Joe," Jane said. "You will be out of here in a few days, won't you?"

"Yes! I sure will. It's going to seem very funny to be working somewhere rather than in the hot sun," Joe said.

"I've got two more summers and I'll be in Greensboro with you," John said.

Joe was planning on going to Greensboro Thursday evening after graduation to get a job. He was going to live with Wayne and Elvie for a short time.

On Wednesday evening after work, Dad was wanting to talk to Joe as he knew that Joe would be gone tomorrow after graduation.

"I appreciate all your hard work over the years, Joe. I know I have worked you hard. I understand why you're leaving. The farm does not have much to offer a young, educated person. If you ever want to come back and farm, I will help you get started. I know you're going to do good in whatever you decide to do. You've been a good, faithful worker and I'll sure miss you," Dad said.

"Thanks, Dad, for everything. I appreciate all that you and Mom have sacrificed to help us youngins get a good education. I know it hasn't been easy for ya'll. I do appreciate it and will always remember the good times that we've had here on the farm. You have taught me how to work. I will not forget it!" Joe said.

At supper, Mom prayed before we ate the Brown family supper of cornbread and milk.

"Heavenly Father, thank you for your goodness, for health and strength you give us. We pray that you'd be with the sick and shut-in, the bereaved, and bless them. Help our family. Be with Elmer, Wayne, Rose, and their families. We pray that you'd be with Joe tomorrow as he graduates and goes on to Greensboro to work. Help him to stay in church and be the Christian that he should be. We're going to miss him. Keep him safe. We pray that you'd bless this food in Jesus' name. Amen. Amen."

Mom and Jane teared up after the prayer. Joe quickly went and gave them both a hug.

"I'm going to miss ya'll," Joe said. "I'll be home every weekend, though. It won't be so bad."

After supper, we sat around and talked. We had worked late in the tobacco field and did not get to the house in time to go to church. The talk was needed by the whole family.

"I'll always remember the neat Christmas gifts I got each year from you, Mom and Dad," Joe said. "We didn't have much, but we always got a toy."

"I always enjoyed our rabbit hunts, Dad, and the rabbit gravy, Mom. It's good to have had the best cook in the whole world for all these years. I will miss these biscuits and cornbread and milk," Joe continued.

"I was so worried about you, Dad, when you got spider bit in the Johnny house. You scared all of us youngins to death. We were afraid you were going to die," Joe said.

"Remember when Danny was afraid Grandpa Proctor was going to give an Eisenhower haircut," Joe added. "Grandpa got a good laugh out of that."

"How about the time when someone asked Danny a question when he was a baby and Wayne told them that Danny couldn't talk cause he don't have any teeth," Jane said as everyone laughed.

Joe and Jane were very close. Joe would really miss her. Joe let Jane play basketball with him. They also sang as she played the piano.

"Jane, do you remember our song?" Joe asked.

"I sure do! It's Bill Grogan's goat," she said. "Let's go sing it!" They headed to the piano. She played and they sang:

"Bill Grogan's goat was feeling fine
Till he ate three shirts off the line.
Now he is sick and almost dead.
Bill Grogan's goat is seeing red."

"I've heard ya'll do that song so many times," Mom said. "Boy, do we have memories? How do people survive without a good family and the Lord? I sure hope that one of ya'll will write a book one of these days about all the good memories at our Little Farm on Brown Road."

"Remember the many blessings over the years. The Lord watched over Elmer and the four years he was gone in the Air Force. Now he is back at work and getting ready to marry Geraldine next week on June 6. We are a truly blessed family," Dad said.

"Joe, I'm the oldest youngin now and it's my job to carry on the good Brown tradition of being Dad's right hand man, now that you're gone. We've had a good time. I'll always remember all the good times playing ball in the cow pasture and then later, football at West Yadkin. Sorry about the missed block on your big reverse play," John said.

"I'll remember all the good times with Leck and Ida Groce. I know they've been your friends for many years. The rabbit hunts with Leck and the visits by their family, Nadine and Justine, their first set of twins, and then, Jane, who was born in 1953. What in the world would good farm folks do without friends like Leck and Ida?" Joe asked about Mom and Dad's longtime friends.

"We'd better get to bed! It's past 10:00 p.m. We don't want to sleep through the graduation tomorrow," Dad said.

Chapter 38
Graduation

The big day was finally here, May 28, 1959, graduation day. Joe, Margaret Allen, Colleen Ashley, JoAnn Brooks, Roger Caudle, Doretha Gardner, Tony Hobson, Hazel Hudson, Donna Johnson, Archie King, James Nicholson, Mildred Pardue, Nancy Reinhardt, Sonja Royal, Tommy Seagraves, Margaret Shore, Willodean Shore, Brenda Swaim, Gail Swaim, Harold Swaim, Sylvia Trivette, Billy Turner, Jerleen Turner, Patty Vestal, Mary Leigh Walker, Carolyn Whitaker, Margaret Wilkins, and Gene Williams would graduate today.

At precisely 11:00 a.m., the processional music was ringing out from Mrs. Caroline Hinshaw, the music teacher. The seniors slowly marched down the aisles for the last time. The audience sang "All Hail the Power."

"All hail the pow'r of Jesus' name!
Let angels prostrate fall;
Bring forth the royal diadem,
and crown Him Lord of all;
Bring forth the royal diadem,
And crown Him Lord of all!"

Mr. Fred C. Hobson, superintendent of Yadkin County schools, prayed and then Mr. Wright introduced the speaker, Rev. Howard Ford, pastor of First Baptist Church in Elkin.

Pastor Ford spoke for a short time on setting goals and for these graduates to continue the learning process that they have used for the past twelve years.

He urged the graduates, "It is not time to quit learning. Even if you do not go on to college, challenge yourself to learn daily. Read your Bible and know what God tells you. Read good books and keep growing. When you quit growing, you will die away. In the modern world we now live in, you are either going forward or you're going backwards. There is no such thing as standing still."

"We must move on from high school to college or to public work and become taxpaying citizens who will raise families to continue to make this country great. Put God first and you will go places in life. Thank you very much and may God bless each one of you," Pastor Ford said.

Mr. Wright again addressed the senior class and presented diplomas to the twenty-eight seniors who had worked hard and reached the goal set by their parents years ago. Like Joe's parents, many other parents in attendance did not have the opportunity to graduate from high school and now they were very proud of their children.

"This achievement of graduating from high school is important and we congratulate you for it. Use this as a stepping stone to even bigger goals in life," Mr. Wright said.

One by one, the seniors came across the stage and received their diploma from Mr. Wright when their name was called. Mr. Wright smiled as he called the names and made the presentation. He had raised this class from the first grade. Now they were graduating.

Mr. Wright spoke, "Margaret Allen, Colleen Ashley, JoAnn Brooks, Joe Brown, Roger Caudle, Doretha Gardner, Tony Hobson, Hazel Hudson, Donna Johnson, Archie King, James Nicholson, Mildred Pardue, Nancy Reinhardt, Sonja Royal, Tommy Seagraves, Margaret Shore, Willodean Shore, Brenda Swaim, Gail Swaim, Harold Swaim, Sylvia

Trivette, Billy Turner, Jerleen Turner, Patty Vestal, Mary Leigh Walker, Carolyn Whitaker, Margaret Wilkins, and Gene Williams."

With diplomas in hand, the graduates returned to their seats to hear the announcement of graduation from the leader, Mr. Wright.

"Class, it is indeed my pleasure to pronounce that you, the West Yadkin High School class of 1959, are officially graduated. You may now switch your tassels on your caps. Let me be the first to congratulate you. God bless you!" Mr. Wright said.

Everyone stood up as the seniors marched out again to the peppy music by Mrs. Hinshaw. It was official. Joe was now graduated from high school.

Once outside, many of the seniors threw the caps into the air in celebration. They were very happy.

"We did it, Joe!" Archie said. "We really did."

"We sure did. I told you we would without any sweat and it only took us twelve years," Joe said.

The Long Friendship

"What are you going to do, Archie? Why don't you go with me to Greensboro today? We'll get a job and get us a place to live," Joe asked Archie as he didn't want their friendship to end after all the good years.

"No! I think I'll go to Winston and get a job at Hanes or Reynolds, one. I'll live at home and catch a ride with my sister," Archie said. "Greensboro sounds like a long way from home."

Joe and Archie went down to the hangout at Brooks and got a hamburger for dinner. Then they drove down to Peggy Ireland's house to see Peggy and Vena Carpenter.

Joe and Peggy liked each other, but Peggy could not date as she was a freshman. Her parents especially didn't want her to be dating a senior. Archie had a similar problem with Vena.

So we sat down at Peggy's house for awhile and talked. We would not be seeing the girls for awhile as Joe would be living in Greensboro. Joe and Peggy would write back and forth all summer, but they never did date.

"I guess it was never meant for Peggy and me to date," Joe would later tell Archie.

"Well, old pal, I appreciate the ride. It's been a fun day and my ride to Greensboro is ready to go. I'll see you tomorrow night after I hopefully get a job," Joe told Archie.

School actually would end on Friday and many of Joe's classmates would go to school one last day, but Joe did not want to go.

"School is over. We have graduated. We've got to move on," Joe said.

Joe's Job

Joe rode to Greensboro with his sister-in-law, Elvie. She had come up for graduation and to give Joe a ride.

"They're hiring at Western Auto. I'll take you by there tomorrow morning," Elvie said. She worked as a telephone operator and was off again on Friday.

On Friday morning at 9:00 sharp, Joe, decked out in his only suit, went in to apply for a job at Western Auto Supply Co. on East Market Street in Greensboro. Mr. Hardy liked Joe's farm background and hired him immediately to start Monday morning at 8:00 a.m. Joe would make a dollar thirty-seven and a half cents per hour. He finally had a job that would get him out of the hot sun.

He would be an order filler. Joe felt like he was making a fortune at that rate. He couldn't wait to start to work on Monday.

Joe did feel a touch of sadness now that he was no longer a farmer. After all of these hard years, he was going to be on his own. He was no longer a student in school. He had a good paying job and would begin a new life.

Without tears, but with a definite attachment to his past, Joe was now leaving the Little Farm on Brown Road.

But his heart would never leave.

Epilogue

The purpose of *Memories, Farm Days, Farm Ways* and *Little Farm on Brown Road* is to leave an account for my children of my childhood on the farm. It was a hard, but rewarding way of life. The long work days of before sunrise to after sunset were just normal for the small farmer. I look back to this hard work as preparation for later challenges in life. Dad was the ultimate hard worker. He believed that all of his youngins should also work hard. He trained them to be a highly productive team.

My life has been greatly influenced by hard-working people, most of whom did not have a lot of formal education but they were educated by having good common sense and the will to work hard to survive. Dad, Mom, Grandpa Brown, Grandma Proctor, Claude Shore, Uncle Nelson Brown and Pastor L. E. Myers all were good country people from whom I learned the values of life and how to strive to use my God-given ability to work hard to achieve goals.

Some outstanding educators helped me get enough education to use with good common sense. Mr. C.C. Wright, one of my heroes, was an old fashioned principal who was always in charge. Mr. Ray Madison, assistant principal and my 6th grade teacher, was one of my favorite teachers. Mrs. Helen Wishon was the perfect English teacher who had her hands full trying to teach us English. Mr. George Holmes was my first basketball coach and my favorite coach in high school.

God used these people to help me, not just while I was on the farm, but throughout my entire life. I am grateful to all of them.

Joe Brown
July, 2005

Also by Joe Brown

Memories – Farm Days, Farm Ways

The author's recollection of his young days on his family's small Yadkin County farm

Price: $15.00, including postage and sales tax.

Available from the author at:

Joe Brown
1042 Bona Court
Kernersville, NC 27284

Telephone: (336) 996-7752

Website: www.HaystackPress.com
Email: Joe@HaystackPress.com

Other Books of Interest
By
Elmer C. Brown

□

100 Bible Studies You Need
(A layperson's guide to growth - $20.00)

Ready to Live
(A guide for Christian Living - $15.00)

The Light Still Shines
(Christians as God's little lights - $15.00)

The Storm Warning
(A Christian adventure novel - $15.00)

The Choice
(A Christian adventure novel - $15.00)

Wonderful
(A study of the names of the Lord - $15.00)

A Time to Weep - America Is Falling!
(A discussion of America's endangered heritage and frightening spiritual decline - $15.00)

All the above books are available from their author at:

Elmer C. Brown
1036 Camelot Lane
Graham, NC 27253

Tel. (336) 226-4695

All prices are postpaid, including sales tax.